DIALOGUE AND LEARNING IN MATHEMATICS EDUCATION

Mathematics Education Library

VOLUME 29

Managing Editor

A.J. Bishop, *Monash University, Melbourne, Australia*

Editorial Board

The titles published in this series are listed at the end of this volume.

DIALOGUE AND LEARNING IN MATHEMATICS EDUCATION

Intention, Reflection, Critique

by

HELLE ALRØ and OLE SKOVSMOSE
Aalborg University, Denmark

KLUWER ACADEMIC PUBLISHERS
DORDRECHT / BOSTON / LONDON

Library of Congress Cataloging-in-Publication Data

ISBN 1-4020-0998-4

Published by Kluwer Academic Publishers,
P.O. Box 17, 3300 AA Dordrecht, The Netherlands.

Sold and distributed in North, Central and South America
by Kluwer Academic Publishers,
101 Philip Drive, Norwell, MA 02061, U.S.A.

In all other countries, sold and distributed
by Kluwer Academic Publishers,
P.O. Box 322, 3300 AH Dordrecht, The Netherlands.

Printed on acid-free paper

Printed in the Netherlands.

CONTENTS

ACKNOWLEDGEMENTS

First of all, we want to thank the involved students and teachers who have made it possible for us to study details of communication in the mathematics classroom. Without their willingness to co-operate our work would not have been possible. We are grateful to every teacher and student who appear anonymous in this book, and to the teachers Bjarne Würtz Andersen, Ane Marie Krogshede Nielsen and Ib Trankjær, who provided us with the material for Chapter 1. We owe a special gratitude to Henning Bødtkjer and Mikael Skånstrøm with whom we have co-operated closely during the whole study. Their teaching has convinced us that dialogue can work in the mathematics classroom.

Many persons have made comments and suggestions for the improvement of the manuscript. We want to thank Alan Bishop, Marcelo Borba, Paul Cobb, Marit Johnsen Høines, Marianne Kristiansen, John Mason and Miriam Godoy Penteado for careful readings, inquiring dialogues and useful comments to previous versions of the manuscript. We are also grateful to H.C. Hansen, Aage Nielsen and Paola Valero for their comments on special issues.

Further, we would like to thank a group of Ph.D.- and MA-students from the State University of São Paulo at Rio Claro: Chateaubriand Nunes Amancio, Jussara de Loiola Araújo, Jonei Cerqueira Barbosa, Telma Souza Gracias, Frederico José Lopes for their important comments on different chapters.

We have had the opportunity to discuss every chapter of this book at different stages within a group of researchers in the cross-institutional Centre for Research in Learning Mathematics. Thanks to Morten Blomhøj, Iben Maj Christiansen, Elin Emborg, Lena Lindenskov and Tine Wedege for valuable comments and support.

Many people have helped us during the process to overcome practical, technical, and linguistic problems. We want to thank Nikolaj Hyldig, Marianne Harder Mandøe and Dana Sandstrøm Poulsen for making the transcripts, and Ebbe Klitgård for translations of transcripts. We are also grateful to Ebbe Klitgård and Marilyn Nickson for correcting our English. Further, we want to thank Erik Nød Sørensen for computer assistance, for drawing the figures, and for setting up the manuscript.

ACKNOWLEDGEMENTS

Chapters 1 and 2 are based on three articles which appeared in *For the Learning of Mathematics*: 'On the Right Track', 16(1), 2-9 and 22; 'The Students' Good Reasons', 16(3), 31-38; and 'That was not the Intention! Communication in Mathematics Education', 18(2), 42-51. We are grateful to the editor of *FLM* for agreeing to the re-use of this material here.

This study is carried out as part of the research initiated by the Centre for Research in Learning Mathematics, which is based on a co-operation between the Danish University of Education, Roskilde University Centre and Aalborg University. The Centre is supported financially by the Danish Research Council for the Humanities.

Aalborg, August 2002

Helle Alrø and Ole Skovsmose

INTRODUCTION

"Today we really learnt something!" Mary exclaimed after she, together with Adam, had concentrated for almost two hours on setting up a spreadsheet. Something significant seems to have happened for Mary, something that should be considered when theorising about the learning of mathematics. In this study we are going to meet with Mary and Adam and many other students in the mathematics classroom. The main purpose of this meeting is to gather empirical resources to gain a better understanding of the role of communication in learning mathematics.

The initial idea that guides our investigations can be condensed in the following hypothesis: *The qualities of communication in the classroom influence the qualities of learning mathematics*. This is not a very original statement and certainly very general. If the statement is to be provided with meaning it is important to clarify at least the two expressions: 'qualities of communication' and 'qualities of learning mathematics'. In this introduction, as well as during the rest of this book, we are going to struggle with clarifying in what sense communication and learning can be connected, and how to conceptualise this connection.

QUALITIES OF COMMUNICATION

In many different contexts, both inside and outside school, special attention is paid to communication. Thus, companies organise workshops and courses on communication in order to improve the way they operate (see, for instance, Isaacs, 1999a; Kristiansen and Bloch-Poulsen, 2000). The improvement of communication is expected not only to have an influence on the atmosphere of the workplace, but also on the way the company operates in terms of business, as expressed in figures and budgets. Communication becomes related to the idea of the 'learning organisation'.

Qualities of communication can be expressed in terms of interpersonal relationships. Learning is rooted in the act of communicating itself, not just in the information conveyed from one party to another. Thus, communication takes on a deeper meaning. In *Freedom to Learn*, first published in 1969, Carl Rogers (1994) considers interpersonal relationships as the crucial point in the facilitation of learning. Learning is personal, but it takes place in the social contexts of interpersonal relationships. Accordingly, the facilitation of learning depends on the quality of contact in the interpersonal relationship that emerges from the communication between the participants. In other words, the context in which people communicate affects what is learned by both parties.

This brings forward the idea that some 'qualities of communication' could be clarified in terms of *dialogue*. The word 'dialogue' has many everyday descriptive references but the important factor common to all is that they involve at least two parties. For instance, it is possible to talk about the dialogue between East and West and about the breakdown of the dialogue between Palestine and Israel. Such references to dialogue are not strictly part of our concern. In philosophical contexts the notion of dialogue occurs in many places. Plato presented his ideas as dialogues; in 1632 Galileo Galilei wrote *The Dialogue Concerning the two Chief World Systems* (which brought him close to the Inquisition), and Imre Lakatos (1976) presented his investigation of the logic of mathematical discovery in the form of a dialogue taking place in an imaginary classroom. Such uses of 'dialogue' refer first of all to analytical forms and presentations of inquiries and of 'getting to know'. As soon as we enter the field of 'getting to know', dialogue becomes relevant to epistemology. However, although our concept of dialogue is also related to epistemology in this way, it will diverge from the traditional philosophical use of the term by being related to 'real' dialogues and not to in-principle dialogues. We use the word 'dialogue' for a conversation with certain *qualities*, and the specification of 'dialogue' is one of the tasks awaiting for us as part of this study.

In talking of qualities related to conversation, we recognise that the notion of quality may have a double meaning. On the one hand, quality may refer to properties of a certain entity. Thus, we can talk (almost in Aristotelian terms) about the quality of a cup as being different from the quality of a glass. In this sense quality refers to descriptive aspects of an entity. However, quality may also contain a normative element. Thus, we can talk about one glass being of a better quality that another glass. Maintaining the distinction between descriptive and normative references to quality is not simple. For instance, we may prefer the quality of a glass to the quality of a cup when drinking wine. In a similar way, we may prefer a dialogue when we think of certain forms of learning, bearing in mind that dialogue refers to certain properties of an interaction.

Paulo Freire (1972) emphasises the importance of interpersonal relationships in terms of dialogue. To Freire dialogue is not just any conversation. Dialogue is fundamental for the freedom to learn. The notion of dialogue is integral to concepts like 'empowerment' and 'emancipation', and from this perspective Freire makes a connection between the quality of what is happening between people and the possibility of pursuing political actions. He defines dialogue as a meeting between people in order to 'name the world', which means talking about events and the possibility of changing these. In this way dialogue is seen as existential. Dialogue cannot exist without love (respect) for the world and for other people, and it cannot exist in relations of dominance (Freire, 1972, 77f.). Further, taking part in a dialogue presupposes some kind of humility. You cannot enter a dialogic relationship being self-sufficient. The participants have to believe in each other and to be open-minded towards each other in order to create an equal and faithful relationship. As the dialogue is directed by the hope of change, it cannot exist without the engagement of the partners in critical thinking (Freire, 1972, 80f.). To Freire the co-operation of the participants is a central parameter of dialogic communication. In co-operation the participants throw light on the world that surrounds them and the problems that connect and challenge them. Freire points out the importance of co-operation between action and reflection (Freire, 1972, 75f.). Hand and head have to go together. Acting without reflecting would end up in pure activism and reflection without action would result in verbalism. However, in a dialogue, reflection and action can enrich each other. According to Freire, the educational dialogue is supposed to examine the universe of the people – its thematic universe – which announces emancipation through education. Freire's program was originally aimed at illiterate people, and it has to be remembered that only in May 1985 did illiterate people in Brazil get the right to vote.[1] To Freire, dialogue clearly refers to a form of interaction with many specific qualities.

In classical philosophy, dialogue first of all refers to a presentation (and confrontation) of two or more different (and contradictory) points of view, with the aim of identifying a conclusion that can be agreed on.

---

[1] Freire makes the revolutionary leaders responsible for the communication remaining dialogic. They should not invade the perspectives of the people and inform or instruct them, nor should they just adapt to the expectations of the people. They should learn about the people's world together with the people – by naming the world (Freire, 1972, 161). The relationship between the revolutionary leaders and the people, as suggested by Freire, can be interpreted in terms of the relationship between teacher and students – an asymmetrical relationship.

Freire and Rogers, however, also viewed dialogue as encompassing interpersonal relationships, where listening and accepting on the part of the participants is fundamental. Dialogue is not just a mode of analysis, but also a mode of interaction. In the following clarification of the notion of dialogue we shall maintain this combination of epistemic and relational aspects of dialogue.

Rogers and Freire have much in common although they work from different historical positions. This is perhaps not surprising as they both relate to the German philosopher Martin Buber (1957), who emphasises the relationship, 'the interhuman', in the dialogue as a certain way of meeting the other with unconditional acceptance. Rogers calls his approach to learning 'person-centered' as opposed to the 'traditional mode', and he describes the two approaches as opposite poles of a continuum (Rogers, 1994, 209f.). He argues that the person-centered mode prepares the students for democracy, whereas the traditional mode socialises the students to obey power and control. In the traditional mode, he argues, "the teacher is the possessor of knowledge and power," and "rule by authority is accepted policy in the classroom". Students are expected to be recipients of knowledge, and examinations are used to measure their receptivity. Rogers emphasises that "trust is at a minimum," and "democratic values are ignored and scorned in practice". In the person-centred mode, he argues, the environment is trustful and the responsibility for the learning processes is shared. "The facilitator provides learning resources," and "the students develop their program of learning alone and in co-operation with others". The main principle is learning how to learn, and self-discipline and self-evaluation guarantee a continuing process of learning. This growth-promoting climate not only facilitates learning processes but also stimulates the students' responsibility and other competencies for democratic citizenship: "I have slowly come to realize that it is in its politics that a person-centred approach to learning is most threatening. The teacher or administrator who considers using such an approach must face up to the fearful aspects of sharing of power and control. Who knows whether students or teachers can be trusted, whether a process can be trusted? One can only take the risk, and risk is frightening." (Rogers, 1994, 214)

Freire contrasts his dialogic approach with 'banking education', where the teacher makes an investment, and where the students are considered boxes and are supposed to preserve what is invested. To both Rogers and Freire, dialogue represents certain forms of interaction fundamental to processes of learning, which, in Freire's terms, can ensure empowerment, and which in Rogers' terms can ensure person-centered learning and students' responsibility. In this sense they find that qualities of communication can turn into qualities of learning, referring to both descriptive and normative elements. When we talk about qualities of communication and qualities of learning, we also have in mind both descriptive and normative elements. We want to locate certain aspects of communication which may support certain aspects of learning, and at the same time it becomes important to support these aspects of learning.

Many studies of communication concentrate on classrooms that are situated in the school mathematics tradition. Here, we refer to a tradition where the textbook plays a predominant role, where the teacher explains the new mathematical topics, where students solve exercises within the subject, and where correction of solutions and mistakes characterise the overall structure of a lesson. We have observed classrooms from a school mathematics tradition where there is a nice atmosphere, and where the teacher-student communication appears friendly. So, by the school mathematics tradition we do not simply refer to the non-attractive features of the mathematics classroom, where a never-smiling teacher dominates the students. However, within the school mathematics tradition we can locate characteristic patterns of communication which have certain qualities, but we are not tempted to refer to these patterns as dialogue.

The form of communication depends on the context of communication, and, like many others, we find that the school mathematics tradition frames the communication between students and teacher in a particular way. In the first chapter of this study we will summarise a few of our observations and analyses of this phenomenon, but in the rest of the book we primarily undertake our investigations in classrooms outside the school mathematics tradition. We are interested in situations where the students become involved in more complex and also unpredictable processes of inquiry. This opens a new space for communication, where new qualities can emerge.

In many cases the mathematics classroom has undergone radical changes. Thematic approaches and project work challenge tradition in such a way that the distinction between learning mathematics and learning something else is not always sharply maintained.

With the exception of Chapters 1 and 2, we describe projects where the planning of the subject matter was a shared process between the teachers and us. Then, when it came to the classroom practice, the teachers were in charge. One reason for this division of labour is simply that the teacher's professionalism in real-life classrooms is much higher than ours. We discussed the interpretations of the observations with the teachers, and we have included their suggestions for possible interpretations. In some cases, we also interviewed the students about their experiences and interpretations. Our concern is to interpret what is happening in the classroom as well as to identify new possibilities for mathematics education. In other words, we are interested in clarifying 'what is the case' in order to find out 'what could be the case' and in this way to clarify what these possibilities may be.[2]

When exploring such possibilities we want to consider the complexity of classroom interaction. For this reason the episodes we refer to are rather extensive and mostly documented in lengthy transcripts. This might seem somewhat long-winded, but it is necessary to include them in order to document our analysis of what is going on. It is only by a careful reading of communication sequences amongst the classroom participants that we can get a glimpse of the reflections and learning processes of the participants that underly their communication.[3]

We include a variety of teaching and learning sequences that have caught our attention. Situations where resistance to learning and to participating dominate the picture can also inform an understanding of

---

[2] A more careful discussion of what it could mean to research possibilities and not simply to provide explanations of what is taking place, has been discussed in Skovsmose and Borba (in press) and Vithal (2000a, 2000b). See also Atweh, Forgasz and Nebres (eds.) (2001); Atweh, Kemmis and Weeks (eds.) (1998) and Jaworski (1994).

[3] Our analysis of classroom interaction refers to pragmatics in the philosophy of language (Wittgenstein, 1953; Austin, 1962; Searle, 1969) and its interpretation in linguistic pragmatics and sociopragmatics (e.g. Maas and Wunderlich, 1972; Wunderlich, 1975 and Levinson, 1983). Thus, the issue of analysis is the use and function of language in context. In this study the speech act interpretation is developed from the utterance level to the level of interaction. The study of the use of language in context includes both verbal and non-verbal language and focuses on qualitative questions like: How are interpersonal relationships and meanings expressed by means of language? What levels of meaning can be interpreted by considering the communication context?

In the analysis we examine what teacher and students actually say and do that shapes a certain mathematics classroom context. We also consider how the classroom and shool context shapes and provides certain meanings and ways of acting to the mathematics classroom.

Our analysis of classroom communication is qualitative and we distinguish between quotations, descriptions and interpretations of what is being said and done (although there might be an interpretation in our selection of described sequences to be analysed). In this way our focus and interpretations can be checked out and perhaps analysed differently from other research perspectives.

In the analysis we look for certain patterns of communication in the mathematics classroom, and our hypothesis is that certain patterns of communication may be related to certain qualities of learning mathematics. Thus our theory of learning mathematics stems from empirical studies from where we generate examples and new theoretical concepts.

qualities of communication and of learning. It is not our intention, however, to look into classrooms where cultural conflicts are presented as, for instance, Renuka Vithal (2000a) does in her study of a pedagogy of dialogue and conflict or Jill Adler (2001a, 2001b) in her study of multilingual classrooms. Nor are we studying learning based on situations with lack of resources. Thus, in our examples it is easy for the students to get access to computers. Similarly, we have not studied learning in a situation in which there are dramatic political threats facing the children as soon as they leave school, as is the case for Palestinian children. The school environment we refer to is a comfortable one. It is Danish. Nevertheless, we believe that the conceptual framework we present can be of relevance in many other situations, including those outside mathematics education. We search for educational possibilities, acknowledging the complexity of real classrooms, and for qualities of communication within this complexity. Our data are not 'sanitised'.[4]

QUALITIES OF LEARNING MATHEMATICS

The Freire approach to pedagogy illustrates the idea that there is a connection between qualities of communication and qualities of learning. Freire wanted to develop certain qualities of learning. The students were not only to learn how to read and write, but also critically to interpret a social and political situation. This was a tremendous and dangerous task, as Brazil was run by a military dictatorship during the period 1964-1984 with the Destacamento de Operações e Informatições de Defesa Interna (Operations and Intelligence Detachments of Internal Defence) serving as the principal center for torture.

Freire identified certain key terms for any reading-writing project, and he paid special attention to how to contextualise these terms. One term could be *tijolo* (brick). By breaking the key terms into syllables like, *ti-jo-lo*, and introducing the elements *ta-te-ti-to-tu*; *ja-je-ji-jo-ju* and *la-le-li-lo-lu*, he found elements for new Portuguese words. About 17 key terms appear to be enough for generating the whole Portuguese language. When choosing the word *tijolo*, Freire would consider also the social relationships related to brick building. All of the key terms came to represent a double opening: towards the grammatical structure of the language, and towards the social structure of society. The key terms

---

[4] The concept of 'sanitised data' is discussed in Vithal (1998a) and Valero and Vithal (1999).

became a nucleus for empowerment. Freire's method was extremely efficient. After 21 hours the participators were able to read simple articles from newspapers, and after 30 hours the course was concluded (one hour per day, 5 hours per week, 6 weeks in total).

A particular reason for this efficiency is that Freire made it possible for the participants to be involved in the process of learning in a powerful way. It is interesting to see how he approached this issue of involvement. In the early 1960s, the Movimento de Culture Popular in Receife launched an elementary textbook intended for adult illiterates. It started with words like: people, vote, life, health and bread, and then proceeded to sentences like 'voting belongs to the people,' 'people without homes live like refugees,' etc. Freire strongly opposed this approach. Although he agreed with the overall political intentions, he considered that it would obstruct the very intention of making people critical citizens. He wanted the themes underlying the reading-writing projects to be open to many interpretations. The learners should be invited into the process of making interpretations. They would then become involved in the decoding of their situation.[5] Learning would be based on dialogue, and the qualities that were associated with dialogue would become qualities of learning.

As already noted, we are particularly interested in certain qualities of communication as constituted by dialogue, and we are interested in certain qualities of learning mathematics. We are not simply considering the most efficient way for students to come to grasp certain mathematical facts. Nor are we only considering the learning of mathematics, where the content of the learning is interpreted strictly in mathematical terms. We are interested in a much broader concept of what can be learnt. Freire, for example, not only concentrated on the reading of *tijolo*, but also considered the social situation of brick-building. In a similar way, we do not want to consider only mathematical concepts and techniques in isolation, we also want to include the social contexts in which they might be operating. This brings us to the idea of *critical mathematics education*. This represents an approach to mathematics where particular qualities of learning mathematics are appreciated.

Activities developed within critical mathematics education cover a broad spectrum and do not represent a single homogeneous approach.[6] It

---

[5] For at description of Freire's work, see Gadotti (ed.) (1996).

[6] The approach of critical mathematics education is developed in studies like Fasheh (1993, 1997); Frankenstein (1987, 1989, 1995); Knijnik (1998); Mellin-Olsen (1987); Secada, Fennema and Adajian (eds.) (1995); Skovsmose (1994, 1998b, 2000a); Skovsmose and Nielsen (1996) and Vithal (2000a). Other notions, e.g. ethnomathematics, have been used, but the overall concern is shared; see, for instance,

is possible, however, to characterise critical mathematics education in terms of different general ideas, one being that the task of mathematics education is more than to provide students with an understanding of the logical architecture of mathematics. Critical mathematics education is concerned with how mathematics in general influences our cultural, technological and political environment, and the functions mathematical competence may serve. For this reason, it not only pays attention to how students most efficiently get to know and understand the concepts of, say, fraction, function and exponential growth. Critical mathematics education is also concerned with matters such as how the learning of mathematics may support the development of citizenship and how the individual can be empowered through mathematics. Remember that Freire developed the most efficient method of teaching reading and writing skills. Similarly, critical mathematics education does not represent turning our backs on mathematics. It also tries to develop the *ta-te-ti-to-tu* of elementary mathematics as well as to illuminate how mathematical techniques and ways of thinking may operate in social and political contexts.

We live in a society where mathematics and mathematical under-standing has become an integrated part of our everyday environment.[7] In fact, we find that mathematics in many different manifestations – as a field of research, as a form of reasoning, as a resource for technological action, as an everyday form of thinking, as a school subject – is po-sitioned in the center of social development. This brings a new challenge to mathematics education and it is one with which critical mathematics education is particularly concerned, i.e. with the possible roles of mathematics and of mathematics education in a world where the com-plexity of technology may provoke unexpected risks. The notion of a risk society was originally coined by Ulrich Beck (1992), and much recent discussion in sociology has evolved around this concept. Risks can be interpreted as natural phenomena, but a risk society emerges when the distinction between nature and culture becomes blurred: "Today, if we talk about nature we talk about culture and if we talk about culture we talk about nature. When we think about global warming, the hole in the ozone layer, pollution of food scares, nature is inexplicably contaminated by human activity." (Beck, 1998, 10-11) We do not live in a natural world any longer, we live in a manufactured world, and risks are

---

D'Ambrosio (2001); Powell and Frankenstein (eds.) (1997); and Stillman and Balatti (2001). See also Apple (1995) and Nickson (2002).

[7] See, for instance, Gellert, Jablonka and Keitel (2001); Johnston and Yasukawa (2001) and Wedege (1999, 2000).

manufactured as well: "Society has become a laboratory where there is absolutely nobody in charge." (Beck, 1998, 9)

For a society to be a well functioning democracy it is important that everybody can read and write. And as Freire has shown, literacy can mean more than just a competence in reading and writing. Literacy can also refer to competence in interpreting a situation as open to change and it can refer to the identification of forms of suppression. Within the framework of critical mathematics education, the notion of *mathemacy* has been presented as a parallel to literacy, as developed by Freire.[8] Thus, the qualities of learning mathematics, with which we are particularly concerned, are represented by mathemacy. Mathemacy is relevant for democracy and for the development of citizenship in the same way as literacy. If mathemacy is to support a critical reading of our social and political environment, it must in particular address the risk society and the roles of science, including mathematics and technology in our everyday contexts.

The idea that guides our studies can now be reformulated in the following way: *Certain qualities of communication, which we try to express in terms of dialogue, support certain qualities in learning of mathematics, which we refer to as critical learning of mathematics manifested by the competence of mathemacy.* In dialogic relationships we hope to find sources for critical learning. (We do not claim that a dialogic relationship is the only resource for critical learning, but it is the nature of this particular ressource we set out to explore.) By investigating dialogic relationships we try to locate elements of critical learning of mathematics.[9]

Stated in this way, the open nature of both 'dialogue' and 'critical' (not to mention 'quality', 'support' and 'mathemacy') will easily drain this formulation of our guiding idea from content. However, during this study we interpret some examples from the mathematics classroom, and in this way we hope to provide a more specific meaning to the thesis and

---

[8] See Skovsmose (1994).

[9] Many recent studies in mathematics education have paid particular attention to the use of computers in the classroom and argued that exactly the computers provide a learning environment which makes it possible for the students to access mathematical ideas more easily (see, for instance, Balacheff and Kaput, 1996 and Blomhøj, 1998). The computers might facilitate experiments and help to relate empirical notions and observations with mathematical ideas. By suggesting qualities of communication as a resource for qualities of learning mathematics, we are not going to negate the possibility that computers are an important resource for learning, but our focus is different. We just take as a natural thing that the students in several of our examples are operating with computers, as they sometimes work with paper and pencil as well.

to the terms by means of which the thesis is formulated. By searching for interpretations of educational situations and of concepts, we try to provide specific input to the conception of learning mathematics critically and to illustrate educational possibilities and potentials. Let us confess immediately that our analyses will not justify the thesis. But, as we have already noted and shall try to show throughout the following chapters, opening the conceptual landscape around the thesis may be a resource for identifying new areas of thought and activity for mathematics education. We begin our investigation by making particular observations in the classroom, and from this platform we try to establish a conceptual framework which may gain a more general significance, maybe also outside mathematics education.

OUTLINE OF THE CONTENT OF THE BOOK

Introduction

In this part (which you have just read) we present the initial idea that guides our investigations: The qualities of communication in the classroom influence the qualities of learning mathematics. Certainly, this thesis not only presupposes clarification via examples and observations, it also presupposes a conceptual development if the thesis is not to be left in a simple rhetorical form.

Chapter 1: Communication in the mathematics classroom

We start by analysing some patterns of communication in the mathematics classroom, observing the school mathematics tradition. *Bureaucratic absolutism* faces students in many such classrooms. It states what is right and wrong in absolute terms. It characterises a learning environment where the handling of mistakes corresponds to a quizzing strategy and with the communication pattern: Guess What the Teacher Thinks[10]. Minimal responses describe a student strategy for operating in such a learning environment. By minimising their answers the students minimise their responsibility for what is happening in the classroom. To identify such qualities of communication is not our main concern, but it serves as background for our study.

---

[10] This term is used by Young (1992).

Next, we describe a classroom situation where students are invited to make open-ended investigations. However, the teacher's intention is not made clear to the students. During the classroom communication the 9-year-old students try to grasp what is the point of solving the presented problem: 'How much does a newspaper fill?' Interpreting this situation brings us to introduce the idea that *learning* (although not all learning) *can be seen as action*. This will be a guiding idea for the rest of our study.

We draw attention to some important aspects of action, in particular to *intention*. Students' intentions are formed on the basis of experiences, prejudices, preferences, expectations, hopes etc. The students' *zooming-in* represents an attempt to relate intentions to a learning activity. In the project 'How much does a newspaper fill?' the zooming-in becomes a trial-and-error strategy of looking for a meaning of the classroom activity. The intensity of the students' zooming-in is in contrast to a minimal response strategy. It is important to establish educational situations where it is possible for the students to associate their intentions with what they are doing, and to establish a culture in the classroom in which the students really want to zoom-in on the activities.

Chapter 2: Inquiry Co-operation

The school mathematics tradition falls within the *exercise paradigm*, but this paradigm can be challenged by *landscapes of investigation*. By leaving the exercise paradigm and entering landscapes of investigation, some patterns of communication are left behind, and new patterns become visible. We see *inquiry co-operation* as a particular form of student-teacher interaction exploring a landscape of investigation.

We follow a conversation between two students, about 12 years old, and their teacher. The students are supposed to make models of the European flags, considering their proportions, stripes, and crosses. As an introduction, they are asked to make a model of the Danish flag. The conversation reveals the elements of what we call the Inquiry Co-operation Model (IC-Model), and the model designates some patterns of communication to which we, in what follows, pay special attention. The elements of the IC-Model are represented by the italicised words in the following paragraph.

By *getting in contact* we understand more than the teacher calling for attention. It means tuning in to each other in order to co-operate. After establishing contact the teacher can *locate* the student's perspective by examining, for instance, how the student understands a certain problem. When the student becomes able to express his or her perspective, it can also be *identified* in mathematical terms, and this provides a resource for further inquiry. Students, as well as the teacher, can *advocate* ideas to be examined, and by *thinking aloud* perspectives become 'visible', which means that they become possible to investigate and to share. The teacher can support the clarification of perspectives by *reformulating* students' formulations. Reformulation can of course also be practiced by the student in order to check out his or her understanding of the teacher perspective. The student can be *challenged* on his or her good reasons in order to support new reflections. On the basis of inquiry the student and the teacher can *evaluate* their perspectives and they might even be able to consider what the students (and the teacher) have learned in the challenging process. These elements of the IC-Model represent certain qualities of communication.

While we expect landscapes of investigation to facilitate inquiry co-operation, the exercise paradigm more likely produces patterns of communication that fit the teacher's quizzing and the students' minimal response strategies. An inquiry process, however, is fragile, and we observe that inquiry co-operation easily becomes interrupted by patterns of communication that are well rooted in the school mathematics tradition. The ghost of classroom absolutism can easily overshadow an inquiry co-operation.

Chapter 3: Further development of the Inquiry Co-operation Model

We follow two 15-16-year-old students, Mary and Adam, who struggle with the problem of organising a spreadsheet which can clarify financial aspects of buying and selling table tennis bats – a task from 'Batman & Co.'. As importers of table tennis bats, Mary and Adam have to consider prices in Swedish Kroner, the exchange rate into Danish Kroner, insurance, freight charges, duty, and profit, not to forget the VAT. And there is also a maximum price to consider. Mary concludes the process by exclaiming: "Today we really learnt something!" We try to analyse the meaning of this statement by reconsidering the whole process in which they have been involved, and we use this analysis in a further development of elements of the IC-Model to become a characteristic also of students' mutual inquiry co-operation.

Getting in contact becomes a preparation for inquiry. Mary and Adam keep this contact during most of the session. It can especially be observed in their continual *inquiring questions, tag questions, mutual confirmation* and *support*. Getting in contact – and staying in contact – is established by many elements, some of which primarily have an emotional

significance. Making an inquiry is not a straightforward logical enterprise.

Locating is a process of discovering possibilities and trying things out.
As a consequence, *what-if questions* become essential. Mary and Adam
ask a lot of such questions. These questions could, for instance, address
the algorithm to be used: What if we do the calculations in this way? The
process of locating opens a space of possibilities for approaching a
certain task, and *what-if* questions are an important tool for doing this.
Thus, locating comes to refer to more than locating each other's
perspectives. It can also mean establishing completely new perspectives
and new learning routes.

Perspectives can be *identified* and made mutually known to the
participants in the inquiry. An identification can include *crystallising
mathematical ideas,* meaning being able to identify a mathematical
subject or algorithm that emerges from the mutual process of locating. A
what-if question can be followed by a *why-question*, and we relate why-
questions to the process of identification. Furthermore, why-questions
lead to attempts to *justify*. Thus, we see a connection between identifying
perspectives and providing justifications – a perspective being a source
for a justification. In particular, the students' good reasons can refer to a
tentative justification, based on an initial perspective.

Advocating[11] can contribute to establishing shared knowledge.
Advocating means speaking what you think and at the same time being
willing to examine your understandings and pre-understandings. Thus,
advocating means tentative arguing with an invitation to inquiry. As
advocating means trying out possible lines of justification, the process of
advocating can lead to suggestions for mathematical proving. Advocating
can represent a suggestion for an answer to a why-question.

Thinking aloud is a particular form of *making reflections public*.
Thinking aloud can also be understood metaphorically, as some thinking
aloud consists of referring to figures or pointing at the screen of the
computer. Thinking aloud helps to ensure a collective process.

Reformulating means repeating what has just been said, maybe in
slightly different words or tone of voice. Reformulating is very close to
paraphrasing and *completing utterances*. We see how Mary and Adam
do this in their efforts to understand each other and it signifies a common
responsibility for the process. Reformulating also has an important
emotive element, as it represents a process of *staying in contact* during
the inquiry co-operation.

---

[11] See Isaacs (1999a) for a discussion of advocacy.

Challenging means attempting to push things in a new direction or to question already gained knowledge or fixed perspectives. *Hypothetical questions* starting with a 'what if' can challenge a suggested justification. A challenge can provide a *turning point* in the investigation. When answers to what-if questions are challenged, it becomes relevant to consider new what-if questions. A challenge can lead to new locating and identifying, and thus it is essential for the construction of new learning possibilities.

An *evaluation* can take many forms. Correction of mistakes, negative critique, constructive critique, advice, support, praise or new examination – the list is unfinished. Mary and Adam continously evaluate their work and so does the teacher. During the process, he pays attention to their ideas, and in the end he gives his unconditional praise of their work.

Chapter 4: Dialogue and learning

This chapter does not include new classroom observations. We discuss the IC-Model with a theoretical reference to the notion of dialogue. By doing so we try to characterise some qualities of communication which we find particularly important. These qualities, referred to by dialogue, we consider a resource for certain qualities of learning. This brings us in the direction of the notions of 'critical learning' and mathemacy.

Not any kind of communication can be characterised as a dialogue. In general terms, we describe a *dialogue* as an *inquiry process* which includes an exploration of participant perspectives as well as a willingness to suspend one's pre-understandings – at least for a moment. A dialogue is unpredictable, as it cannot include given answers to questions beforehand. Thus, it also includes *running risks*. Entering a dialogue cannot be forced upon anybody. In a classroom this means that the teacher can invite the students into an inquiring process, but students have to accept the invitation for the dialogue to take place. In a dialogue *equality* must be maintained. In these terms we try to clarify an idealised concept of dialogue.

Speech act theory emphasises that many different things can be done by means of language. Austin (1962) considers 'How to do things with words' while we consider 'How to do things with dialogue'. In our interpretation, a dialogue cannot consist of just any kind of speech acts, and for that reason we introduce the notion of *dialogic act*. Such an act involves making an inquiry, running a risk and maintaining equality. However, we find that a 'dialogic act' is not only a conceptual ideal. In particular, we find that the elements of the IC-Model – getting in contact, locating, identifying, advocating, thinking aloud, reformulating, challenging, and evaluating – all exemplify dialogic acts.

The idea presented in Chapter 1 that (some) learning can be seen as action, is now elaborated into the idea that (some) learning can be seen as dialogic action, constituted by dialogic acts as exemplified by the elements of the IC-Model. However, dialogic acts are fragile. As already indicated in Chapter 2, we can observe that such acts easily turn into other patterns of communication, which hardly can be labeled dialogic. The school mathematics tradition contains many rituals and 'contracts' which prevent dialogic acts from taking place. Consequently, dialogic based learning is difficult to realise.

Chapter 5: Intention and learning

In this, as well as in Chapter 6 and Chapter 7, we include new empirical studies. All situations are set in landscapes of investigation. We do so in order to clarify connections between 'dialogue' and 'critique'. By exploring these connections we try to relate qualities of communication with qualities of learning. Some connections between dialogue and critique will be expressed in terms of intention while others in terms of reflection. In this chapter we concentrate on the notion of intention.

It sometimes happens when the class is split up into groups that members of one of the groups do not engage themselves in the presented task, but occupy themselves with other kinds of activities. In many other situations as well, it is possible to observe a resistance towards learning. In the project, the 'Travel agency', the students' task is to plan for a holiday trip, considering possible destinations, prices, travel routes, etc. In this project we observe a *resistance group* in action. Their surprising, humorous, sexist, bizarre and self-ironic remarks establish provocative *zooming-outs*.

This observation brings us once more to consider *intention* as a basic underlying need for the dialogic acts included in the IC-Model. And, consequently, intention becomes a key-concept for the further development of the notion of learning.

We try to clarify the notion of intention by commenting on three aspects. We see *intentions-in-learning* as essential if the learner is to be involved in the process of learning. Intentions-in-learning are also essential if the students are to obtain ownership of the learning process. However, intentions connected with learning are far from the only set of intentions that the students may have. A student can have intentions about avoiding being noticed by the teacher, about sitting next to somebody, about joining the game in the next break, etc. Some *underground intentions* refer to the students' zooming-out of the official classroom activity. Such intentions also flourish in the classroom. More often underground intentions are not explicitly addressed in the classroom, but they can nevertheless guide the students' activities. The students may still be acting, but not necessarily any longer as well adjusted learners. They may act as a resistance group. The *resources of intentions* can be located in the students' background as well as their foreground, which we refer to as their dispositions. Dispositions make up raw material for establishing intentions. One of the ideas of inviting students into landscapes of investigation is to establish their resources for intention as part of the classroom activities. Making an inquiry presupposes involvement.

Chapter 6: Reflection and learning

In the project 'Caramel boxes' the students are going to plan a factory production of caramel boxes. As a beginning they have to construct two boxes, one twice as big as the other. We use this example as a reference for a further discussion of *reflection*. Students can reflect on the result of some calculations. They can be worried if the result seems to be wrong. Reflections may concern the reliability of the solution in a specific context. Reflections can concern a variety of issues. 'Caramel boxes' is full of such examples.

Reflection cannot be forced upon anybody. Instead it is an act carried out by the reflecting person. This emphasises the importance of investigating intentions and reflections together. This is what we suggested in Chapter 1 when we talked about learning as action, and in Chapter 5 we continued this discussion. In this Chapter 6 we try to clarify how reflection becomes the second concept by means of which we conceptualise links between dialogue and critique.

We try to clarify the notion of reflection by commenting on three of its aspects. The *scope of reflections* refers to what is addressed in a reflection. Thus, the scope of reflections can be narrow and address only particular aspects of a calculation. The scope can be broadened and include issues of reliability of a calculation. The *subject of reflections* refers to who might be doing the reflection. Naturally, this can be an individual person, but it is also possible to consider collective reflections, when the reflections are grounded in interaction. It is of particular importance to consider to what extent collectivity of reflections may expand the scope of reflections. The *context of reflections* can naturally not be ignored when we consider what is addressed in reflection. The school mathematics tradition makes one frame of reflection, and so does schooling in general. One function of entering a landscape of investigation is to change the context of reflections. And this change may help to broaden the scope of reflections.

Chapter 7: Critique and learning

Several sociological and political considerations highlight the relevance of reflections in order to counterbalance the blind development of (mathematically based) technology that accompanies a risk society where 'wonders' as well as 'horrors' are waiting in a bewildering mix. This more fundamental notion of reflection brings us to the notion of *critique*. Is it possible for mathematics education to support a critical learning of mathematics where the students are involved and where the reliability of mathematics is not taken for granted but raised as a question? Facing the *challenge of critique* means trying to struggle with this question.

The project, 'Terrible small numbers', concentrates on a discussion which often accompanies the introduction of new technologies. Terrible small numbers can be used in support of a claim that, say, an atomic power plan is 'hardly dangerous at all'. The calculated probability that an accident may occur in a particular year can be estimated to be p, a number, whose difference from zero appears so small that it can be claimed not worth considering. This project concentrates on the phenomenon of salmonella. The project takes place in a 9th grade with 15-16-year-old students. It involves experiments with samples and probabilities.

The intention is to illuminate two different issues related to the use of mathematics. *Reliability* refers to questions like: If we have to investigate a certain population, how reliable is it then to investigate just a sample? In what sense can a sample tell 'the truth' about the whole population? Naturally, the discussion of reliability need not just consider the reliability of conclusions drawn from investigations of a sample. It can concern the reliability of any statistical information or, generally, any information put in numbers. In this sense, reliability opens a fundamental discussion about 'trust in numbers'.

Responsibility refers to actions and decisions based on mathematical calculations: How are we supposed to act in a situation where we only have a limited knowledge of the risks involved? What does responsibility mean in such a situation? We cannot imagine any of the basic structures of today's society functioning without mathematics being an integral part. For that reason it becomes a fundamental aspect of modern society that actions are decided upon by reference to numbers. What does responsibility include in this case?

With reference to the example, we reconsider the basic conceptual relationships, which we have explored. The fundamental notions throughout our study are *dialogue, intention, reflection* and *critique*, and they are closely interconnected. Dialogue represents a collective action, exemplified by dialogic acts. These collective acts (this inter-action) is a ressource for critique and for critical learning. The two main links between dialogue and critique are constituted by intentions and reflections. Both dialogue and critique is carried out by somebody, so intentions are involved. And something is addressed in a dialogue and by a critique, so reflections are involved as well.

By providing this clarification of the relationships between the notions dialogue, intention, reflection and critique, we have tried to provide more substantial meaning to the formulations of our initial guiding idea: The qualities of communication in the classroom influence the qualities of learning mathematics. We have emphasised certain qualities of communication in terms of dialogue, and in particular of dialogic acts and the inquiry co-operation model. And we have emphasised qualities of learning mathematics in terms of critique, and the connection between dialogue and critique we have tried to clarify in terms of intention and reflection. This brings us to the notion of *mathemacy*, which we see as a competence 'parallel' to literacy as presented by Freire. In this way we argue that a dialogue-based learning of mathematics may lead to a critical learning of mathematics.

Chapter 8: Critical epistemology and the learning of mathematics

In this chapter, we relate our discussion of learning mathematics and of learning in general to other interpretations of learning. Although our examples make reference to mathematics, our interpretation of learning might be broader than just learning mathematics. We try to clarify where in the epistemological landscape our journey, via examples and conceptual clarifications, has taken us to.

We characterise one group of learning theories as *mono-logic*. By this notion we refer to theories where learning is conceptualised as an individual undertaking. Jean Piaget's genetic epistemology is mono-logic, and similarly radical constructivism (in its original radical formulation) concentrates on the 'lonely learner'. The emergence of these mono-logic learning theories are inspired by relating learning to natural and biological growth, and Piaget aimed at explaining steps in learning which could be compared to other natural processes of growth. Contradicting the mono-logic paradigm, we find the *dia-logic* paradigm, where learning is considered first of all in terms of interaction. We see

the inspiration from Lev Vygotsky as supporting a dia-logic epistemology.

Although contrasting each other, the Piagetian and the Vygotskian
paradigm also maintain a basic similarity. Both paradigms accept the
basic assumption of modernity, i.e. that the development of science and
of scientific concepts takes place in harmony with social, political,
cultural and personal progress in general. John Dewey is a strong
proponent of this assumption, as he explicitly claims that scientific
methodology provides the best possible guideline for learning for
democracy. As a consequence, the main aim of education is to provide
access to scientific thinking – maybe by careful scaffolding, maybe by
supporting the child in his or her zone of proximal development.
Concentrating on simply providing access to scientific thinking defines a
non-critical aspect of an epistemology, and both Dewey- , Piaget- as well
as Vygotsky-inspired learning theories contain such aspects.

We do not rely on the Dewey-assumption, and consequently it
becomes important to develop a theory of learning (and of learning
mathematics) which in particular faces the challenge of critique. The
challenge is provoked by the idea that mathematical thinking and science
in general are not only a resource for critique, but also a form of thinking
that should be addressed by a critique. This means that mathematics is
not only an object for learning, but also an object for critique. A *critical*
theory of learning mathematics tries to illuminate how critique and
learning mathematics can be connected and how the competence of
mathemacy can be supported.

CHAPTER 1

COMMUNICATION IN THE MATHEMATICS CLASSROOM

The purpose of teaching mathematics is to point out mistakes and correct them! This seems to be a common understanding of mathematics education among many students.[12] We have even seen examples of pre-school children expressing the same view in a role play about teaching mathematics.[13] One child was playing the role of the teacher the rest were 'students'. One 'student' was supposed to do an exercise on the blackboard and wrote some serious-looking symbols in a long row. Afterwards, the 'teacher' erased a couple of those symbols and wrote some others while accusing the 'student' of being mistaken. Thus, even before having any school experiences of their own and without having an understanding of what symbols might mean, the children showed an understanding of mistakes and of the correction of mistakes as being a central parameter in mathematics education.

One reason why the notion of 'mistakes' seems so important in mathematics education can be related to the search for 'truth' in mathematics. A main task of a philosophy of mathematics has been to give an adequate explanation of 'truth'. Absolutism in epistemology is associated with the idea that the individual has the possibility to acquire absolute truth. This idea connects with the Euclidean ideal in epistemology. Relativism, though, maintains that truth is always located by someone in a certain context at a certain time. Thus, truth cannot be grasped in absolute terms. With mathematics in mind, relativism has been put forward by both radical and social constructivism.[14]

---

[12] Alrø and Lindenskov (1994). This chapter is a rewriting of Alrø and Skovsmose (1996a, 1998).

[13] See Fosse (1996).

[14] See, for instance, Glasersfeld (1995) and Ernest (1998a).

Somehow the philosophic discussion of mathematical truths, becomes reflected in a discussion of mistakes in the mathematics classroom.[15] Like the concept of 'truth', the concept of 'mistake' has two extremes – one absolutist and one relativistic. The absolutist interpretation apparently has a sound basis. For instance, to think that 12 multiplied by 13 equals 155 seems a simple mistake. But the situation looks somewhat different if we come to the applications of mathematics. If we measure one side of a play ground to be (about) 12 m and the other side to be (about) 13 m, its area may well be 155 m^2 – the ground looks rectangular. Relativism may have a bearing when the application of mathematics is considered. Nevertheless, it often seems possible to make absolute mistakes when applications of mathematics are presented in mathematics textbooks. (We will return to this point in the section 'From exercises to landscapes of investigation' in Chapter 2.)

In the first section of this chapter we discuss mistakes and correcting of mistakes on the basis of classroom observations.[16] We suggest the notion of bureaucratic absolutism to characterise the type of learning environment, where mistakes are handled in absolute terms. Mistakes are simply *mistakes* and have to be elimininated. This learning environment corresponds very well with the communication pattern: Guess What the Teacher Thinks.[17] Further, referring to a non-bureaucratic classroom, we introduce the notion of perspective in order to describe student understandings and pre-understandings as resources for learning. Here the

---

[15] Normally the (theoretical) discussion of mistakes in the mathematics classroom has concentrated on the mistakes of the students. We could as well look at teacher mistakes, teacher ways of interpreting own mistakes, student ways of interpreting teacher mistakes, teacher ways of hiding mistakes, etc. The study of mistakes can take a variety of directions. Nevertheless, we shall follow the mainstream and concentrate on student mistakes, and teacher ways of interpreting and correcting these.

[16] The observed mathematics lessons we refer to in Chapter 1 and Chapter 2 were part of the normal teaching programme. Many analyses of traditional mathematics classrooms have from different theoretical perspectives pointed to the fact that communication plays an important role for the dynamics of the classroom. We are especially inspired by the microethnografic approach of the German group of symbolic interactionists and their studies of routines, relationships and patterns of communication that can be found in the traditional mathematics classroom, e.g. Bauersfeld (1980, 1988, 1995); Krummheuer (1983, 1995, 2000b) and Voigt (1984, 1985, 1989).

Other important contributions to this field of analysis are Cestari (1997); Cobb and Bauersfeld (eds.) (1995); Jungwirth, H. (1991); Lemke (1990); Pimm (1987); Sfard (2000) and Steinbring (1998, 2000). For a discussion of the culture of the mathematics classroom, see also Brown (2001); Lerman (ed.) (1994); Nickson (1992); Seeger, Voigt and Waschescio (eds.) (1998) and Wood (1994).

[17] The term 'Guess What the Teacher Thinks' is used by Young (1992, 106f.).

students' guessing can be understood as their zooming-in on the class-room agenda. Finally, we discuss learning in terms of action, including the crucial notion of intention.

MISTAKES AND CORRECTIONS

As 'truth' is a key term in the philosophy of mathematics, so are 'mistakes' a key to grasp an implicit philosophy prevailing in many mathematics classrooms. Correction of mistakes opens a backdoor to the classroom philosophy of mathematics.

Philosophical absolutism maintains that some absolute truth can be obtained by the individual. Classroom absolutism comes about when (students') mistakes are treated as absolute: 'This is wrong!' 'You have to correct these calculations!' Thus, classroom absolutism seems to main-tain that mistakes are absolute and can be eliminated by the teacher. Our point is not, however, that no mistakes in the mathematics classroom should be stated as real mistakes. We do not want to maintain an absolute relativism. But it seems like absolutism in the philosophy of mathematics automatically leads to absolutism in pedagogy that justifies certain forms of classroom interaction.

We can conceive of different types of mistakes found in mathematics education. In what follows we talk about 'mistakes' in the broadest way to include 'real' mistakes, other sorts of (mis)conceptions, as well as simply alternative conceptions. The mistake could concern the output of some algorithm: 'This calculation is wrong!' The mistake could concern the used algorithm: 'You should not add these numbers but do a subtrac-tion!' The mistake could concern the sequence in which things are done: 'When drawing a graph you first have to calculate some values of the function!' The mistake could have to do with the way the text is inter-preted: 'No, when the exercise is formulated like this, you first have to find the value of x!' Or it could have to do with the organisation of the tasks for the students: 'No, no, those exercises are for tomorrow!'

Although the content of these mistakes is quite different, the correc-tions can be expressed in the same absolute terms. The basic assumption is that the aim of a correction is to correct a mistake. The phenomenon that all sorts of mistakes are treated as absolute, i.e. as real mistakes, we refer to as classroom absolutism.

In our observations of traditional mathematics classrooms[18] we find many examples of explicit corrections. We shall try to illustrate the nature of these mistakes by a few examples of teacher statements:

(1)   Teacher: This is wrong, you have to calculate once again.

(2)   Teacher: There is a tiny mistake in both of them.

In (1) the teacher rejects the result and tells the student to try once again. Example (2) differs in form although it certainly is an explicit correction. The correction is modified by the word 'tiny', which indicates that the student might be on the right track or that the teacher wants to encourage the student to continue without caring too much about the mistake. In neither of the situations in which these teacher statements occur, though, does the teacher argue how the student is mistaken, he just states it. Neither is there any advice or information about what the student is expected to do.

Implicit corrections can take several forms, e.g.:

(3)   Teacher: You have to erase those numbers… you are not going to
                 use them at all.

The teacher does not tell the student directly that he has made a mistake, but as one only erases something that is incorrect or insufficient, the student can easily understand the utterance as a correction of a mistake. But still the teacher does not say anything about what kind of mistake the student has made or how it should be corrected.

(4)   Teacher: Ellen, what was it, how much is 3/4 plus 3/4
      Ellen: 6/8. [4 sec.]
      Teacher: Don't you remember, I took these [pieces from a fraction
                 game] this 3/4 and this 3/4, and that equals 6, and what
                 are they still…? [5 sec.]
      Ellen: Mmm… 3/4.

In this example the correction is made implicitly with a certain questioning strategy by which the teacher tries to make Ellen guess the answer.

---

[18]   Young (1992, 86f.) uses the term 'the method classroom' to describe a strongly teacher ruled classroom communication. More generally we can refer to the 'school mathematics tradition'. See, for instance, Cobb and Bauersfeld (eds.) (1995); Cobb and Yackel (1998) and Richards (1991).

Concerning the content of the correction, our observations show that the teacher focuses either on the algorithmic procedure or on the result of the students' investigations.

(5)   Teacher: Your numbers could be right, if you handle them right.

The teacher tells the student that he is wrong, by telling him that he "could be right, if...". What he is wrong about is the algorithmic procedure: "if you handle them right." The mistake concerns a wrong algorithm or a wrong use of the algorithm.

(6)   Teacher: The last two numbers are wrong, Jeanett, you must try to correct them.

In (6) the mistake pointed out by the teacher obviously concerns the result of the student's work.

Corrections refer, explicitly or implicitly, to an authority. It could be the teacher, the textbook, or the answer book.

(7)   Teacher: I would rather have you drawing a line than putting a cross up in the air. [to show which numbers he has already used in the calculation]
      Tim: This is just as easy.
      Teacher: It isn't always just a question of easiness.

(8)   Teacher: The first condition for calculating correctly is that you put it down correctly.

(9)   Teacher: If they made the exercise, they are the ones to decide whether it is right, aren't they?

In (7) the teacher wants a different marking of the numbers used by the student in an exercise. The student writes his proposal on the blackboard. He argues that his marking method is quite as easy, which is indirectly rejected by the teacher. But the teacher does not argue why drawing a line should be a better or more correct way of marking than putting a cross above the numbers. The teacher can represent the authority.

In (8) the teacher's correction indirectly refers to the textbook: "that you have put it down correctly," i.e. that you have written exactly what is prescribed by the textbook. The argument is naturally that it is a mistake not to solve exactly the exercise spelled out in the textbook. The textbook becomes the authority.

In (9) the student's result is compared to the answer book, which states a different result. The teacher argues that the answer book must be correct, because the authors of the exercise are the ones to decide whether the result is right or wrong. This might be right, but it might not necessarily help the student to an understanding of the problem and the way of solving it.

BUREAUCRATIC ABSOLUTISM

The corrections we have put forward in the examples above illustrate absolutism in the classroom. The teacher, the textbook, and the answer book make up a unified authority, which hides the nature of the sources of the correction. The students are not met with argumentation but with reference to a seemingly uniform and consistent authority, even though the sources of corrections might be very different. Some rest upon mathematical features, some upon practical matters of organising the educational process, etc. Nevertheless, all mistakes are treated as absolute; they are pointed out by the teacher with no explanation or argumentation as to what should be done differently or why. Furthermore, the generality of the corrections seems never to be questioned. This is caused by the fact that the correction is not contextualised but stated in general terms, not referring to the context of the problem solving process.

A student facing the classroom authorities may have a similar experience as a client, facing bureaucracy. For instance, the bureaucracy might have different reasons for refusing an application: The client may not really need the favour; the application may be handed in too late; some information is missing; there is no money left, etc. These reasons for refusing the application can be quite different. But when the client faces such bureaucracy, the denial of the application turns out to be of the same 'logical form' whatever reason the bureaucracy might have: the application is refused. Good reasons or bad reasons, moral reasons, administrative reasons, logical reasons and other reasons – all appear in the same way. Either things fit into the schemes of the bureaucracy or not.

Students meet the same phenomenon in some mathematics classrooms. For that reason we characterise classroom absolutism as a *bureaucratic absolutism* that appears to draw on unlimited resources for stating in absolute terms what is right and what is wrong. And this absolutism does not explicate reasons for this distinction. Furthermore, bureaucratic absolutism is characterised by the difficulty of getting in contact with the 'real' authority: 'We cannot do anything about this, it is outside our reach. Sorry about this.' Things are as they are according to rules and standards: It is not possible for the person behind the desk to alter things. The client could quarrel, but it is not possible to change things all the same. Similarly, the absolutist mathematics teacher is not supposed to change the fact that students have to deal with a certain kind of exercises, and that the formulae they have to use are those put on the top of the page. Bureaucratic absolutism faces students in many mathematics classrooms.[19]

We also find that even if teachers show great sympathy to alternative forms of teaching they may have difficulties in practising their own ideas, because bureaucratic absolutism has taken hold of them as it fits the school organisation. It is built into basic structures of communication in the classroom. This puts teachers in a paradoxical situation. On the one hand they might want to educate students to be open and critical, and on the other hand they feel that they have to follow a textbook to lead the students into the best possible situation to cope with the described questions. In many situations teachers experience a strong obligation to prepare students for tests and exams that are based on bureaucratic absolutism.

Normally classroom communication is characterised by an asymmetrical relationship between teacher and students. As Michael Stubbs (1976, 99) puts it: "Anything the pupil says is sandwiched in anything the teacher says."[20] The teacher asks a question, the student answers, and the teacher evaluates the answer:

Teacher: How much is 3/4 + 3/4?
Student: 1 1/2.
Teacher: Very good.

Not every sandwich is as simple as this one, but the student would often answer with one single word filling out the teacher's monologue.[21] The

---

[19] Lemke (1990, 137) describes this phenomenon as an "ideology of objective truth" that radiates "an aura of total objectivity". Other studies also reveal the existence of bureaucratic absolutism, see for instance Naidoo (1999) for her study of some South African mathematics classrooms. This absolutism appears as a cross-cultural characteristic of mathematics education.

[20] The aspect of control shows itself in the so-called I-R-F structure (Initiation - Response - Feed-back) of the classroom communication (Sinclair and Coulthard, 1975). Lemke (1990) calls this pattern of communication the 'triadic dialogue'.

[21] See Pimm's (1987, 52 f.) 'cloze'-procedure. Bauersfeld (1988, 36) analyses a certain kind of dialogue, which he calls the 'funnel pattern'. The teacher's way of asking questions is narrowing the answering possibilities. The student cannot guess what the

'sandwich' is a pattern of communication that emphasises the existence of an authority in the mathematics classroom, and it can be seen as the interactional manifestation of classroom absolutism.

The teacher knows the answers to his questions beforehand, and the students are supposed to guess what the teacher has in mind. This procedure gets repeated; thus, a right answer gives rise to a series of new teacher questions. The teacher knows the direction of his or her questions, but the students might get a rather fragmented experience, because they do not have an idea of the whole purpose. They have to make a great effort to follow the teacher in order to gain that. Thus, guessing their way through implies the possibility that the students will concentrate on guessing rather than on the mathematical content of the subject.

In previous studies we have seen, how student responses to the teachers' quizzing communication are most often limited to minimal responses.[22] Some of them are:

- questioning answer: 'Is it 4?'
- immediate refusal of own answer: 'Is it 4? No.'
- denying to know an answer: 'I've never heard about that!'
- asking for help: 'Would you please explain it to me again?'
- arbitrary guesses: '4, no 5, oh no 8!'
- echo-answering: 'I've got the same result as Peter!'
- silence!
- being occupied with other things.

In other words, the students take a minimal responsibility for their learning process. However, we have also observed the opposite student behaviour, namely that they insist on following the teacher track. We will return to that point.

PERSPECTIVE

Bureaucratic absolutism is not a feature of every situation that we have observed within the school mathematics tradition. There are other patterns of communication. The essential point is, however, that it is not

---

teacher is aiming at, and he does not reply at all or only by one-word sentences. In the end the teacher is most likely to answer the question by himself. This form of communication signals also that every mathematical question has one right answer, which has to be stated.

[22] See for instance Lemke (1990) and Alrø (1995, 1996).

possible to change communication simply by some sort of educational decision. The possibility of taking this step depends on a change in the educational situation and a change of perspective. We are going to use the notion of perspective in the presentation of other notions, so let us here make some clarification of 'perspective'.

A perspective is normally not presented by an explanation. It is part of the background for communication. Normally, nobody finds it necessary to communicate a perspective explicitly. In fact it is not obvious how one should do this. Where to begin? A perspective often belongs to the tacit dimension of communication, but it is from this background that statements find their meanings. A perspective is a source of meanings. Without a perspective no communicative act will take place. The perspective is decisive of the things one chooses to see, to hear, and to understand in a conversation, and it manifests itself through our use of language, in the things we choose to talk about and not to talk about, and in the way we understand each other.

The purpose of a conversation can be to explain one's perspective, to understand the perspective of the other person and perhaps to agree upon a shared perspective or upon the fact that you have different perspectives on which you want to insist. For example the students and the teacher could share the perspective that the whole educational task is to come to master some techniques and to be able to pass an examination. Teacher and students could also have different perspectives, like for instance if the students focus on the result of an exercise, while the teacher wants them to explain the algorithm.

A shared perspective can be established even in case nothing much has been said. Nevertheless, the perspective becomes, so to say, the factory for the production of meaning. The converse may also be the case: Even if everything seems to be stated explicitly, it may be difficult to communicate if the communicators cannot understand or accept each other's perspectives or if no perspective is shared. In this case, the wheels of the factories of meaning production run for no use.[23]

It is a common situation that one perspective dominates another. When the teacher points out mistakes he or she maintains a perspective which the students are supposed to accept to the extent that they try to avoid new mistakes. To ask for a correction of mistakes is a normal way of maintaining this perspective. Corrections mould a perspective. Correc-

---

[23] The notion of 'meaning production' has been developed by Lins (2001). We use the expression, although without trying to implement Lins' elaborated interpretation of the notion.

tion of mistakes, then, maintains the existence of an authorised perspective, which it seems impossible to discuss. The existence of an authorised perspective, although not public, provides an authorised source for meaning production in the absolutist classroom.

A first step in trying to overcome bureaucratic absolutism is the teacher and the students coming to locate and examine their perspectives. Although formulated as simple advice, examination of perspectives and meaning is not a simple activity.[24] These activities will be met by an obstruction from 'the logic of schooling', which is part of the tacit dimension that sets the agenda for much classroom discourse. And, as indicated, one of the obstacles in overcoming bureaucratic absolutism is the students' already established implicit philosophy of school mathematics, which says that the correction of mistakes is an essential teacher task in the mathematics classroom. It is not a simple educational task for a teacher to create a 'climate of inquiry'. To change bureaucratic absolutism does not simply presuppose a change in the teacher attitude. This absolutism is not only rooted in an attitude but in the whole logic of schooling.

In the following example, we see how the students try to get hold of the points of the educational process. They want to be part of the process and to adjust their perspectives to the teacher intentions. We observe a situation where the logic of schooling is challenged, because the situation in the classroom is open. This makes it possible to observe students in new roles as well as other patterns of communication. The students do not follow any minimal-response strategy. They become active.

'HOW MUCH DOES A NEWSPAPER FILL?'

Our teaching example starts with the following question: 'How much does a newspaper fill?' [25] The textbook *MATEMA*[26], from which the topic

---

[24] 'Negotiation of meaning' is a related term that is used by Voigt (1994).

[25] The sequence we are going to present makes part of an observation material made by a teacher team in Randers Kommune in Denmark. It consists of three video tapes containing observations from a 3rd and a 7th grade. Bjarne Würtz Andersen and Ane Marie Krogshede Nielsen are the teachers and Jan Boserup has taped and edited the video in cooperation with Ib Trankjær who has also coordinated the project. We were not present at the lesson we describe. The lessons were videotaped as part of a project of making examples from classroom practice available to the public. It was not the idea to produce 'perfect' lessons, but to provide material which makes is possible for outsiders to discuss what takes place in the classroom: students, teachers, colleagues,

has been taken, is marked by a process-oriented idea, which involves the students developing mathematics through a working process rather than through instruction. *MATEMA* seeks to create opportunities for teacher and students to enter a mathematical educational interaction. One way of doing this is to create a situation that on the one hand is determined by certain structures and premises, but on the other hand partly leaves the generating of concepts to the students.

MATEMA does not declare any overall mathematical intention with the unit 'How much does a newspaper fill?' All that appears from the teacher's manual is that the topic contains 'lots of mathematics'. It is suggested that work can be done with items such as weight, height and breadth, but also with the comparison of different newspapers with respect to content and size. The textbook thus leaves it to the teacher to choose an angle. The students' book for *MATEMA* launches the question, 'How much does a newspaper fill?' Judging from pictures of laid out newspapers and matrices for marking the height and breadth of newspapers, it is reasonable for the teacher to assume that the topic is meant to throw light on the concept of 'area'.

The concept of 'filling', however, is not precise: 'You fill too much on that chair', 'It fills my consciousness', 'The pie fills my stomach', 'The picture fills most of the wall', 'The tabloids fill people with gossip', 'Reading the newspaper fills all of my mother's morning'. Nevertheless, it is a clear educational idea to initiate mathematical activities with such an open concept. 'Fill' is a many-valued term in the question, 'How much does a newspaper fill?' It could refer to time, volume or area. 'Fill' demands specification.

First lesson on Monday morning

The teacher enters the 3rd form. He carries a plastic bag and has a smiling, although perhaps a somewhat stiff smile on his face as he looks at the class. He has some difficulty gaining the attention of the students, which is focused on the cameraman. This is the first lesson videotaped.

---

parents as well as researchers. We have had the opportunity to discuss details of the video and our analysis with the persons involved.

[26] *MATEMA* is a textbook series from the 1st to the 10th form, prepared and edited by Peter Bollerslev, Vagn Harbo, Viggo Hartz, Peter Olesen, Leif Ørsted Petersen and Ib Trankjær. *MATEMA* can be seen as a Danish interpretation of some of the intentions which, on the international scene, have been promoted by Hans Freudenthal's activity perspective on mathematics education.

The light in the room has been measured several times, and as everything seems to be working the lesson can start.

The situation takes place in a classroom that can be characterised by many positive terms. Teacher and students have a friendly relationship. The students have a great confidence in the teacher. They seem interested in mathematics and, generally, they are active. In this energetic atmosphere we meet the teacher and the students when the teacher introduces a new topic.

At first it is unclear to the students what it is all about. Naturally it is not easy for the teacher to clarify the situation with a direct statement of the whole idea, i.e. that 'it is about 'area' and 'volume', but that is something we will have to find out as we go along'. Furthermore, the question 'How much does a newspaper fill?' is not integrated in a situation that provides a context for answering the question. The unit has no frame of reference available for the students. Consequently they have to follow the lead of the teacher. They have to find an answer to how much newspapers fill without understanding why they need such an answer.

It is possible to talk about vantage points, which are established through the teacher setting a scene. Vantage points represent possible perspectives on classroom activities. A vantage point provides an overview of the task and indicates some meaning to the task. (Naturally, the meaning indicated by the vantage point need not be found relevant by the students.)[27] A vantage point may clarify an overall idea, such as e.g. 'collecting newspapers': How many newspapers is it possible to collect during an afternoon? Has anybody been involved in collecting newspapers? (A common source of income for scouts in Denmark.) A scene setting may define a number of tasks, and if these make sense to the students so they can discuss and describe them, vantage points are established. In this sense setting the scene for vantage points can give content to a discussion about the meaning of the proposed activities. Vantage points may help to illuminate certain perspectives or to open new perspectives.

However, certain ways of setting the scene does not 'justify' activities in the classroom. But by presenting a perspective on the mathematical content, students get the possibility to associate new meaning to the related activities – acceptable or not. From the vantage point students and teacher can prepare for the direction of the teaching-learning process.

---

[27]   See Skovsmose (1994) for a discussion of 'vantage point' and 'scene-setting'.

Openness from the start

One overall purpose (for the textbook and the teacher) with 'How much does a newspaper fill?' is that the students learn something about 'area', but how does the teacher lead the students on the track:

Teacher:	Now, the topic we are going to work on this week is right here in this bag. [putting a pile of newspapers on the desk] What do you say to this?
Several students:	Are we going to read?
Teacher:	Are we going to read? …What?
Peter:	No, we are going to play. Yes, play.[28]

The teacher starts by introducing the newspaper as the topic the class is going to work with. The students are not quite sure where the teacher is heading with his question "What do you say to this?" Are they going to read... or to play? This can of course also be understood as joking comments, since the students know well enough that first lesson Monday morning says mathematics. The teacher maintains his openness about the subject by asking whether the students have newspapers in their homes, and if so which newspaper, and what is the difference between a newspaper and a local commercial paper, and if any of the students can spell the word 'commercial'. In this indirect way the teacher reaches the question: 'How much does a newspaper fill?'

Teacher:	Newspapers like these, do they fill much? Do they *fill* much?
Sally:	[Shaking her head.]
Teacher:	They do. They fill an awful lot, look here. Look here, how thick it is. If you have papers from, say, a fortnight, you would have a pile like this all of a sudden. [measures with his hands] I have a basket at home, you know, where I put my papers. A basket… that looks something like this. [illustrates a box with his hands] Then I put my papers in that when I have read them, and sometimes I take them up if I want to read them again. Then they sit like this. [makes a downward

---

[28] In order to understand the transcript it is necessary to add some information about the indexicality of the spoken dialogue, i.e. a description of, for instance, the paralanguage, the bodylanguage, and the deixis of persons, time and place, all of which the teacher and students use and understand quite well in the shared context of communication, but which we as analysts and readers of communication have to interpret in order to reformulate the meaning of the words outside the original context. The English transcript is a translation from Danish, which is naturally an important source of inaccuracies.

movement with a newspaper] Then all of a sudden it is quite full, and it *pours* out with papers, and then I get annoyed with them. Then all of a sudden I just take them and collect them in a pile, and then I take them down to the bin, you know. They *fill* a lot, newspapers. [...] We are going to try to measure newspapers. We will measure them in various ways. I have three different papers for you. I have the county paper and I had... have this one called 'Politiken', and then another one called 'Aktuelt', it looks like this. It looks a little different from the other two, as you can see. Now look at it, you can see there is a difference, can't you?

Tim: It is smaller. [about 'Aktuelt']

Teacher: Yes, it is smaller. Yet maybe there is no less in it.

Tim: Right.

Teacher: It may be that there is as much text in it, it depends on the number of pictures. By the way, you can see the weather forecast here on the back. Can you see? You are going to measure in the groups you are in at the moment...

If you take his words on face value, it appears as if 'to fill' is to be related to something about volume: The papers are filled into a basket or a bin. The students are told that they are going to measure, but what are they really going to measure: How many papers a bin can hold? Which paper is the thickest? Or is it only the weather forecast that is going to be measured? "By the way, you can see the weather forecast here on the back. Can you see? You are going to measure in the groups you are in at the moment..." The message appears obscure, and the students seem to be confused.

Why do the students not react? Most likely because they already know that if they follow the teacher all will be well. Thus, it is a matter of finding out where he is going. And when you are not told by asking, then you have to make guesses. Through this the students express an intention of taking part in the classroom activities. They are searching for the teacher perspective. Another possibility is that the students know the teacher and his way of communicating so well that they are able to make an understanding of a message that to outsiders looks absurd.

The openness could mean that the students could lose their interest in taking part in the class altogether. That they could stop trying to make sense of the teaching and just follow the instructions that seem unavoidable. When the students persist with their attempts to define a purpose it can thus be interpreted as a vote of confidence for the teacher. The students stay as partners in the process of finding a perspective. They are keen to make sense of what is going to happen. The scene setting established by bringing newspapers to the classroom has not been successful in the sense that no helpful vantage points have been constructed. But the students continue to search for the meaning of the suggested activities.

Guessing what the teacher has in mind

Some students have a formidable faculty for guessing what the teacher is getting at and an elegant way of appropriating his thoughts. That does not mean, however, that any learning is going on.[29] Rather it may be a technique that the student has learned to be able to get on in class.

The guessing pattern we are going to study from 'How much does a newspaper fill?' is of a different kind, because the students are trying to work themselves into the teaching topic. Their interest does not appear instrumental, but rather directed towards content.

Teacher:	There are two things you have to measure at any rate. That is: how much does a newspaper fill, and then you have to [ic][30] then you have to find out which paper fills most. And how do we get about finding out how much a newspaper fills? How much does a newspaper fill? And then you can try and study the picture of the student there, who is measuring... you know that student there. [pointing at the overhead showing a picture from the textbook] is measuring how much the newpaper fills. And what does the student do... Camilla?
Camilla:	She opens it.
Teacher:	She opens it. Because what does it mean to fill? What does it mean to fill? That a newspaper fills something – what does that mean? What does it mean, what does a newspaper fill? What... what... what? [John raises his hand]
John:	It can fill a room.
Teacher:	How?
John:	If you... [teacher interrupts]
Teacher:	What do you have to do then?
John:	If you take a lot of newspapers.
Teacher:	Yes, if you... well, you are only allowed to use one.
John:	Then you can spread it out.
Teacher:	You can spread it out. You can take the pages apart and spread them out and then find out how much it fills.
John:	Yeah...

---

29 See Voigt (1984, 232).

30 [ic] means 'incomprehensible talk'.

Teacher:	But can't it… can a newspaper not fill in other ways? [John is looking away]
Laura:	You can weigh it.
Teacher:	That's true, but that's something different. That has not got to do with filling, has it? That is different, that will appear later on this. [pointing at the overhead] But first you have to find out: Which newspaper fills the most? And you have to use these three for that. Which one fills the most?

John's idea that newspapers "can fill a room" seems straightforward – it can be understood as analogous to filling a basket or a bin which was also the perspective introduced by the teacher from the very beginning. The suggestion is both logical and viable, but it is not what the teacher was getting at now, so John makes another guess: "Then you can spread it out." This time he hits the target, but apparently he loses all confidence when the teacher asks if a "newspaper can fill in other ways". After all, this is what John just suggested and the teacher had turned down. He pulls out and Laura suggests that you could weigh newspapers to find out how much they fill. But again the teacher turns the student down by noting that weighing is different, and that it is not on the agenda till later.

We will never know where John was going with his idea: "It can fill a room." Was he approaching a suggestion about measuring the volume of a bunch of newspapers? If this is the case, then John's suggestion could be an accurate step in clarifying the concept of 'filling'. Only if it is pre-supposed that 'filling' is to be interpreted in terms of area, John's idea can be turned down along with Laura's about weighing newspapers. But the rejection means that the educational idea of introducing the open concept of 'filling' gets partly lost.

The communication indicates that the teacher has one perspective or one intention that he pursues, while the students have to guess their way. This results in two different ways of communicating. The teacher has already prepared the topic and has a certain understanding that he wants to realise. The students are only trying to clarify what the unit is all about. Thus the directed communication of the teacher is confronted with the circularly searching communication of the students.

The ambiguity of 'to fill' is productive if seen as an opportunity to make the students clarify concepts (do we have 'area' or 'volume' in mind?). It is an important insight to reach that you must have common concepts to be able to talk consistently about how much newspapers fill. However, the significance of this clarification is lost as the effort to find out how much newspapers fill is replaced by an attempt to find out how much they weigh. Neither in the workbook nor in the discussion in class is it revealed what could be the purpose of comparing the weight of the newspaper with what it fills.

Realising that the student might have something different in mind

The newspaper is put on one of the scales of a balance, and the teacher points at the other scale.

Teacher:	What do we need in this one over here, Michael?
Michael:	Another newspaper.
Teacher:	[Promptly] No! [3 sec.] Well it would be possible. We will do that then… There Michael, I did that now, then. And what did I find out by doing that, Michael?…
Michael:	That it was heavier.
Teacher:	That is right. It is possible to do what Michael suggests. That can make us find out which one is heavier… 'Politiken' is heavier than 'Aktuelt'… The two newspapers there do not weigh the same.

Apparently, the teacher has a clear answer to his question about what to put in the scale, so he promptly rejects Michael's proposal of "another newspaper". After a short hesitation he seems to realise that the student might have something different in mind, then he corrects himself: "Well it would be possible." In this situation the teacher changes the direction of his questioning. He follows the student perspective and co-operates in the examination of the comparison of weight. Furthermore, he points explicitly to the student perspective when concluding: "It is possible to do what Michael suggests." The perspective of comparison, however, is not what the teacher had in mind, so he continues:

Teacher:	But what can we also find out, if we put something different in that thing there, John? [Pointing at the scale.]
John:	Put a weight in it.
Teacher:	We can put a weight in it. Here they are, both in plastic and brass. What can we find out then, John?
John:	Then if we know how much they [the weights] weigh, then we can find out what they [the newspapers] weigh.
Teacher:	What can I find out? What am I finding out now, John? [Puts a weight in the bucket, which tips.]
John:	Now you are finding out that the weight is too heavy.
Teacher:	Right, I maybe need to take off some weight, but now I will find out how much the newspaper weighs, and the figure… now I get a figure… and I can write down that this newspaper here weighs for instance 100 g.

John guesses the right answer, i.e. that newspapers can be weighed on the scale by means of weights. But the teacher also wants John to say what the teacher will find out by that. That John knows this strategy can be seen from his way of phrasing his answer: "Now you are finding out that…" but still he does not quite hit the target by focusing on the weight itself. The teacher wants to say something about the weight of the newspaper, but in principle they are talking about the same thing – only from different perspectives. The result is that teacher and student do not meet in their communication. The meaning of the different approaches (weighing the newspaper versus considering the heaviness of the weight) is not verbalised, and no mutual understanding is established on the basis of the different perspectives of the two parties. However, the interpretation of 'to fill' in terms of volume and weight is now abandoned. From now on 'to fill' becomes approached in terms of 'area'.

Which unit to use?

After the introduction in the classroom the students are now to go into groups and start measuring. One group (Camilla, Malene and Thomas) is working in the corridor, measuring how much newspapers fill when they are spread out. This is where a problem of finding a unit of measurement arises. The teacher arrives next to the group:

> Teacher: …well you see, what fills is what you can walk upon, touch… But are there other ways? You can also measure how much they fill with a metre rule, that would be a possibility. You decide how you want to tell the others how much this newspaper fills when it is spread out.

The exercise consists of two things – first to find a unit of measurement: "you decide," and secondly to measure the newspapers: "how much this newspaper fills when it is spread out." The teacher does not reveal how or with what purpose they are to measure the newspapers, but suggests that the students can use a metre rule. However, the group decides to count the pages of the newspaper, first (in consultation with the teacher) having turned down measuring in steps as an unreliable way of measuring. But then another problem arises. The pages of the different papers are not the same size. (While 'Amtsavisen' has the regular size of, say, the 'Times', 'Aktuelt' has the half-size of the 'Sun'.)

> Teacher: But look at this, here is another newspaper. You remember that small one, but look at this page, a page like this in this paper here, in fact it fits, as you can see, it fits right here.

[puts a double page from 'Aktuelt' on top of a single page from 'Amtsavisen'] And that means that when you spread out that newspaper like this, when you tear it apart, then that is a page, then you have to count how many pages there are of this kind here, not of that kind there, that is a double page, then, isn't it? So now you are to count how many there are of that kind, so just count how many there were and write down how many.

The group is then left to its own devices, and it turns out that it is not so simple to decide what a page in a newspaper is. Camilla takes the teacher's offer of deciding about the size of a newspaper for themselves on face value: "Then we can just say, this is a page of a newspaper," but Malene refers to the definition provided by the teacher:

Malene:	No, no, that is no good. No, if we spread out the paper like this…
Camilla:	Then we can just say, this is a page of a newspaper.
Malene:	No. [very determined/irritated tone of voice]
Camilla:	There is one.
Malene:	Well, no, that is two pages. There, now look at this. [takes the newspaper from Camilla] There are two pages, one, two. [counting and pointing at the newspaper page]
Camilla:	[making objections, which cannot be heard clearly on the tape]
Malene:	There *are* two pages, do you not remember what the teacher said, that then we could… [ic] …well, it *is* two pages.
Thomas:	I can't see whether this one is 'Aktuelt'.
Malene:	'Aktuelt'? Oh, but it says so on the front, doesn't it? [taking the newspaper from Thomas and beginning to study it]

We see a disagreement between Camilla and Malene. Whereas Camilla makes her proposition in a timid voice, Malene has a determined and evidently irritated tone of voice in her rejection and explanation. At the same time she is very much engaged with solving the exercise.

In the discussion of 'which unit to use' the teacher and the students at least obtain an agreement on the notion 'to fill': It has to do with area. This partial clarification of perspective may provide the students with new 'learning energy'.

The students take control

Malene presents her argument with a certain authority by referring to what the teacher has said. The authority is strengthened further as she is capable of rejecting, arguing, explaining and directing at the same time.

Not only is she able to argue against Camilla, she also directs Thomas, who is trying to find out where the different newspaper pages belong. It looks as if Malene is taking control,[31] and this tendency is strengthened in the following sequence:

Camilla:	Is this not the way to count: One, two? [pointing at the pages]
Malene:	No. One, two. [irritated tone of voice and pointing in a different way]
Camilla:	One, two. [Sticking to her suggestion.]
Malene:	No! […]
Thomas:	Now, look at this.
Malene:	There were only these small pages, so he says: a page like this, this is a page.
Thomas:	No.
Malene:	That's what he said.
Camilla:	No.
Malene:	Yes.
Thomas:	He said, one like this was one.
Malene:	No, listen: In this paper… which one was it we had a moment ago? What was it called?
Thomas:	'Aktuelt'.
Malene:	Aktu… 'Aktuelt', O.K. There were only these small pages, what can we do?
Camilla:	Can't we try to do like we did?
Malene:	No, please listen, will you? There were only those small pages, they cannot make up a big page.

Camilla sticks to her own position, however. They all laugh at the situation, but the discussion continues:

Malene:	That is why I say: In that one it has to be… it has to be twice the size, because it is not a page like this [Camilla laughs], listen will you, now then it can't be the same, because there were twelve pages, and it was only small pages like this.
Thomas:	It was not.
Malene:	Then fetch the newspaper.
Camilla:	I will go and ask the teacher.
Malene:	But he would not know, would he?
Camilla:	Yes he will.
Malene:	If there are two papers like that, well, let us see… I will go and get that paper, and then let us see, let us see if it was a

---

[31] According to the teacher, Malene is normally not the one to take the lead in class.

            page like this [Malene gets the newspaper], can't you see? It
            is not at all like this, can't you see?

Thomas: Right.

Malene: Then we cannot measure it, can we, because they are not the
            same.

It is noteworthy here that Malene in fact steps in to assume an authoritarian teacher role.[32] She argues and explains, but she also gives out orders: "Then fetch the newspaper," she disciplines: "listen will you" and she asks questions, which she (partly) knows the answers to: "Which one was it we had a moment ago? What was it called?" When the others question her authority, she refers to what the teacher has said: "That's what he said." Thus, the teacher is invisibly present in the communication, and Malene is his advocate.

In the sequence here, however, the rest of the group oppose to Malene as an authority, and in the end they fetch the real authority to settle the disagreement. "I will go and ask the teacher," Camilla says. However, we shall leave the group before Camilla returns with the teacher.

Malene's taking control can be understood as a reaction to the lacking teacher control. A possible student logic can be that when the teacher will not decide, then somebody else has to do it. It may express the student's attempt to create clear guidelines for the direction of the course. The situation can also be seen as an example of a group dynamic 'law', which takes effect when the official authority is absent. In such circumstances there is often a battle about who decides, and in the end there is one to take over. Apart from the power struggle it is noteworthy how involved and serious the students are in their work with the problem, even though they are working in the corridor and without the presence of the teacher. This observation underlines an essential aspect of learning.

LEARNING AS ACTION

We can interpret the student activities in 'How much does a newspaper fill?' in terms of *zooming-in*. Let us describe it in general terms. The students enter a classroom. They have some expectations. They are curious about what is going to happen. The teacher indicates some tasks and some activities, but although the mathematical concepts and tasks are

---

[32] With reference to Bakhtin, Høines (2002) uses the concept of an authoritarian teacher voice to describe such a pattern of communication.

contextualised no useful vantage points are established from where the students could assign meaning to the suggested activities. The students become tricked and confused. The activities seem interesting but the students want to understand more clearly what is going to happen. They ask questions. The teacher explains, but the students do not get the point. They try, nevertheless, to accommodate their 'learning concerns' to the situation. They perform a zooming-in. This can be seen as a collective activity performed by the students.

We can imagine that the students and the teacher reach an understanding. The students do see what it is all about. They get the point. Such a situation can be described in terms of shared perspectives. The students grasp the proposed teacher perspective. The teacher grasping the students' perspective may also be the case. A zooming-in designates a searching for a useful perspective. A not successful zooming-in can naturally also be observed. It was in fact a not successful but persistent zooming-in, which drew our attention to the phenomenon of zooming-in itself. We conceive zooming-in as an interesting phenomenon that reveals structures of the actual classroom practice. It also provides elements to a discussion about the nature of learning activities.

Zooming-in is not a common phenomenon. We can mention two factors that tend to eliminate a zooming-in. First, the classroom can be organised in a way that makes it clear what all tasks are about. The second factor is that the students do not care about what they are doing or the students may be submerged in a well-defined instrumentalism.[33] These two factors can be combined in the traditional mathematics classroom: The teacher explains the new topic, the teacher introduces which exercises to do next, the students do the exercises, and the teacher 'ticks' the results. In a classroom practice that is structured along this pattern there is not much need of zooming-in.

Besides that, something is out of focus, a zooming-in indicates that the classroom practice is not routinised.[34] It indicates that the students in fact are concerned about what is going to happen. We interpret the two student communication patterns: 'guessing what the teacher has in mind' and 'the students take control' as their active attempts of zooming-in on the whole purpose.

We find that zooming-in activities indicate a fundamental aspect of learning. The students' zooming-ins indicate that (at least some) *learning can be seen as action*. This idea is fundamental to our interpretation of

---

[33] For a discussion of instrumentalism, see Mellin-Olsen (1977, 1981).

[34] See Voigt (1984, 1989) for a discussion of routines in the mathematics classroom.

learning, and accordingly for how we see teaching. Naturally, we are not going to claim that all kinds of learning can be seen as action. Some forms are more precisely described as forced activities, as the soldiers drill and practice by which they learn to go marching. Other forms of learning may be better described as assimilation or enculturation, as for instance the child's learning of the mother tongue. A habit can be assimilated, also in cases where the learner has no clear intention of adopting the habit. We find, however, that learning as action can be associated with certain qualities, and we want to elaborate on this notion.

Action can be associated with terms like aim, decision, plan, motive, purpose and *intention*. A person is 'involved' in his action.[35] This means that we will try to separate action from, say, 'biologically determined behaviour'. In fact, we are all doing a lot of things that hardly can be classified as actions, such as, for instance, nervously scratching one's forehead while trying to solve a tricky problem. In order for an activity to be classified as action, a certain intentionality must be part of it. A second requirement for being able to act is that one is not forced into a situation where no alternatives exist. It is not possible to act in an over-determined situation, choice must be possible. In short, action presupposes both an involvement of the person and an openness of the situation.

We want to interpret some learning in the same way as action. Such learning presupposes both an openness of the situation and the involvement of the students.[36] We have characterised the introduction to 'How much does a newspaper fill?' as openness from the beginning. This openness has a good and a bad side to it. The students get a possibility to find out what purposes the unit might have. To the extent that they are able to recognise the intentions and to identify with them, they can be joint owners of their education.[37] Joint ownership also means having shared perspectives. As learners they can be acting and involved. On the other hand the openness can lead to confusion, which makes it difficult for the students to take part in a joint effort.

In the sequence 'Guessing what the teacher has in mind' the students may search for a purpose with their education, and in this way they try to direct their intentions to learning. In the sequence 'the students take con-

---

[35] For a discussion of 'intention' and 'action' see Searle (1983) and Skovsmose (1994).

[36] Viewing learning as action is on a par with constructivism as it has emerged more and more clearly in the discussion about mathematics education (see e.g. Glasersfeld (ed.), 1991). This also involves a complete departure from 'empty vessels' pedagogy.

[37] Mellin-Olsen (1987, 1989) who is inspired by activity theory has often used the phrase that the pupils have to own the aims of their education.

trol' the teaching unit will be given new energy, although it may lead the students on the wrong track. These actions, 'guessing' and 'taking control', we have characterised as zooming-in, and we can interpret a zooming-in as an observable token of students' directing their intentions to the learning process. A zooming-in indicates a search for shared perspectives. It indicates a wish for ownership, and it represents action.

Intention and action are closely related, but not in the sense that the intention of doing something comes first to be followed by a certain behaviour that is expected to fulfil the intention. The intention of the action is present in the action itself. The same goes for learning. The students do not first have an intention to learn before they let themselves be involved in learning. The intentions have to be present in the process of learning. The fact that the students in 'How much does a newspaper fill?' continue the intense discussion of what is meant by a newspaper page – even after they have left the classroom and the teacher domain – we see as indicative of their wish to see the purpose of the exercise. They want to be acting.

A zooming-in may appear as a trial-and-error strategy of looking for meaning of a suggested classroom activity. It also becomes clear to us, the importance of establishing educational situations in which it is possible for the students to zoom-in and to establish a 'culture' in the classroom in which the students really want to try out a zooming-in activity. This means making space for the students to be owners of the educational process.

The teacher is also an acting person. This claim is of course not particularly novel. In many descriptions of educational situations, education has been described as a process subjected to planning and structuring. Teaching has been described as a complicated action, at times in management terms, whereas the receiving end, the students, have often been described in terms that place them as objects for educational planning. In our terminology education is characterised by two 'agents' meeting each other. One of the problems is thus to co-ordinate two different types of actions, i.e. learning and teaching. For that reason it is of special interest to see how teacher and students meet about the educational content. One kind of meeting we have characterised as quizzing and guessing patterns of communication. In the following chapters we will discuss some other patterns and their consequences for learning. In fact we intend to characterise the student-teacher communication in terms of co-operation, and this brings new qualities to the process of learning.

CHAPTER 2

INQUIRY CO-OPERATION

What counts as traditional mathematics education will naturally vary during time, and also from country to country. Thus, it is difficult to provide any general characteristic of 'tradition'. We shall, however, suggest that the school mathematics tradition is characterised by certain ways of organising the classroom. For instance, a mathematics lesson can be divided into two parts: First, the teacher presents some mathematical ideas and techniques. This presentation is normally closely related to the presentation in the given textbook. Secondly the students work with selected exercises. These exercises can be solved by using the just presented techniques. The solutions are checked by the teacher. An essential part of the students' homework is to solve exercises from the textbook. The time spent on teacher presentation and on students doing exercises can naturally vary. Other elements can be included as for instance students' presentations of selected topics and solutions.[38]

In the school mathematics tradition the patterns of teacher-students communication can also become a routine, and much research has tried to identify the communicative patterns that dominate this tradition. We are interested in possible causes for such communicative patterns, as for instance the quizzing pattern of communication we described in Chapter 1, and here we shall pay attention to one particular aspect of the school mathematics tradition, the *exercise paradigm*. This paradigm has a deep influence on mathematics education, concerning the organisation of the individual lessons, the patterns of communication between teacher and students, as well as the social role that mathematics may play in society, for instance operating as a gatekeeper (the mathematical exercises fit nicely into processes of exams and tests). Normally, exercises in mathematics are formulated by an authority from outside the classroom. It is neither the teacher nor the students who have formulated the

---

[38] See Blomhøj (1995) for a similar characteristic of traditional mathematics education.

exercises. They are set by an author of a textbook. This means that the justification of the relevance of the exercises is not part of the mathematics lesson itself. Most often, the mathematical texts and exercises represent a 'given' for the classroom practice, including the classroom communication.

The exercise paradigm has been challenged in many ways: by problem solving, problem posing, thematic approach, project work, etc. To put it more generally, the exercise paradigm can be contrasted by investigative approaches.[39] We see the activities of solving exercises as being much more restrictive for the students than being involved in investigations. We want to elaborate on learning as action and not as a forced activity, and this makes us pay special attention to students being part of an investigative approach. In order to create possibilities for making investigations, it is important to consider possibilities outside the exercise paradigm. 'Openness from the start', illustrated by the project 'How much does a newspaper fill?' shows what it could mean to leave the well known frame of the exercise paradigm.

In this chapter we try to characterise more generally challenges to the exercise paradigm in terms of *landscapes of investigation*. We will discuss what it would mean to enter such a landscape. And by discussing an episode from the project 'What does the Danish flag look like?' we try to clarify the notion of *inquiry co-operation* as a particular form of student-teacher interaction when exploring a landscape of investigation. This co-operation we will specify into an *Inquiry-Co-operation Model* (IC-Model) that designates a significant pattern of communication. Such a pattern cannot easily be identified within a classroom practice located in the exercise paradigm.

FROM EXERCISES TO LANDSCAPES OF INVESTIGATION

Let us look at an example of an exercise in mathematics education: Shopkeeper A sells dates for 85p per kilogram. B sells them at 1.2 kg for

---

[39] An investigative approach can take many forms. One example is project work, as exemplified for primary and secondary school education in Nielsen, Patronis and Skovsmose (1999); Skovsmose (1994) and for university studies in Vithal, Christiansen and Skovsmose (1995). See also Cobb and Yackel (1998).

£1. (a) Which shop is cheaper? (b) What is the difference between the prices charged by the two shopkeepers for 15 kg of dates?[40]

Clearly we are dealing with dates, shops and prices. But most likely the person who constructed this exercise neither made any empirical investigation of how dates are sold, nor interviewed anyone to find out under what circumstances it would be relevant to buy 15 kg of dates. The situation is artificial. The exercise is located in a semi-reality. Solving exercises with reference to a semi-reality is an elaborated competence in mathematics education, based on a well specified (although implicit) agreement between teacher and students.[41]

Some of the principles in the agreement are the following: The semi-reality is fully described by the text of the exercise. No other information concerning the semi-reality is relevant in order to solve the exercise, and accordingly not relevant at all. The whole purpose of presenting the exercise is to solve the exercise. Asking any other questions about the specific nature of the semi-reality is similar to any form of disturbance of the mathematics lesson. A semi-reality is a world without sense impressions (to ask for the taste of the dates is out of the question), only the measured quantities are relevant. Furthermore, all the quantitative information is exact, as the semi-reality is defined completely in terms of these measures. For instance, the question whether it is OK to negotiate the prices or to buy somewhat less that 15 kg of dates is non-existing. The exactness of the measurements combined with the assumption that the semi-world is fully described by the provided information makes it possible to maintain the one-and-only-one-answer-is-correct assumption. The metaphysics of the semi-reality makes sure that this assumption gets a validity, not only when references are made exclusively to numbers and geometric figures, but also when references are made to 'shops', 'dates', 'kilograms', 'prices', 'distances', etc.[42]

---

[40] The example is taken from Dowling (1998), where he describes the 'the myth of references'. The following presentation and discussion of landscapes of investigation is based on Skovsmose (2000b, 2000c, 2001a, 2001b). The notion of 'virtual reality' referring to the world set by the mathematical exercises has been used by Christiansen (1994, 1997).

[41] See Brousseau (1997) and Christiansen (1995) for a discussion of 'the didactical contract'.

[42] If it is not realised that the way mathematics fits the semi-reality has nothing to do with the relationship between mathematics and reality, then the ideology of certainty finds a place for growing. For a discussion of the ideology of certainty, see Borba and Skovsmose (1997).

We can easily find examples of exercises without any references to a semi-reality, but with references only to pure mathematical entities. Just think of the imperative formulations: 'Solve the equation...', 'Reduce the expression...' and 'Construct the figure...'. The school mathematics tradition can be characterised in terms of operating along an almost infinitely long row of exercises.[43] So, whether or not the exercises refer to mathematical notions only or to a semi-reality, the one-and-only-one-answer-is-correct assumption is maintained. Not surprising then, that the idea of making absolute mistakes, included in bureaucratic absolutism, is nourished by the exercise paradigm.

We can also find examples where the constructor of the exercises has made a great effort formulating exercises with references to real-life situations.[44] Such references help to break away from the school mathematics tradition and the associated patterns of teacher-student communication. As soon as we have to do with real-life references, it makes sense to consider the reliability of the calculations. It also makes sense to check the information that the exercise presents (to check the correctness of the information presented in exercises referring to a semi-reality would be nonsense). For instance, figures concerning unemployment can be presented as part of the exercise, and based on such figures questions can be asked about the decrease or the increase of the employment, comparison can be made between different periods of time, different countries, etc. Still, the activities are part of the exercise paradigm.

The school mathematics tradition is closely linked with doing exercises referring to mathematics or to a semi-reality. And as soon as we have to do with references of this type, a certain pattern of communication between teacher and students becomes dominant. Thus, bureaucratic absolutism goes along with the metaphysics of the semi-reality. In fact, this metaphysics permeates the whole form of communication between teacher and students. Exercises with real-life references open a route out of the school mathematics tradition and challenge bureaucratic absolutism. For instance, it becomes difficult to maintain the assumption that one-and-only-one-answer-is-correct, as it becomes relevant to question the information provided in the exercise.

---

[43] As Mellin-Olsen (1991) has observed, this has caused the development of a certain set of metaphors, referring to travelling, for instance: 'having a delay', 'speeding up' and catching up'.

[44] See, for instance, Frankenstein (1989).

The whole metaphysics that dominates the school mathematics tradition begins to break down.

We can try to leave the exercise paradigm and to enter a different learning environment, which we refer to as *landscapes of investigation*. Such landscapes have an open nature. Exercises are substituted by some kind of scene setting that introduces the landscape. Students can formulate questions and plan different routes of investigation. They can become part of an inquiry process. In a landscape of investigation, the teacher's: 'What if...?', can be substituted by the students' 'What if...?' And the teacher's: 'Why is it so that...?' can turn into the students': 'Yes, why is it so that...?'

As is the case with the exercise paradigm, the meaning of the activities carried out in landscapes of investigation can be related to a semi-reality. Thus, projects can be developed referring to, say horse races, taxi-geometry, rock concerts, etc., without having much to do with real horse race, real taxi driving or real rock concerts. The project 'How much does a newspaper fill' also refers to a semi-reality. Clearly there were real newspapers distributed among the students, but the tasks were somehow artificial. The students' initial question: "Are we going to read?" was obviously not relevant. The newspapers, presented by the teacher, were not going to maintain their real-life significance.

We can also see landscapes of investigation being developed with, first of all, reference to mathematical entities. Thus, much activity in dynamic geometry, as supported by programmes like Cabri and Geometricks, refers to issues with a purely mathematical content. Here the students can explore properties of reflections, rotations, and translations. Using spreadsheets, the students can investigate the convergence of series. But, naturally, computers are not essential elements in operating in landscapes of investigation of a purely mathematical nature.

Finally, we can observe landscapes of investigation with a large degree of reference to real-life situations. The tradition of doing project work in mathematics education has supplied a richness of examples of this type.

Putting these observations together in a single diagram we reach a simplified overview of possible learning environments, each of which we for short shall refer to as a milieu of learning (see Figure 2.1). The milieus (1), (3) and (5) represent the exercise paradigm, with (1) and (3) providing the kernel of the school mathematics tradition and framing certain patterns of teacher-student communication. The milieus (2), (4) and (6) represent landscapes of investigation, but with different sorts of meaning producing references. Such references can also provide vantage points to the extent that they make it possible for students to overview what they are doing or asked to do. In milieu (1) and (2) references are made only to pure mathematics. In (3) and (4) references are made to a semi-reality, while milieu (5) and (6) include real-life references.

	Paradigm of exercise	Landscapes of investigation
References to pure mathematics	(1)	(2)
References to a semi-reality	(3)	(4)
Real references	(5)	(6)

Figure 2.1: Milieus of learning.

The model in Figure 2.1 is very simplified. Many more elements have to be considered in a clarification of milieus of learning, but for our purpose this simple model will do. In particular, the model emphasises that different forms of references provide different milieus of learning. Proposing possible references, we previously referred to as scene setting. A vantage point makes it possible for students to perceive the learning activities from a certain perspective, and in this way students can assign new meaning to their activities.

A landscape serves as an invitation for the students to get involved in a process of investigation. However, a landscape only becomes accessible if the students in fact accept the invitation. The possibilities of entering a landscape of investigation are dependent on relational qualities. Acceptance of the invitation depends on the nature of the invitation (the possibility of exploring and explaining pure mathematical topics might not look so attractive to many students); it depends on the teacher (an invitation can be presented in many ways, and to some students an invitation from a teacher might appear as a command); and certainly it depends on the students (they might have other priorities for the time being). What might serve perfectly well as a landscape of investigation to one group of students in one particular situation might not provide any invitation to another group of students. In the project 'How much does a newspaper fill?' the invitation was not presented in terms of specific tasks for the students, but it was clear that the students accepted the invitation. They tried to zoom-in on the possible purpose of the activities, and when needed they seemed eager to take over responsibility and ownership of the inquiry process.

There are different aspects involved in moving from the paradigm of exercises to landscapes of investigation. The patterns of communication may change and open for new types of co-operation and for new learning possibilities.[45] We shall pay particular attention to the inquiry processes that are made possible in landscapes of investigation. Especially, we are interested in the possibility for the students to be active in their learning. Both teacher and students may experience uncertainties in coming to operate in landscapes of investigation, not protected by the well-defined 'rules' for how to operate in an exercise paradigm. Thus, leaving an exercise paradigm also means leaving a comfort zone and entering a risk zone.[46]

ENTERING A LANDSCAPE OF INVESTIGATION

What are the possible gains of operating in the risk zone associated with a landscape of investigation? We see this very much related to the emergence of new possibilities for students' involvement, for different patterns of communication, and consequently for new qualities in learning. Landscapes of investigation, as for instance developed with reference to constructivism and ethnomathematics, make it possible to pay special attention to the experiences and to the activities of students. The understandings and pre-understandings of the students can come to play a significant role in the classroom communication, and this means that they can provide learning with new qualities.

---

[45] See, for instance, Bartolini Bussi (1998); Bauersfeld (1992); Burton (1996); Burton (ed.) (1999); Clark (ed.) (2001); Christiansen (1994, 1995, 1997); Cobb (1995); Cobb, Yackel and Wood (1995); Høines (2002) and Yackel (1995).

[46] We return to the notion of 'risk zone'. As we shall see in Chapter 5, landscapes of investigation may also provide new opportunities for students to distance themselves from the learning process. The notion of risk zone has been presented and discussed in Penteado (2001).

We suggest the concept of *inquiry* as referring to processes of exploring a landscape of investigation. By the term inquiry we also refer to the work of John Dewey.[47] According to Dewey, it is essential for the learner to be involved in a process of 'finding out'. The sort of inquiry that is relevant is similar to that of a scientific investigation, because the way of learning is similar to the way of studying any phenomenon. An inquiry-based education is completely dissociated from the idea of transferring knowledge. Knowledge is not to be delivered, it must be developed. A process of inquiry must start from where the students are: "Anything which can be called a study, whether arithmetic, history, geography, or one of the natural sciences, must be derived from materials which at the outset fall within the scope of ordinary life-experience." And Dewey adds: "It is a cardinal precept of the newer school of education that the beginning of instruction shall be made with the experience learners already have; that this experience and the capacities that have been developed during its course provide the starting point for all further learning." (Dewey, 1963, 73-74)

Dewey has developed his educational ideas in great detail, and provided the notion of inquiry with particular interpretations. We are not going to follow Dewey into his particular interpretation of the nature of research and inquiry (in fact, in Chapter 8 we shall provide a critique of one of Dewey's perspectives on science and education), but we are going to acknowledge the importance of the notion of inquiry and of the significance of relating processes of learning to processes of researching. Thus, entering a landscape of investigation also means entering an area to be researched. And, like Dewey, we do not see any important difference between processes of learning and processes of research. Both are processes of inquiry.

We find that there are two basic elements that cannot be ignored when making an inquiry. An inquiry process cannot be a forced activity, it presupposes the involvement of the participants. Furthermore, it must be an open process. Results and conclusions cannot be determined in advance. In our characteristic of 'action' in Chapter 1, we emphasised that an action cannot be a forced activity. It presupposes an involvement of the acting person, and also a degree of openness. Thus, we find that 'learning as action' and 'learning as inquiry' fit nicely together.

Students must be invited into a landscape of investigation in order to become owners and active participants of the inquiry process. The notion

---

[47] A general overview of Dewey's educational ideas is found in Archambault (1964). See also Dewey (1938, 1966).

of invitation is important.[48] An invitation can be accepted or not – an invitation is not an order. For that reasons it is important that the teacher becomes aware of the students' 'good reasons' for bringing themselves into the process of inquiry, or for staying outside. Zooming-in reveals that students may have good reasons for accepting the invitation, although a zooming-in does not necessarily reveal the nature of these good reasons. Accepting an invitation means that the students can locate themselves in the activities, and that they can locate a perspective which provides 'good reasons' to take part in the activities.[49]

'Good reasons' refer to reasons that count as serious – although not necessarily offered as reasons. Good reasons might be implicit. Mostly they are only possible to locate by reading between the lines of communication. The students' good reasons are very complex. Good reasons for being part of an inquiry process can be related to mathematics: The students can be interested in the topic. The reasons can also have to do with the contextualisation: The students may feel familiar with the topic as it is presented. Good reasons can be very personal, as the student's involvement can have to do with his or her relationships with the teacher or with other students. Thus a strong involvement can be an expression of a wish to co-operate with somebody, or with a fear of becoming excluded. Naturally, the school setting cannot be ignored, and many reasons for being engaged in learning activities can be related to organisation elements, like a student's wish to perform well in mathematics (independent of whether this is organised in terms of exercises or landscapes of investigation).

This complexity of reasons can bring the students into landscapes of investigation, or make them stay as spectators. We find it important that the students find reasons to enter an inquiry process. In this way we have to do with a process of learning in which the students are acting. It is important that students find good reasons for bringing their intentions into the learning process. Learning as action presupposes intentions in learning.

The personal interrelationships among students and between teacher and students manifest themselves in patterns of communication. To operate in a landscape of investigation (with good reasons) means to co-

---

[48] The notion of invitation seems to indicate that the landscapes of investigation are constructed somehow in advance and not together with the students. This need not be the case. Nevertheless, the notion of invitation is still important, as the process of entering or learning in a landscape of investigation, is an on-going process. Making an invitation can include that students and teacher set up or identify a landscape together.

[49] For a further discussion of 'students' good reasons', see Alrø and Skovsmose (1996b).

operate, and co-operation is supported, or obstructed, by certain forms of communication. In particular, we do not find that the patterns of communication, which characterise the school mathematics tradition will support an inquiry process.

Literature on mathematics education has described fascinating co-operations between students and teacher taking place in landscapes of investigation. The students are deeply involved in the process of making discoveries, and the teacher, operating as the sensitive supervisor, facilitates the students' way on the route. Suddenly the teacher also experiences new mathematical properties, of which he has previously not been aware. We have to do with an *inquiry co-operation*. Such a co-operation will be of particular interest to us, as we see inquiry co-operation as an essential part of developing certain qualities of communication and of learning mathematics. An inquiry co-operation is a manifestation of some of the possibilities that emerge when entering a landscape of investigation. Thus, our task in the rest of this chapter is to describe in more detail some of the qualities of communication and learning in such an inquiry co-operation.

We will present such details in the IC-Model. We extract the elements of this model from a specific conversation between a teacher and a group of students. The notion of 'model' is used in a rather neutral way. The IC-Model is not intended to prescribe a simple pattern of communication that we recommend; in fact we could also have chosen to talk about an IC-pattern of communication. Our identification and presentation of the model is based on a conversation between teacher and students that takes place in a landscape of investigation, which can best of all be characterised as being of type (4) – references to a semi-reality – although also including references to the real Danish flag.

'WHAT DOES THE DANISH FLAG LOOK LIKE?'

The following sequence is part of an introduction to a course of approximately twelve lessons in a Danish 6th grade mathematics class. The students work in groups of 2-5 participants. They are supposed to make models of the European flags, while being careful about the proportions of flags, stripes, and crosses. As an introduction, the students are asked to make a model of the Danish flag (see Figure 2.2), just as they recall it. Afterwards the groups have to argue and comment on their results and see which model is most similar to the real flag. We follow this work with the construction of the IC-Model in mind. Thus, we are searching for a first answer to the questions: What does it mean to operate in a co-operative manner in a landscape of investigation? How does such co-operation manifest itself in patterns of communication?

Alice and Deborah have cut out some white strips to make a cross.

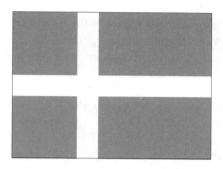

Figure 2.2: The Danish flag.

But when they are about to place the cross on a piece of red paper, they are not quite sure how to do it (see also Figure 2.3). They ask the teacher to help.[50]

Getting in contact, locating, identifying

Teacher:	Alice, if we decide that it should be this broad. [the red paper for the flag] Let us decide that…
Alice:	Yes.
Teacher:	…in order to have something to look at.
Alice:	Yes.
Teacher:	Then we can estimate it, can't we? How would you place this [the cross] here in the middle?
Alice:	I would measure.
Teacher:	…if you think that it should be placed in the middle. Do you think so? Is this [the white cross] right in the middle or is it a little up or a little down?
Deborah:	It is a little up.
Alice:	It is in the middle.
Teacher:	Okay, and then how would you carefully place it right in the middle?

---

[50] The following transcript constitutes an unbroken sequence, but we divide it into smaller parts in order to facilitate the presentation of the IC-Model.

Alice: Measure.
Teacher: Yes but... oh, yes. You could do so. How would you meas-
            ure, then?
Alice: I borrow a ruler.
Teacher: [laughs] Yes, okay.

First, the teacher suggests that they use the original size of the red paper for the flag, and Alice accepts his suggestion. So far they talk the same language – they are *getting in contact*. The teacher uses the personal pronoun "we" in his opening of the conversation, which indicates they are working together.[51]

He changes his way of communicating when addressing them as "you" in his first question: "How would you place that here in the middle?" The teacher is no longer part of the team, but he has a wondering attitude towards the students, trying to *locate* their perspective. Alice proposes a method for the solving of the problem: "I would measure," but before listening to this suggestion the teacher corrects himself and asks again. His first formulation presupposed that the students would actually place the cross right in the middle, but his reformulation questions this presupposition and allows for other perspectives: "Do you think so?" We interpret this as the teacher's way of trying to locate the students' perspective about what it could mean to place the cross on the red paper in a proper way.

Alice and Deborah have different ideas about the placing of the cross, and the teacher uses a kind of selective hearing when ignoring Deborah's proposal and repeating Alice's (identical with his own?). Still, he continues his examination of the students' ideas of solving the problem: "How would you carefully place it right in the middle?" The teacher tries to *identify* what procedure the students would use. By the words "carefully" and "right" the teacher implicitly claims that the procedure should be based on mathematical calculations, and not just by eye.

Alice repeats her proposal of measuring, which is accepted by the teacher, who wants to know how Alice would proceed. This could bring about an identification of a proper method. While Alice has a practical approach (I borrow a ruler), the teacher is waiting for some calculations to be carried out. The teacher's laughter indicates that he is aware of this. But still he encourages Alice to continue: "Yes, okay."

---

[51] The use of 'we' can naturally also be understood as the teacher pretending a co-operation (majestaetis pluralis).

Advocating, thinking aloud, reformulating

When Alice has borrowed a ruler, she goes on *advocating* her suggestion about measuring. She makes her proposal in an open way: "I would measure" which does not exclude other possibilities:

Alice:	…and then I would measure that one.
Teacher:	[points out] first you measure the breadth of the red piece, and then you measure the breadth of the white piece, and what do you do after that?
Alice:	That is… 22.4. [the breadth of the red piece]
Teacher:	22 1/2 or is it 22.4?
Alice:	22.4.
Teacher:	Yes, and this one is… ? [the breadth of the white strip]
Alice:	It is 5 1/2, no! Yes 5.4.
Teacher:	5.4 okay. What then?
Alice:	What is half of 22.4, that is 11.2. [Deborah interrupts]
Deborah:	…and then we have to find the middle.
Alice:	Yes, then we find the middle.
Teacher:	Yes, but when you put this [the white cross] on you cannot see your mark in the middle.
Alice:	No but then I just put the dot a little farther out. [outside the red paper]
Teacher:	I see, okay.
Alice:	It shouldn't be that difficult.

Alice is about to measure both the breadth of the red piece of paper and the breadth of the white strip for the cross. Her expressions "this way" and "that one" are reformulated and pointed out by the teacher. The teacher still pursues Alice's ideas of an algorithm which can be seen in his persistent questioning: "and what do you do after that?" and "What then?" During this examination Alice is thinking aloud: "It is 5 1/2, no! Yes 5.4" and "What is the half of 22.4? That is 11.2." The last example of thinking aloud indicates that Alice has begun solving the problem before she has answered the teacher's question about what to do next. That may be the reason why Deborah interrupts to point out the algorithm: "and then we have to find the middle" (see Figure 2.3).

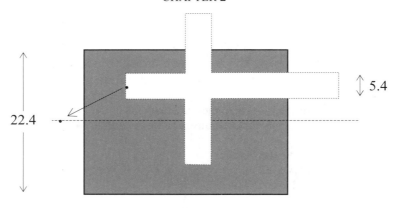

Figure 2.3: Placing the strips.

At this point the teacher objects that they will not be able to see their own marking on the middle of the red paper, which means that they cannot place the cross accurately. But still Alice has a solution to the problem: She just puts the mark outside the paper so that she can still see it when placing the cross. She seems quite happy with this solution herself, and the teacher accepts it in the first place: "I see, okay," although this would mean that the idea of identifying a proper mathematical procedure is given up.

Here the story might have ended. The students have located a problem, they have identified an algorithm after some *thinking aloud* and *reformulating*, and they have produced a result. So they are done with the job. But the teacher wants them to consider the possibility of identifying a more strict procedure for placing the white strips.

Intermezzo: Challenging or quizzing

Teacher:	Look here. Why don't you instead… couldn't you calculate how much that piece should be, [pointing at the piece of red paper] I mean the breadth of the red piece above. How much should it be, when the whole piece is 22 point… [Alice interrupts]
Alice:	This one is 5 1/2.
Teacher:	This one was 5 1/2, and this one was 22 1/2, wasn't it?
Alice:	Yes.
Teacher:	…approximately.
Alice:	How much is that? It is… [3 sec.]
Teacher:	Yes, it is the math teacher asking.
Deborah:	It is 8 point something.

Alice: No, it certainly isn't 8 point something, it is…
Teacher: It is the same as 22 minus 5.
Deborah: Yes, sure.
Alice: It is 17.
Teacher: How much is it going to be, the red piece up here?
Alice: It is going to be…
Deborah: Then you just take half of it.
Alice: Then it is going to be half of 5 1/2.
Deborah: No the half of 17.
Teacher: No the half of 17, isn't it.

The teacher *challenges* the students by introducing another algorithm: "Why don't you instead… couldn't you calculate how much that piece should be?" He wants the students to calculate in order to be able to place the cross precisely in the middle of the red paper. The teacher question is formulated in a cautious hypothetical way that, in principle, leaves it up to the students whether they want to follow his track or not. But in this sequence a radical change in the character of the conversation can be observed. From being an open dialogue where the teacher was curious about the students' perspective of the problem, it changes to a *quizzing* pattern, where the students are supposed to guess what the teacher is aiming at. The teacher is aware of that change himself, which can be seen in his meta-statement: "Yes, it is the math teacher asking."

Obviously the teacher wants the students to subtract 5.5 from 22.5 and divide by 2 in order to calculate the size of the red pieces on each side of the white stripe. Deborah seems to follow this idea more quickly than Alice, as can be seen in Alice's rejection of Deborah's proposal "It is 8 point something". The teacher presents the algorithm step by step: "It is the same as 22 minus 5" and "How much is it going to be the red piece up here?" Deborah explains the algorithm to Alice: "Then you just take half of it," but Alice does not seem to follow her ideas. Instead she wants to take the half of 5 1/2. We do not get to know of the students' reasons for their different proposals, and the teacher once again makes use of his selective hearing by repeating Deborah's suggestion.

In this part the teacher's questions are not inquiring about the students' perspectives. He wants the students to grasp a particular idea, and he knows the answers to the questions himself. In this step-by-step procedure the teacher tries to show the idea of the procedure. It seems difficult for Alice to follow the teacher perspective and it seems as though this causes a temporary stop to her own involvement. We have called this sequence an intermezzo because the quizzing communication interrupts the inquiring process. Still, it leads to the identification of a procedure. Or does it? After this the teacher changes his way of communicating once again.

Challenging

Deborah:	We don't measure in that direction, do we?
Alice:	No sure, it is… no what is half of 5 1/2?
Deborah:	What the hell are you doing?
Alice:	It is 2.75.
Teacher:	Yes.
Alice:	Then you have to subtract 2.75 from 17. That is uh… 15 point something.
Teacher:	Yes it is 15 point something, that is right. [laughs]
Alice:	But 15 what?
Teacher:	But what are you going to use them for, those 15?
Alice:	But I would measure down there…
Teacher:	…and then down to 15 and then put all of it [the cross] down in the bottom. I will be back in a moment, then you can try to tell me what you have done.

What is conspicuous in the above sequence is that the students have recaptured the lead. Alice cannot give up her idea of taking half of 5 1/2, and she is *challenged* by Deborah: "What the hell are you doing?" There is no shared perspective on the procedure. Deborah has in mind taking half of the 17, while Alice intends taking half of the 5 1/2. Both steps make sense, but as part of two different procedures. Alice goes on searching for an answer to her own question, and the teacher lets her, although it is not clear where subtracting 2.75 from 17 would lead them. He does not interrupt the student inquiry until Alice has come up with a cautious proposal: "15 point something." Then the teacher *challenges* her perspective (not the result of her calculation): "But what are you going to use them for, those 15?" Alice makes a suggestion of measuring from the top of the red paper, but the teacher challenges again by (ironically) pointing out that this would place the white cross at the bottom of the flag. The teacher leaves the students for a moment, and the two girls get the chance to examine certain positions by themselves.

Evaluating

We do not know what the two girls have been talking about while the teacher has been away.[52] But as he returns a couple of minutes later, they have got an algorithm and a solution.

Teacher:	Yes Alice, have you found out?
Alice:	Yes.
Teacher:	How did you manage it?
Deborah:	We measured 8 1/2 down and 8 1/2 down.
Alice:	The half of 17.
Teacher:	Yes 17, it was the difference between the red and the white piece, wasn't it?
Alice:	No half of the red piece.
Teacher:	Yes of the red piece when you have subtracted the white one, isn't it?
Alice:	Yes, and then the half of 17, that is 8 1/2.
Teacher:	Yes.
Alice:	And then we have measured 8 1/2 inwards and that is there.
Teacher:	Good.
Alice:	And then we have measured 8 1/2 inwards there, too.
Teacher:	Yes, that is right. You dropped the idea about 15?
Deborah:	Yes, because it turned out to be wrong.
Teacher:	Okay.

The teacher questions the students' methods: "How did you manage it?" Deborah's idea was used: 8 1/2 was measured from the top of the red paper, and Alice stresses her participation in the process by emphasising that 8 1/2 is half of 17. The teacher *evaluates* their work by responding: "Good" and "That is right". Finally he wants to know what came out of the proposal of 15. "You dropped the idea of 15?" and Deborah concludes: "Yes, because it turned out to be wrong." Of course, the teacher could have examined the student proposal of 15 and how it turned out to be wrong. Further, it would have been interesting to listen to the students' co-operation in order to get to know how they found another algorithm in the end. But the point is that they actually found out by reflecting and acting on the basis of their own perspectives.

---

[52] The microphone of the audiotape was placed on the teacher, and the video sound was not good enough to catch the dialogue between Alice and Deborah.

INQUIRY CO-OPERATION MODEL

In our comments to 'What does the Danish flag look like?' we emphasised the elements: getting in contact, locating, identifying, advocating, thinking aloud, reformulating, challenging, and evaluating. These elements we condense into the IC-Model (see Figure 2.4).[53] In what follows we will argue that the IC-Model consists of communicative acts among teacher and students that can support learning in a particular way.

A main condition of communication in the IC-Model is active listening: "It is called 'active' because the listener has a very definite responsibility. He does not passively absorb the words which are spoken to him. He actively tries to grasp the facts and the feelings in what he hears, and he tries, by his listening, to help the speaker work out his own problems." (Rogers and Farson, 1969, 481) Active listening means asking questions and giving non-verbal support while finding out what the other is getting at. Active listening means that teacher and student get in contact. By the term *getting in contact*, we thus understand more than the teacher calling for attention. 'Getting in contact' means tuning in to each other in order to prepare for co-operation. This is the first condition of mutual inquiry. After establishing mutual attention the teacher can *locate* the student's perspective by examining, for instance, how he or she understands a certain problem. Naturally, various possible perspectives and different ways of approaching a task or a problem can be located. Perhaps it is difficult for the student to express his or her mathematical idea, or in general to express the perspective that he or she tries to establish on the problem. The teacher could function as a facilitator by asking in an inquiring mode, trying to participate in the student's way of interpreting the problem. When the student is able to express his or her perspective, then it can possibly be *identified* in mathematical terms – identified not only by the teacher, but also by the student. Thus, the process of identification will provide a resource for further inquiry. Naturally, the process can also take the opposite direction, and the students can try to identify the teacher perspective.

---

[53] Sigel and Kelley (1988) present a similar way of thinking in their 'Spiral Learning Cycle', that contains elements of focusing, exploring, restructuring and refocusing to describe the patterns of teacher questioning techniques (distancing strategies) that challenge the students' mental operations in the learning process.

Advocating means putting forward ideas or points of view not as the absolute truth, but as something that can be examined.[54] An examination may lead to a reconsideration of perspectives or to further inquiry. Advocating means proposing arguments for a certain position, but is does not mean sticking to a particular position at any cost. In particular, advocating can take the form of *thinking aloud*. By thinking aloud, perspectives become public because they become visible on the surface of communication. This means that it becomes possible to investigate them. The teacher can support the clarification of perspectives by *reformulating* students' formulations. For instance, perspectives can be reformulated by the teacher so that he makes sure that he understands what the student says. Reformulation can, of course, also be practised by the student in order to check out his or her understanding of the teacher perspective. In this way the perspective can be clarified for both teacher and students and this makes it possible to prevent misunderstandings. Again, it is essential that the students have the opportunity to reformulate

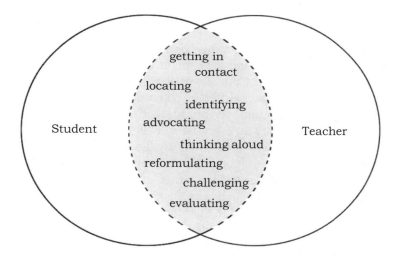

Figure 2.4: The Inquiry-Co-operation Model.

---

[54] See Isaacs (1999a).

the teacher statements. This is a process of reaching a shared understanding.

Clarification of perspectives is a precondition for making a 'qualified' *challenge*. Here the teacher could play the role of opponent as well as the role of partner. It is important that the teacher is able to do both in order to strengthen the student's self-confidence. The challenge should be adjusted to the student's conceptions – not too much and not too little.[55] And quite different patterns of communication may emerge if the challenge turns into 'quizzing'. Furthermore, it is important that the teacher, as well, is ready to be challenged. Making challenges can happen both ways.

Evaluating teacher and student perspectives is part of the inquiry process. Did they see the same problem? Did they look at the problem from the same point of view? Did they try to solve it the same way? Misunderstandings and other differences may occur explicitly in the teacher-student communication. For instance, the participants may locate that the teacher perspective relates to a general analysis of the problem, while the student thinks of the problem as a concrete, practical one. The point is not to obtain the 'right perspective', but to obtain a shared responsibility for the inquiry process. This does not mean that 'everything is right'. The point is that 'right' and 'wrong' cannot dominate an inquiry process. On this basis the student and the teacher can evaluate their perspectives and they might even be able to discuss what the student has learned in the process of challenging.

The IC-Model designates different communicative acts, which make up a pattern of co-operation between teacher and students in which the students' perspectives play an essential role. Patterns of co-operation can be facilitated by landscapes of investigation. Participation and co-operation cannot be forced upon students. Inquiry co-operation involves actions that we have described in terms of communicative acts. The possibility of carrying out such acts depends upon how the students' perspectives become integrated in the process.

One reason for examining student perspectives in the mathematics classroom is that they can be seen as important resources for learning. Examining the student's perspectives not only helps the teacher to know the student's way of thinking, it also helps the student to an awareness of his or her own way of acting in the classroom. The important thing is that the student's perspectives and not the teacher's explanation can become the starting point for inquiry co-operation. Put more generally: The

---

[55] This refers to Bateson's (1972) notion of 'the difference that makes a difference'.

communicative acts included in the IC-Model bring the students and their perspectives into the classroom public arena. New resources for learning become available, and new qualities in learning become possible.

OBSTRUCTIONS TO INQUIRY CO-OPERATION
(LEAVING A LANDSCAPE OF INVESTIGATION)

If the thesis is put forward that teachers in their normal practice pay attention to students' perspectives, then it ought to be possible to find some evidence of this in an empirical investigation. However, our observations of classrooms, following the school mathematics tradition, do not have much to offer on this point. The absolutely dominant structure of communication between students and teacher (as well as between students) is that of quizzing, explaining the right algorithm and correcting mistakes.[56] It must be emphasised here that in our case, we have a liberal interpretation of inquiry co-operation. We have outlined it as a pattern of communicative acts, but we do not suggest that all the elements have to be present or that they should take place in a prescribed order. Instead, an IC-Model can be seen as a characteristic of a communicative co-operation in which (some of) these elements, explicitly or implicitly, are brought together in a cluster. Only in a very few cases within the school mathematics tradition have we identified a fully developed IC-Model. Sometimes we can identify mini-IC-Models; but more often the phenomenon of IC-Model-deformation is observed. We find situations in which inquiry co-operation seems to be initiated yet it soon becomes fragmented and gradually eliminated.

We have identified different forms of degeneration of the IC-Model. Thus, inquiry co-operation, not least the element of challenging, can degenerate into 'quizzing'. This was indicated in the example above when the teacher wanted the students to try an alternative procedure for placing the white cross. However, inquiry co-operation can be obstructed in many other ways.

For instance, inquiry co-operation can be defeated by the time schedule: 'Sorry, we do not have time. Do something like this and this.' Inquiry co-operation thus becomes substituted by the language of bureaucracy. This can be caused by the fact that the teacher experiences an obligation to teach what is needed for the students to follow the

---

[56] Talking about 'our observations' we refer to classroom observations made in the spring of 1993 in one 5th and two 6th grade mathematics classes in Denmark.

prescribed curriculum. The 'logic of schooling' can also come to dominate what is taking place in a particular lesson and provide communicative acts with particular meaning. If students have to pass an examination by the end of the year, then the teacher seems obliged to make sure that the students have acquired the mathematical skills that constitute the basic object for examination. An elaborated process of inquiry co-operation might appear to be so time-consuming that it has to be interrupted. A kind of teacher self-censorship might obstruct inquiry co-operation.

We can think of many reasons for the teacher *not* trying to locate the students' perspectives and *not* using them as a resource for learning purposes. As mentioned, one is the fact that it takes time to explore the individual student's perspectives. To pay much attention to students' perspectives demands use of time taken from other classroom activities. Consequently, the teacher, who is responsible not only for the students who might be the most eager to present their ideas, but for the whole classroom community, chooses to ignore students' perspectives. A different reason for not taking notice of the students' perspectives is to assume they do not exist, or, in slightly different terms, that the students' perspectives are not considered worth discussing by the teacher.

Obstruction of inquiry co-operation cannot simply be interpreted as an obstruction caused by the teacher acting in a traditional way. It is important to realise that students are brought up within a certain school discourse that influences their pre-understandings and expectations of classroom activities. For instance, students often expect the teacher to present the knowledge that he or she wants them to gain. They are not going to insist on their own ideas because they expect to be controlled and evaluated by the teacher. Thus they do not have to be responsible for their own contributions. The teacher will always give the right answer or come out with the right algorithm in the end.[57] Such a pre-understanding of teacher and student roles prevents the teacher from practising inquiry co-operation. The student self-censorship might obstruct inquiry co-operation. The student may have an idea about how to handle a certain problem, but he or she does not want to articulate this when the teacher is present. The student does not want to reveal him- or herself by making a (maybe silly) suggestion, which could spoil the teacher's good impression of him or her. Instead the student replaces the initiated inquiry co-operation by official classroom discourse.[58]

---

[57] See Voigt (1989, 31).

[58] See Christiansen (1995).

The final reservation with respect to inquiry co-operation that we want to point out is that the communicative acts inherent in the IC-Model make demands on the students' verbal abilities. Thus, the pattern might favour those students who express themselves willingly and easily and disadvantage others, for instance serious but quiet students, who are just as interested in learning mathematics by working by themselves.

These points illustrate some of the difficulties of an inquiry based mathematics education and some of the risks involved in travelling in a landscape of investigation. It is not a simple task to realise inquiry co-operation. However, moving from the exercise paradigm and into landscapes of investigation may open the way for patterns of communication such as those in the IC-Model. We find this step important because it means a change of learning milieu. The IC-Model not only represents qualities of communication, it also constitutes an important resource for learning. New qualities of learning become possible when new possibilities of communication become realised. As a consequence we want to take a more careful look at the elements of the IC-Model.

CHAPTER 3

FURTHER DEVELOPMENT OF
THE INQUIRY CO-OPERATION MODEL

The IC-Model has been developed with reference to a particular example of communication between a teacher and a group of students. The following key notions describe elements of inquiry: *getting in contact, locating, identifying, advocating, thinking aloud, reformulating, challenging and evaluating.* In this chapter we will reconsider these elements by looking at students' mutual inquiry co-operation.

We analyse group work that contains several new inquiring elements that seem to relate to the notions of the IC-Model. In the final section we will summarise these elements in order to develop the IC-Model to become not only a model of teacher-student communication, but a general model of inquiry co-operation in teaching and learning mathematics that aims at concretising inquiry as a communicative practice. This also includes a discussion of observed communicative patterns that seem to be an obstacle to inquiry co-operation.

'BATMAN & CO.'

We are in a 10th grade mathematics class. This week the students have two lessons in mathematics from 10 to 12 o'clock every day. In this particular school it is possible to set up a different schedule every week, so the students are used to special arrangements. We look at a course of inquiry that takes place in a classroom environment of group work where the teacher plays the role of a consultant. There are no given exercises, but the teacher introduces the students to a landscape of investigation with clearly defined vantage points that allow the students to raise mathematical questions and to solve mathematical problems. This means that they should be able to obtain an idea of what they could be doing in this landscape. Naturally, this does not prevent them from having to face difficulties. The presented landscape includes references to a semi-reality, but it also includes real-life references.

The class is going to imagine to be the Danish division of an American factory, 'Run for Your Life', that makes sports articles. Every day they get new information and orders that they have to consider. The first day the introduction is: "For the coming promotion campaign we need a large amount of balls. We have bought some black and white leather – 25 m^2 of each colour…" and a big shopping trolley with many sorts of balls is placed in the 'factory hall'. Cardboard, scissors and glue are also available. Some students begin to examine the well-known black and white handballs and soccer balls. They consist of 12 pentagons and 20 hexagons each. How can the factory begin a production? Later they get this fax: "Our sports centre has burnt down. We have rented a bubble hall of 25×40 meters. We need grounds for handball, basketball, badminton and volleyball. Please help us!" There is a lot of serious (and non-serious) work in the classroom. The students define their own tasks, they produce a lot, they calculate a lot.

A particular job is requested from 'Batman & Co'. This company needs bats for table tennis. The price must be no more than 89 Danish Kroner, and the Danish division of 'Run For Your Life' has no bats of that price in stock. However, a Swedish supplier is able to sell the bats at 70 Swedish Kroner. Naturally, the students also have to consider insurance and freight charges that are estimated to be 1.5 %. They are informed that the exchange rate between Danish and Swedish Kroner is 82.14; another source says 81.29. Duty is 8% and the profit is expected to be 25%. Finally, the VAT (Value Added Tax) in Denmark is 25%. As mentioned, 'Batman & Co' only wants to pay 89 Danish Kroner per bat. How to handle this situation? We will see how two students cope with this and how the teacher tries to facilitate their progress in work.

Mary and Adam from one of the groups get a computer and find a spreadsheet to solve the problem. They struggle hard and concentrate on this work during the two-hour lesson without any break.[59] A couple of times they are interrupted and challenged by the teacher. The 'factory hall' is filled with humming and shouting voices of the other 'workers',

---

[59] This is especially remarkable in the case of Adam, who is considered a problem child by many teachers. He has not done much during the first days of the project, but before today's lesson the math teacher, with whom he obviously has a respectful relationship, has kindly asked him to pull himself together and show his capability. The teacher has confidence in Adam, and his idea was to challenge him by bringing the computer into the classroom. See also Alrø, Skovsmose and Skånstrøm (2000).

but Mary and Adam do not allow themselves to be disturbed, not even when other group members try to interfere in what they are doing.[60] On this day the whole class is going on an excursion, and the bus will leave a few minutes after the lesson. But Mary and Adam keep working, and they do not stop when the teacher ends the lesson (in this school there is no bell ringing). They remain all alone in the room working at the spread-sheet.[61]

After some time they realise that they have to stop in order to join the others: Mary: "Well, should we give this up?" Adam: "Yes, no, we'll save it, won't we?" Mary: "Yes, it's actually very interesting, we have been quite clever, don't you think?" Leaving the classroom, Mary blushes when she addresses the teacher: *"Today we really learned something!"*

Prices in Danish Kroner

Mary and Adam have not been in a group together before, but they seem enthusiastic about what they are going to do. They start trying to set up a spreadsheet with the information from the teacher's introduction.[62] They start with the cost price of one bat, $C1$, which is 70 Swedish Kroner. Then they add insurance and transport which is 1.5 % of the cost price. They construct the formula $C2 = C1 + 0.015C1$. Then follows the transaction into Danish Kroner. Mary clears her throat:

Mary: OK, then there's the rate of exchange if you are to work out what it is in Danish Kroner, right?

---

[60] Actually the surrounding voices disturb the tape recorder, so that it is difficult to hear what Mary and Adam say. That is one of the reasons for many incomprehensible utterances [ic] in the transcript.

[61] We present and analyse the whole course, but in what follows some sequences of the transcript are omitted.

[62] Mary and Adam are going to construct the following sequence of formulae (in principle):
$C1$ (the original price)
$C2 = C1 + 0.015C1$ (insurance and freight is added)
$C3 = 0.8129C2$ (transaction into Danish Kroner)
$C4 = C3 + 0.08C3$ (duty is added)
$C5 = C4 + 0.25C4$ (profit is added)
$C6 = C5 + 0.25C5$ (VAT is added)
Our numeration is a bit simplified compared to Mary and Adam's. The conversation is strongly indexically anchored which means that the situational context including the computer gives meaning to the large number of features like deixis, pointing, facial expressions etc. This meaning can (easily) be understood by the students in the situation, but it needs translation or explanation when presented in another context.

Adam: Right… [looks down] Rate of exchange, then you write the
            rate there, don't you?
Mary: No, then you write 70 [the original price in Swedish Kroner],
            and then it's plus the rate, isn't it?
Adam: What if there's another rate and not 70 Kroner?
Mary: Then you write that box there plus the rate, I suppose?
Adam: We are not supposed to… we are only supposed to write the
            rate, we are supposed not to… we aren't supposed to write
            anything in that box.
Mary: Aren't we?
Adam: Not as I understand it. [4 sec.] It's just meant to be there so
            that… [4 sec.] It's just meant to be there so that we can go
            and change the rate. Otherwise we can't… Well, we can, but
            then we need to enter the formula or something, right?
Mary: Yes right, that's what I thought we might do.
Adam: Yes, but that would be more troublesome, if we were to
            change the rate instead of just having a place where we could
            write what the rate is.
Mary: It doesn't even say what the rate is, it says what…
Adam: …the rate is.
Mary: No.
Adam: Yes, it's 14.
Mary: That's not the rate.
Adam: Yes otherwise it wouldn't say exchange rate.
Mary: Wasn't it plus that one there? …It can't be true that 100
            Swedish Kroner cost 72 or 82.
Adam: Well OK, it does say 82.14.
Mary: Christ, is it that low? Well OK, that seems to be true then. [4
            sec.] But why does it say 82 Kroner down here then?
Adam: Because it's another… something right… 98-11-09, it's 3
            days since it was calculated, right? [4 sec.] Mikael [the
            teacher]… there are 2 different rates there and there. [points
            to the paper] What then?… that [points to the paper] and
            that…?

In this sequence Mary and Adam discuss how to operate with the rate of
exchange in the spreadsheet and what to do about the original price in
Swedish Kroner. They ask a lot of *inquiring questions*, which indicates
that they are mutually interested in *locating* the perspectives of the other
or in locating a possible perspective, which could be useful in trying to
cope with the problem of transaction into Danish Kroner. Some questions
are formed as arguments with a tag question at the end.[63]

---

[63] Lakoff (1975) introduced the term 'tag question' in order to describe women's use of
language when avoiding asserting their opinions. Eggins and Slade (1997, 86) state

Mary takes the lead and opens the question of the exchange rate: "OK, then there's the rate of exchange if you are to work out what it is in Danish Kroner, right?" She ends up with a tag question "right?" that can be interpreted as 'asking for confirmation', and she gets it. Tag questions can be seen as a way of *getting in contact*. They serve, too, as an invitation for co-operation. Tag questions can also be part of a personal way of communication or a demographically influenced habit. Anyway, tag questions can be observed as a dominant way of communication for both students, and they actually get and give each other confirmation in most instances. So, in the very beginning Adam confirms Mary's proposal and states a new one with a tag question: "Right... Rate of exchange, then you write the rate there, *don't you?*" This time Mary objects to his proposal and suggests writing the exchange rate in the formula. This proposal is not rejected but *challenged* by Adam who poses a hypothetical question: "*What if* there's another rate and not 70 Kroner?" (As "70 Kroner" does not refer to an exchange rate, a slight confusion occurs in this formulation. However, this is not referred to later, and it does not cause any particular problems.) We see this as an open and inquiring way of coming to an understanding which is followed by Mary's hypothetical questioning suggestion: "Then you write that box there plus the rate, *I suppose?*" *Hypothetical questioning* can be understood as a wondering attitude, as an openness and willingness to examine possibilities, instead of just rejecting or leaving the subject.

Adam argues that they just have to write the actual rate, and, as mentioned, Mary continues her asking attitude: "Aren't we?" Instead of just turning Mary's proposal down, Adam argues in an advocating way: "Not as I understand it." He puts his arguments forward, not as the absolute truth, but as something that can be examined. This can also be seen in the pauses in his speech. He acts respectfully to Mary's perspective as well as to his own, and we see this kind of behaviour as promoting a continuing process of inquiry. Mary confirms Adam's argument: "Yes right, that's what I thought we might do," and Adam continues his argumentation for a space to write the actual rate. This sequence can be seen as the students *advocating* their points of view while showing their openness to inquire about their own contributions.

They look for the information about the foreign currency which causes some difficulty for Mary, who wonders if the Swedish Krone is really of so little value: "It can't be true that 100 Swedish Kroner cost 72

---

that tag questions have ambigous functions as invitation and asking for confirmation in dialogue.

or 82. [...] Christ, is it that low?" The students are not operating with tasks simply referring to a well-defined semi-reality; they are also considering the real-life references. Could it really be that the rate is that low? Mary accepts this and goes on in her examination: "Well OK, that seems to be true then..." She continually asks inquiring questions and Adam continually tries to answer and challenge. Then he also *locates* two different exchange rates due to the change of exchange rates over three days. He addresses the teacher who does not answer him right away, and they go on the two of them, apparently without waiting for an answer.

After solving the problem with the exchange rate they have to consider how to make the spreadsheet calculate the price in Danish Kroner.

Mary:	Write C2.[64]
Adam:	C2?
Mary:	plus...
Adam:	Er... no, not plus, right?
Mary:	Well, yes.
Adam:	No, multiplied by the figure we found, right?
Mary:	But then you have to convert that figure there into zero point because that is in 100 Kroner. Then you have to convert it into a Krone... in a Krone, right? Then it's 0.82, no 0.8125.
Adam:	Then that's what you write when you write the rate, isn't it?
Mary:	Well OK, we'll do that then.
Adam:	We can also just write what happens first. C2 divided by 100, we have divided that there [4 sec.] up to 100 [ic]
Mary:	And then multiplied by that figure or what? So that it's 81.0, so...
Adam:	No multiplied by, no multiplied by that figure.
Mary:	Of course, multiplied by that figure, right? No, well...
Adam:	Yes.
Mary:	Of course, that's right, yes that's true, it's 0, because there is no exchange rate.
Adam:	Well, if we fix it at 81.29. [4 sec.] Then we get this amount of money, and that's quite likely, isn't it?
Mary:	Well yes.
Adam:	...I mean that our rate is a bit less?

They have to start with *C2*, and then do something to this figure. Mary suggests that the exchange rate could be added. Adam objects and suggests multiplication. Mary seems to feel her way through, fishing for Adam's confirmation, for example: "Of course, multiplied by that figure,

---

[64] Here, and in what follows, we have renumbered so that the references to the cells of the spreadsheet in the dialogue follow the numbering presented in note 62.

right? No, well…" She rejects her own proposal immediately which indicates that she is not so very sure. Mary follows Adam's suggestions in this sequence, meaning that she gives up advocating her own suggestion as soon as Adam objects to it. It might be because she trusts Adam's authority. It might also be that she has realised that adding the exchange rate would not bring the calculations in any promising direction. Adam: "Then that's what you write when you write the rate, isn't it?" Mary: "Well OK, we'll do that then."

Adam on the other side seems rather sure of what he is doing. He objects to Mary's proposals and asks for her confirmation, and he finally concludes that he is right by referring to their calculation from before. He ends up with a another tag question that makes Mary confirm: "Well, if we fix it at 81.29. [4 sec.] Then we get this amount of money, and that's quite likely, isn't it? […] I mean that our rate is a bit less?"

The construction of the formula is difficult. Mary suggests 'addition', but Adam hesitates. The conclusion is 'multiplication'. Finally, the uncertainty of multiplying by 81.29 and dividing by 100 becomes clarified. So, although the process appeared confusing, it resulted in a proper *identification* of the formula: $C3 = 0.8129C2$. Mary and Adam are both open to inquiry.

Profit

The formula: $C4 = C3 + 0.08C3$ (duty is added) is constructed, and Mary and Adam come to the question of profit. The profit suggested is 25%, but maybe this ought to be moderated in order to keep the price low. How to make the computer comprehend that?

Adam:	Profit is 25, isn't it?
Mary:	Then you just enter 25 over there.
Adam:	What?
Mary:	Then you just enter 25% over there.
Adam:	Yes.
Mary:	But that's only the profit
Adam:	But we have to be able to change the profit.
Mary:	But why do you want to write it in per cent then? Have you considered writing the percentage then, over there?
Adam:	Yes.
Mary:	Well OK. [4 sec.] How will you enter it?
Adam:	How will I enter what?
Mary:	Just try, then we'll reconsider.
Adam:	Then you write there, what… how much the profit is in per cent, right?
Mary:	And then you write 25%?

Adam:	Yes exactly, then you write [5 sec.] in all... and there you write equals...
Mary:	...that one, right?
Adam:	...that one.
Mary:	Plus profit, right?
Adam:	What?
Mary:	That one plus profit, right? That one [ic]
Adam:	No, not plus.
Mary:	Yes... oh no, it's, oh no, it's per cent. How the hell does one do that?
Adam:	That one... times... oops... times...
Mary:	...that box on top... and then you have to write it in...
Adam:	No wait a minute, multiplied by that one
Mary:	...and then divided by...
Adam:	di... divided by... 100... will it do that then?
Mary:	Should we try and find out?
Adam:	I mean if perhaps we ought to put it in parenthesis, then we are sure, aren't we. I don't know...

Adam is about to make a box in the spreadsheet for percentage of profit. Mary follows his actions by asking him a lot of questions about how to do it: "But why do you want to write it in per cent then? Have you considered writing the percentage then, over there?" and "How will you enter it?" Adam verbalises his reflections and Mary continually tries to follow what he is doing. She has a proposal about adding the profit, which is rejected by Adam, and she does not *advocate* her suggestion but withdraws it immediately. The process is intensified after Mary's question: "How the hell does one do that?" when Adam almost *thinks aloud* and they mutually complete the utterance of one another. We understand this as their efforts to understand each other and as their common responsibility for solving the problem. At the same time Mary and Adam seem to realise that neither of them has located an adequate perspective. It is not enough to understand each other. They need to do something more.

There seems to be some uncertainty about how to calculate the profit. Mary: "Plus profit, right?" Adam: "What?" Mary: "That one plus profit, right?" Adam: "No, not plus." Mary: "Yes... oh no, it's, oh no, it's per cent. How the hell does one do that?" Here Mary and Adam clear up various possible confusions. To calculate the profit you have to multiply by 0.25 and not by 25. There is also confusion about addition or multiplication? Thus, it is 'common knowledge' that profit has to be added. However, this does not simply mean adding 25% or adding 0.25. Several times they *reformulate* each other's formulation. By this process of reformulating and changing they try to *identify* a useful mathematical procedure.

Most likely such questions would not have caused any difficulty had Mary and Adam been presented with the problem as part of an exercise. The situation is, however, quite different when Mary and Adam themselves have to identify the formula. In a pre-constructed exercise the mathematical ideas have, in advance, been 'crystallised', and when the students then 'know the game of doing exercises', they can operate more directly with the mathematical formulae. But when mathematisation has to take place, certain difficulties emerge. They face the problem of *crystallising mathematical ideas* for themselves. Thus, they have to translate the task of transacting Swedish Kroner into Danish Kroner in terms of mathematical operations, and to translate 'adding profit' as an operation that includes multiplication.

One interesting detail at the end of this sequence is Adam's words about the capacity of the computer: "...will it do that then?" He does not question if they themselves can find out, but if the computer can. So he suggests including a bracket to be sure that the computer will accept it. We interpret this as his mildly ironical self-assurance at this part of the course. Mary on the other hand is more likely to wonder whether they can find out themselves: "Should we try and find out." And looking at the whole course it becomes evident that "try" is a key word in Mary's approach.

Almost completed

After some more advocating, locating and thinking aloud, the spreadsheet becomes almost completed, and they are about to see the whole picture:

$C1$ (the original price)
$C2 = C1 + 0.015C1$ (freight and insurance is added)
$C3 = 0.8129C2$ (transaction into Danish Kroner)
$C4 = C3 + 0.08C3$ (duty is added)
$C5 = C4 + 0.25C4$ (profit is added)
$C6 = C5 + 0.25C5$ (VAT is added)

When $C1 = 70$ DKr the result will be:

$C1 = 70.00$
$C2 = 71.05$
$C3 = 57.756545$
$C4 = 62.377069$
$C5 = 77.971336$
$C6 = 97.46417$

This result, however, would certainly not be acceptable for 'Batman & Co', who was only willing to pay 89 Danish Kroner for a table tennis bat.

Until now, Mary and Adam have been working all alone to set up the spreadsheet. It has not been easy, but they have supported each other a lot, and they have helped each other to move forward. *Inquiry co-operation* is taking place during the whole process. Thus, we can observe some interesting student patterns of communication that seem to progress their work. They are mutually interested in the perspective of the other – they ask inquiring questions. These questions lead to explanations, hypothetical questions, crystallising of mathematical ideas, and confirmation. They use a lot of tag questions that lead to mutual confirmation. They complete the utterances of one another and they treat each other and the perspectives of one another very respectfully. We have witnessed a dialogue where the elements of the IC-Model – getting in contact, locating, identifying, advocating, thinking aloud, reformulating, challenging and evaluating – all have been present.

We can, however, also observe some patterns of communication – a few only – that seem to obstruct their co-operation and prevent them from getting further. Sometimes they reject their own proposals before having examined them, and sometimes they object without argumentation.

Teacher interference

Mary and Adam have almost finished the spreadsheet set up when the teacher calls for their attention. He sits down next to Adam on his right side so that he can look at the screen. Mary sits next to Adam on his left.

Teacher:	You had a question, Adam.
Adam:	When?
Teacher:	I thought I heard you…
Adam:	Er… when you were over there. [points down the classroom]
Teacher:	No, er, I don't know… I just thought I heard you [ic]
Adam:	Maybe, but then I think we've figured it out… yes.

However, the teacher does not leave. He wants to get an idea about what they are doing. They are about to add the VAT when Mary explains:

Mary:	OK, the VAT is written in percentage… then there is the figure in total, it's just plus VAT. […]
Adam:	9… times, right? [ic]
Teacher:	What er…?

Mary interrupts the teacher in a loud tone of voice:

Mary:	Yes, yes, but actually what, what we have done, what's right… all we have to do is just change something to make it correct.
Adam:	We also have to write the price in total.
Teacher:	Look at that, isn't tha… isn't that a er…?
Mary:	But that's price in total.
Adam:	Yes, I know.
Teacher:	Isn't there a problem somewhere?
Mary:	Just copy, Adam.
Adam:	What, no, right? No just [ic]
Mary:	It's actually the same price, that one, right?
Adam:	Yes yes, it'll be there twice.
Mary:	Yes.
Teacher:	Could we ca… can you get that, all those decimals away… or is it possible to, at the end…?
Mary:	Oh yes, it's possible to do…
Adam:	Oh yes, it's possible to do…

They obviously become aware of the teacher's concern about "all those decimals".

Teacher:	How long can we carry on with the many decimals? How long can we justify them and say…?
Adam:	How long we can use them? [...]
Teacher:	How far down in er… [4 sec.] is it all right to calculate with 57.756545 Danish Kroner *there*, in line three?
Adam:	Yes that's all right, but it's not necessary.
Mary:	But otherwise it can't be really precise, but you can't have… that small, I mean you can't pay that small amount, can you?
Teacher:	But do you pay here?
Adam:	But that is multipl…
Mary:	But it doesn't matter, because you don't pay anything there, right?
Adam:	It does matter, because it is multiplied with… It'll be in the percentages, too.
Mary:	Mmm… it's only at the end you have to… to round it off, right?
Teacher:	Yes.
Mary:	That is where we are paying… what is it? [looks at the teacher]
Teacher:	Er… maybe, but that's because I don't know myself either…

In this sequence the teacher interferes in the students' work. He addresses Adam in the first place, reacting to his calling for him some time ago (when they had to choose between two different rates of exchange): "You had a question, Adam." But Adam tells him that they have found out in the meantime. Mary takes the lead to continue with Adam and indicates that they can manage without the teacher: "OK, the VAT is written in percentage." So when the teacher takes a turn, she interrupts him immediately in a very loud tone of voice: "Yes, yes, but actually…" She thinks they are on the right track and indirectly she rejects his interference: "what we have done, what's right… all we have to do is just change something to make it correct." The downgrading "all" and "just" indicates that she cannot see a problem, and she does not seem willing to follow the teacher's attempts to make them reflect. She interrupts him and gives her own explanation once again without listening to what he is trying to ask: "But that's price in total." She apparently ignores the teacher's *challenging* question: "Isn't there a problem somewhere?" and returns to Adam with a request to go on: "Just copy, Adam." In this sequence Mary continues to reject and counter-argue with everything the teacher says.

Mary seems irritated. She has changed from an inquiring attitude towards Adam before the teacher came in to an offensive attitude towards the teacher. She interrupts him, denies or refuses his proposals in a determined tone of voice, and she does not look at the teacher for a long time while talking to him. It seems like she would rather be without him.[65] The teacher, on his side, has sat down next to Adam, which might intensify the feeling of distance for Mary.[66] He asks a lot of inquiring questions: "Isn't there a problem somewhere?", "How long can we carry on with the many decimals?" and "But do you pay here?" etc. The teacher's questions relate to what the students have already done, and as the teacher does not explicate his intentions Mary might hear these questions as controlling or critically evaluating. This might be a reason for Mary not to accept the teacher's invitation. They do not *get in contact*, and at this stage it is not possible for the teacher to be a facilitator for Mary. They do not attune their expectations to each other, and this may be an obstacle to a common process of inquiry. The teacher tries to get in contact, but although Adam, previously, has asked for the teacher's attention, his presence is not really welcomed now. His presence appears more

---

[65] She confirmed this in a conversation four months later, saying that the teacher introduced a problem they had already solved. So they were at a quite different step of the process.

[66] The teacher said that he had the feeling that Mary pulled herself away from him.

like a disturbance. One reason could simply be that they are almost ready to start the experimental work with the spreadsheet.[67]

The teacher has not succeeded in making the students listen to his questions, so he goes directly to the point: "How long can we carry on with the many decimals?" and "How long can we use them?" We interpret this as an indirect request that he wants them to make a change, although his question starts out hypothetically with a general address "we" – later to become a "you". Adam concentrates on the screen, and he reacts to both Mary and the teacher. He does not seem to take anybody's part. To the teacher's question he argues that it is OK but not necessary to have many decimals, and that the decimals mean something to the result: "It'll be in the percentages, too." Mary supports this argument and adds another: "Mmm... it's only at the end you have to... to round it off, right? [...] That is where we are paying... what is it?" Her tone of voice indicates an offensive position towards the teacher, whose acceptance is cautious: "Er... maybe..."

Here they are getting closer to the point of the teacher interference. If the different steps in the spreadsheet represent real financial transactions, then it does not make sense to use more than 2 decimals. Thus, although freight and insurance are stated in terms of per cent, the actual payment of freight and insurance cannot result in any amount of money including more than 2 decimals. However, if the spreadsheet just serves as 'experimental reasoning' then there is no real point in being troubled with the number of decimals. Two different perspectives are present, but serious advocating does not seem relevant. Adam and Mary are about ready to do some experimenting with the spreadsheet. It appears not productive to occupy themselves with the teacher's queries. The getting in contact has not been successful.

However, at this point the teacher, referring to the decimal issue, makes a meta-statement: "I don't know myself either," which indicates a symmetry in the student-teacher relation. This remark changes their way of communication – not immediately, but it certainly makes a difference. The remark supports a new getting in contact. It signifies that the teacher is present and open to inquiry. Equality has been re-established. "I don't know myself either" serves as an invitation for inquiry and little by little Mary gives in and starts to co-operate. After sorting out some computer-technical problems, the teacher is about to leave:

---

[67] Later, this interpretation is supported by Mary's remark as the teacher leaves the group: "We are only half an hour late."

Teacher:	...now you ought to be able to work with that.
Adam:	Yes, we sure know that.
Mary:	Then we can go in and change... our profit shouldn't we try?
Adam:	Yes...
Mary:	We are only er... we are only half an hour late. [6 sec.]

The teacher seems to believe that his interference has clarified things to the students: "...now you ought to be able to work with that." But Adam's comment: "Yes, we sure know that" indicates that there has been no doubt for the students about what to do. At worst, the teacher might have wasted their time or his own. As Mary says: "We are only half an hour late."

Mary suggests a strategy for solving the problem: They can change their profit, as they have realised that buying the bats at 70 Swedish Kroner would result in a price of 97.46 Danish Kroner (or should we say 97.46417 Danish Kroner), which is not acceptable to 'Batman & Co'. Mary and Adam make an attempt, but it seems that the profit has to be reduced too much, in case the sum should be reduced to, at most, 89.00 Danish Kroner. They struggle for a while with the problem, but they are in need of a new idea of how to tackle the Batman condition.

What about turning it upside down?

At this point the teacher, who has returned, *challenges* the students. The co-teacher is by now also present:

Teacher:	What if, you could say... we want to make 25 per cent...? How much are we willing to pay for it then?
Mary:	Are we willing to what?
Teacher:	How much can we afford to pay...What are we agreeing to, what Swedish offer are we agreeing to?
Mary:	What, wh... what do you mean now? [looks down at her papers]
Teacher:	What is the maximum Swedish we can pay?

Mary, Adam and the teacher try out different things on the screen and they laugh together.

Co-teacher:	What did you want to pay for it?
Mary:	93.
Co-teacher:	What did you say?
Teacher:	89.
Co-teacher:	Really, well OK it was a bit more than 89... 93.
Teacher:	It's that department.

Mary:	63.75.
Co-teacher:	63.75 yes. [laughs]
Teacher:	OK.
Adam:	No, I just think 63.60.
Mary:	Ah… good [ic]

The teacher introduces a different idea. They need not reduce their profit, they could also try to 'make business'. They could simply give the Swedish supplier a different offer. But which? How much could they pay the Swedish supplier, and still offer the bats to 'Batman & Co' for 89.00 Danish Kroner without reducing the expected profit? The teacher initiates this possibility through hypothetical and challenging questions that almost appear as *thinking aloud* and serve as an invitation for locating a different possibility. The idea has not been indicated previously, and it represents a *turning point* in the investigation.

Here the communicative relation between the teacher and Mary changes. The teacher opens some new possibilities: "What if…?" And Mary wants to understand, so she asks him to explain further: "Are we willing to what?" and "What, wh… what do you mean now?" As she seems to understand, the three of them start non-verbal co-operation with the computer. We cannot hear what they mumble here, but as they all laugh they might have found some interesting or funny clues.

The co-teacher asks how much the students would pay, and she confirms Mary's proposal of a result, 63.75. It is not clear from where Mary gets the idea of 63.75 Swedish Kroner. It might be a result that has been calculated by the co-teacher. However, the following concentrated work shows that this proposal has no influence on Mary and Adam's approach. They are far away from the exercise paradigm where the basic element is the result. In fact, in this situation the result might appear irrelevant to them. The suggestion, 63.75 in Swedish Kroner, is not considered.

In the following exchange the teacher *challenges* the students again by suggesting that they turn the spreadsheet "upside down" and "calculate backwards". This combination of locating a new possibility and challenging the students becomes a *turning point* in the whole process of investigation.[68]

---

[68] Four months later Adam made the following comments about this: "It wasn't that exciting having to set up the spreadsheet. Turning it upside down was the big challenge. It was difficult and we came to a stop several times. It was difficult for instance when taxes had to be subtracted and not added."

Teacher: Now we can play around with it. [4 sec.] Could you er...
             could you make the spreadsheet in a way so you typed in the
             Danish Kroner from the start... this is how much we want to
             pay... I mean, kind of turning it upside down?
Adam: You mean... that we want to pay this much?
Teacher: If we from the start say 89 Danish Kroner, this is what we
             know... and then make a spreadsheet saying: then we know
             exactly what we want in that foreign country we are entering?
Adam: In a way that it will... so we could make *this* adjust?
Teacher: Yes, so we, so we know [ic] the nature of the problem...
Adam: Yes, yes.
Teacher: ...to 89... and what does that mean then, when we come
             down to Sweden... but could you make a spreadsheet that,
             let's imagine we could move to another country, say, wh...
             what does it mean in Switzerland in...? I know I'm a bit
             vague... if we were to try...
Mary: ...what... I don't quite understand what you mean?

The teacher continues the explanation.

Teacher: But if you could try it out precisely in a way so you could
             write 89 down there and then correct it.
Adam: If you... yes, then it would, yes.
Mary: This is what you mean, right?
Teacher: That is what I mean.
Adam: Yes, you could do that.
Mary: You *could* actually do that.
             [...]
Adam: Then we'll just make a new one.
Teacher: Do you want to do that?
Mary: Should we try it... shouldn't we then... couldn't we just...
             can't you go in and change this one...?
Adam: Then we can just go in and change the rate and...
Mary: ...in a way so we'll go up and say, that one er... that one
             should equal... something there?
Teacher: Give it a try.
Mary: Yes, should we give it a try?
Teacher: What you said before...
Adam: What?
Mary: What this here?
Teacher: What you said before was what I meant.
Mary: Yes, yes, by the way I just explained it. [laughs]
Teacher: Yes, you just explained it a bit better than me... yes...
             [laughs]
Adam: I'm lost!

The teacher introduces the idea of making an inverse spreadsheet that takes the maximum price in Danish Kroner as an input, and then determines what can be offered the Swedish company. "If we from the start say 89 Danish Kroner, this is what we know... and then make a spreadsheet saying: then we know exactly what we want in that foreign country we are entering?"

The teacher's hypothetical questions are followed up by the students' widening, clarifying questions to the teacher perspective: "You mean... that we want to pay this much?" and "so we could make *this* adjust?" Adam especially tries to understand what the teacher is getting at. Mary is momentarily put off: "what... I don't quite understand what you mean?" The teacher explains and suddenly Mary gets the clue. She completes the teacher's utterance at this place and states: "This is what you mean, right?" which is confirmed by the teacher. They are still talking 'what-if'-language. They are reflecting what they could possibly do, but still they have not decided anything, until Adam suggests: "Then we'll just make a new one [spreadsheet]." They agree to give it a try and quickly Mary verbalises her approach: "Should we try it... shouldn't we then... couldn't we just... can't you go in and change this one...?" She gets hooked on the idea: "Yes, should we give it a try?" and she gets full credit from the teacher: "Yes, you just explained it a bit better than me... yes..." They laugh together and it seems like the two of them have established a positive *contact* which is likely to be of importance to Mary's willingness to participate in (and learn from) the long and troublesome journey which is waiting for them. Compared to the previous teacher interference (addressing the number of decimals) this one challenges the students by introducing a new perspective: It is possible to do business with the Swedish supplier! Given this possibility it makes sense to try to turn the spreadsheet 'upside down'. Mary might experience this as a positive challenge, and this can be another reason for the regained positive relationship. Perhaps it is this alliance between Mary and the teacher that provokes Adam's reaction "I'm lost!" (spoken out in English).

The teacher certainly runs a risk by making this challenge. First, he cannot know beforehand if the students will accept his invitation, and he runs the risk of spoiling their engagement in the inquiry co-operation, which could have included experimental work with the spreadsheet they have already done. This experimentation could naturally also include the idea of 'doing business', and they would probably get to the conclusion that about 63 Swedish Kroner could be offered to the Swedish supplier. Secondly, the teacher runs the risk of over-challenging the students. The whole idea of the challenge is dependent on the students grasping the idea.[69] However, they do. We do not know exactly why this happens. Things have been somewhat cloudy to both Mary and Adam, but certainly they come to realise that there is something to go for. They face the challenge. A new approach is possible, turning the investigation around becomes a success.

Mary, Adam and the teacher begin to reflect together upon what would be the possibilities of turning the spreadsheet upside down – or rather what they are able to do when turning it upside down – then 'what-if' is replaced by another key term 'then we can'. They eagerly support each other by repeating what the other says, by questioning and by confirming. They end up in a good laugh together before the teacher leaves the group. So Mary and Adam are left in good humour and keen to continue for themselves.

Besides clarifying new possibilities, the last part of the dialogue might also have the important function of bringing back the ownership of the process of inquiry to the students. The teacher provides a turning point, and if the process is supposed to be owned by Mary and Adam, they should not only accept this, but also take over the responsibility for the process. Mary and Adam are now on their own.

Divided by… or is it just minus?

In what follows Mary advocates the idea of turning the spreadsheet upside down with a hypothetical *what-if question* and invites with a *tag-question*: "If we then try saying… that one, this box, right? It has to equal er… 89, and then minus all the stuff we went through… minus, divided by and all the stuff we went through, right?" They have to find some kind of algorithm. Mary outlines a possible procedure, and this calls for a crystallising of mathematical ideas. The agenda is set, and Mary and Adam set out on a long walk. They start with the last step in the original spreadsheet, the adding of the VAT:

$$C6 = C5 + 0.25C5$$

---

[69] We asked the teacher what he would have done, if the students had not accepted his challenge, and he said: "Well, there is a prelude to the course. I embrace Adam on his way to the classroom and ask him to accept my invitation. But then you can never tell, what will happen. The risk that the students do not accept your invitation is an occupational risk. Then you try another suggestion, coax the students, threaten them, give it up… or perhaps I would have tried another challenge."

What would the inverse process then mean? Mary explains again to Adam that they are going to subtract everything that they added before, and she checks with a question if he follows her: "...do you see what I mean?" But Adam is not quite sure, he wants Mary to show him.

For the first time he leaves the control of the keyboard to Mary, but the keyboard obviously causes Mary some problems, so shortly after the roles change again when Adam offers to show her what to do. Mary uses trial and error, and she invites Adam to co-operate, because, as she says, she does not think she can make it out herself. She seems to be insecure about the mathematical operations.

Mary:	Divided by... er... or is it just minus?
Adam:	Minus.
Mary:	25%, right?

The VAT needs to be taken away. But what could be the mathematical operation behind removing the VAT?

Because it is something you learn from

Mary wants to put the percentage of the VAT in the formula of the spreadsheet. But, obviously, Adam has a different way out of this problem. His next turn is a series of *challenging questions* followed by a reformulation of Mary's perspective. They are *thinking aloud* together, trying to *identify* the principles of the hidden algorithm. In what follows we can observe some individual differences in the students' approach that surface in their argumentation.

Mary:	...we have to be able to change everything, I mean, if there were to come er... the Prime Minister suddenly thinks that now it should be 26% [the VAT]... then we have to be able to write 26%...
Adam:	[ic]
Mary:	There, then we have to be able to change it up there too.
Adam:	Why does it have to be...?
Mary:	It has...
Adam:	...really, it's not relevant.
Mary:	It has something to do with, no, but it has something to do with spreadsheet, it's like, I mean we cannot... then we might as well just have written.
Adam:	No, because we don't have to go in and foresee all contingencies and make it be... over and beyond... [gesticulates] because then we could spend the rest of our lives on this crap.

Mary:	No, but it isn't difficult, it's just finishing up that formula.
Adam:	Yes, yes, but why do it, when you can skip it?
Mary:	Adam, because it is something you learn from… having to calculate all of it backwards… that's the hard part, if you just say er… the last figure we have… er… I mean that's not the pri… the price… right? Minus, then… it would be easy.
Adam:	Then all of it would be a lot easier.
Mary:	Yes, but then you don't learn the thing about calculating backwards, and how to do it on a spreadsheet… the point is that you are able to go in and change everything… I mean in theory, right, I mean why don't we just write plus 25% instead of writing plus that one, right… when we were calculating downwards?
Adam:	We didn't.
Mary:	We didn't, no, so we should, we shouldn't do it this time, should we?
Adam:	Why do we need to be able to change everything?
Mary:	That is actually the whole *point* with a spreadsheet, to be able to change everything, or we might as well just write, whatever we wanted there. [turns the computer to face herself]
Adam:	Well, by all means go ahead.

Adam has an *easy-way-out, product-oriented perspective*: They ought first of all to concentrate on what is necessary in order to solve the problem. You can see it in his arguments about what might be irrelevant: "…really, it's not relevant," "Well, but there's just no reason to do it, that's what the problem is." and "Yes, yes, but why do it, when you can skip it?" and he stresses the simple: "Then all of it would be a lot easier." Adam is also concerned about saving time: "because then we could spend the rest of our lives on this crap."

Mary has a *meta-learning, process-oriented perspective*: They should reflect on all possibilities in order to learn from their work. Her first argument refers to a possible change in the VAT: "[…] we have to be able to change everything, I mean, if there were to come er… the Prime Minister suddenly thinks that now it should be 26%… then we have to be able to write 26%…" She expresses a direct aim of learning: "Adam, because it is something you learn from… having to calculate all of it backwards," "Yes, but then you don't learn the thing about calculating backwards, and how to do it on a spreadsheet… the point is that you are able to go in and change everything… I mean in theory, right?" and "That is actually the whole point with a spreadsheet, to be able to change everything…" The easy-way-out perspective, as maintained by Adam, is overruled by a 'teacher' voice that can be heard in Mary's argumentation, for instance in her meta-statements: "Adam, because it is something you learn from" and "that is the point with a spreadsheet."

Mary and Adam reveal two different perspectives on what is the task, they argue without dealing with the perspectives of the other and without being willing to examine their own perspectives. This seems to block the inquiry temporarily and may have prevented them from identifying the principles of the hidden algorithm. It almost comes to a quarrel, when Adam suddenly pushes the key board away: "Well, by all means go ahead." This is one of the few times where the mutual respect is not maintained. They seem frustrated. They have not found a clarifying idea. Their long walk continues (and at this place we have left out a longer part of the transcript).

Yes, yes, you're right, no, it doesn't work

The two students go through a long and concentrated process of extracting the VAT. It appears to be very difficult for them to figure out how to write the formula. Trial and error is their predominant way of acting in the following excerpt. They verbalise their thoughts and actions. They continue to *think aloud* along their road.

Adam:	Minus 0.25. Then it just takes *C1* and subtracts 0.25... that's not really useful to us.
Mary:	No.
Adam:	If we had taken 0.25 from something.
Mary:	We can't just minus 0.25?
Adam:	If you have a figure and say minus 0.25, then you subtract 0.25, not 0.25%?
Mary:	Yes.
Adam:	We have to in fact subtract 25%, right?
Mary:	Yes.
Adam:	Are you saying 0.25?
Mary:	Yes, yes, you're right, no, it doesn't work.
Adam:	Then it subtracts...
Mary:	Then *divided* by 0.25%. Don't you think you can write that?
Adam:	It is times 0.25.
Mary:	No, because it is, yes, it is. Then we add 25%, right? Oh no, we don't. Oh no, we don't, then we have to say times. [ic]
Adam:	We don't?
Mary:	Yes, otherwise we had to say divided by 1.25, right?
Adam:	Times 0.25.
Mary:	Why are you dividing by *C2*?
Adam:	I'm not... times 0.25 then we have a figure... that...
Mary:	Oh yes.

Adam: ...that figure we then have to...
Mary: This one, this figure without VAT, that's the figure we have
           now, right?
Adam: No.
Mary: Isn't it?
Adam: That one is how much VAT we *pay*.
Mary: Yes, you're right. Then say times 100... no.
Adam: No, no, not at all. Then we have to say...
Mary: Then say... divide... divided by 1.25. Then we still have it.
Adam: No, but take a look. This one, now we actually have how
           much it is minus VAT, then we just take er... then we just
           take...

The idea of subtracting the VAT could lead to the formula:

$$C2 = C1 - 0.25$$

This possibility is scrapped by Adam: "Minus 0.25. Then it just takes *C1*
and subtracts 0.25... that's not really useful to us." The percentage must
be the percentage of something. Mary confirms: "We can't just minus
0.25?" They have, if not located the problem, then made a step towards
clarification.

Some clarification of the percentage and decimals is also needed.
Adam explains to Mary, who agrees: "If you have a figure and say minus
0.25, then you subtract 0.25, not 0.25%?" And as the VAT has to be subtracted, Adam suggests: "We have to in fact subtract 25%, right?" There
still is an agreement. Or is there? Mary is not quite sure: "Yes, yes,
you're right, no, it doesn't work." She suggests division instead of subtraction: "Then divided by 0.25%. Don't you think you can write that?"
But Adam comes up with the proposal of multiplication: "It is times
0.25." This is certainly not easy.

Mary tries to recapitulate. How is the VAT calculated: "...we add
25%, right? Oh no, we don't. Oh no, we don't, then we have to say
times." Mary then locates a new possibility. Could it be the opposite operation: "divided by 1.25, right?" Adam seems to ignore that a new
perspective is presented. Maybe he does not even hear the remark. He
just continues: "Times 0.25." Once again Mary tries to advocate her idea:
"Then say... divide... divided by 1.25. Then we still have it." Adam objects to her idea, it is left before being examined, and it is not stressed
again. The suggestion that they could divide by 1.25 is presented by
Mary without obvious forethought in the previous dialogue. This possibility has not been touched upon previously. This indicates that what is
made public in a dialogue is only part of the learning process. It may relate to former experience, reflection and learning. Further, some

processes of locating may not be linked to language in the same way as processes of clarification and justification.

In this process Mary seems quite confused and doubtful. Thus, we are not sure whether her suggestion about dividing by 1.25 should be seen as an expression of a well-considered identification of a method or as an arbitrary suggestion. She has a lot of suggestions, which she often regrets immediately: "Yes, yes, you're right, no, it doesn't work," "Then we add 25%, right? Oh no, we don't. Oh no, we don't" and "Plus, no minus total, no... yes, plus total." At the same time her repeated questions and tag questions ask for Adam's support and confirmation. She does not take responsibility for her own proposals, she does not *advocate* further her point of view, and this may be an obstacle to their inquiry. Adam, on the other hand, seems more secure about what to do, as he explains to Mary: "No, but take a look. This one, now we actually have how much it is minus VAT, then we just take er... then we just take... plus total." The apparent insecurity of Mary and the seeming security of Adam may have prevented them from considering Mary's suggestion of dividing by 1.25 that could have brought them immediately on a viable track. Some *locating* made, some locating lost.

Are you making it in one line only?

In what follows, the students struggle along the road to construct the inverse spreadsheet. They do not make things easy for themselves, trying to insert the formula in one line. But they do not lose courage during the process. They keep concentrating on the job, and they seem to insist on solving the problem.[70] But as Mary says with a laugh: "Oh my goodness, this is hard." The first element in their long formula is:

$$C2 = C1 - 0.25C1$$

They act like they are making progress. Next, the profit and then the duty also have to be subtracted, somehow. Things seem to be possible to handle. The formula they have now constructed contains the following elements:

---

[70] Some months later Mary confirmed this: "It is great to have the opportunity to finish the job, and it is very satisfying when one is able to reach one's goals."

$C1$ (the maximum price)
$C2 = C1 - 0.25C1$ (VAT subtracted)
$C3 = C2 - 0.25C2$ (profit subtracted)
$C4 = C3 - 0.08C3$ (duty subtracted)

However, the actual expression they are struggling with can be represented in the following way:

$$((C1 - 0.25C1) - 0.25\,(C1 - 0.25C1)) - 0.08((C1 - 0.25C1) - 0.25\,(C1 - 0.25C1))\ldots$$

It is not so clear to what extent they are convinced about the reliability of their approach. At this point the teacher shows up again.

Teacher:	Are you making it in one line only?
Adam:	Yes, yes. Then plus duty, then we need the reverse of…
Teacher:	Yes, apparently you have to do that right, or is it, it is difficult to distinguish the errors? Is that an error in the editing of the spreadsheet? [ic]
Adam:	Oh no, but it's just because er… We haven't, we are not done yet.
Mary:	It doesn't make sense yet. [laughs] We are not done with it, you see.
Teacher:	You are not done with it? Do you think it's a problem, I ask…
Mary:	Yes, it's extremely difficult.
Teacher:	…you mean the changing part?
Adam:	Minus…
Mary:	We have gone backwards now. Now we begin in a way so it goes backwards, right? That's what we're talking about, right?
Teacher:	Yes…
Mary:	Minus…
Teacher:	Can I, can I…?
Adam:	Do you think it'll work at all in the end?
Mary:	I don't know… I'd think it would.
Teacher:	I'll gi… I would, I had to, I would have to take it in smaller portions.
Mary:	How so? You have to have it all in one.
Adam:	He wants to make more boxes, make more boxes, you could do that, you could have done that there, that one, there, that one, there and so on.
Teacher:	How do we get from…?
Mary:	But then we should have done it the other way.

Teacher:	...how do we get from $C6$ to $C5$? Let's go over that first. [71]
Mary:	From $C6$ to $C5$... from $C6$ to total, we have it there, right?
Teacher:	How do we get from $C6$ to $C5$?
Mary:	No, we have written C there, we have put them together
Teacher:	Yes.
Mary:	Minus.
Teacher:	What is the VAT then... of the total?
Adam:	25%
Mary:	No, no, hey, we have taken... yes, yes, we have done it there. That figure er... $C5$ times 0.25, right?
Adam:	We can't say what it is.
Mary:	No, we can't say what it is, it doesn't say anywhere.
Teacher:	Can't you begin by writing 89, can't you begin by writing 89 there?
Mary:	Why should we begin by writing 89 there? What are you do-ing now?
Teacher:	[ic] Now I'm ruining everything for you. What happens if you go down into $C6$ and write 89? That's what we'd like it to end up with, you see.
Mary:	Yes, but that's what we'll do at the end, that's actually... yes, yes, oh, but that's... if we write 89 there, right? But that's what we are doing, but it doesn't matter, we don't have to write 89 in our er... our er... formula, do we? We have to be able to change that too, right? [4 sec.]

First, the teacher tries to intervene in Mary and Adam's attempt to write the formula in one single line: "Are you making it in one line only?" This could be understood as an implicit criticism, but the students do not let themselves be disturbed by this at once. As the teacher observes that Adam's attempt does not work he tries to *locate* what is the problem: "...is it, it is difficult to distinguish the errors? Is that an error in the editing of the spreadsheet?" Just like the first time he interfered, the teacher seems more concerned with what they have already done than with their on-going activity. And just like the first time, the students seem to get a little bit impatient or irritated here. Apparently they interpret the teacher's questions as implicit objections as they immediately reject his initial *challenging questions* by interrupting: "Yes, yes..." and by defending themselves. Adam says: "Oh no, but it's just because er... We haven't, we are not done yet." And Mary supports him with the same argument: "It doesn't make sense yet. We are not done with it, you see."

---

[71] Here, $C6$ and $C5$ refers to the numbering of the cells in their first spreadsheet.

The teacher paraphrases this go as to show that he has heard the argument. "You are not done with it?"

But the teacher does not give up that easily. He can probably see that they are in trouble and he asks: "Do you think it's a problem, I ask…?" Mary admits that it is "extremely difficult," but she does not ask for help. Instead she explains to the teacher that they are about to calculate backwards while continuing the process together with Adam.

The teacher still wants to intervene and he cautiously asks: "Can I, can I…?" As this obviously does not work he makes a suggestion formulated as a personal statement about what he would do, if he was in charge: "I'll gi… I would, I had to, I would have to take it in smaller portions." Adam begins to question their own strategy: "Do you think it'll work at all in the end?" and to follow the teacher perspective instead: "He wants to make more boxes, make more boxes, you could do that…" Mary on the other hand is not likely to give it up: "I don't know… I'd think it would." She challenges the teacher's proposal: "How so? You have to have it all in one," and she uses the subjunctive when talking about what they did not do, "but then we should have done it the other way," meaning that she is not likely to do things in another way now.

Until now the teacher has used an inquiring way of questioning, but here this is replaced by a quizzing questioning: "How do we get from $C6$ to $C5$?" and "What is the VAT then… of the total?" The teacher tries to lead the students on a new track, and the students do try to follow the teacher perspective here. Mary still seems unlikely to accept it, so she challenges the teacher's proposal of starting with the price: "Why should we begin by writing 89 there? What are you doing now?" The teacher takes responsibility by admitting that he is going to destroy their work: "Now I'm ruining everything for you." It must be hard for the students to accept that their efforts would not work. Adam poses questions about the teacher's proposal and tries to answer his questions. Mary, however, keeps objecting to the teacher's ideas, but he seems to ignore her when illustrating on a piece of paper what he would do.

In this context the teacher's quizzing questions and drawing on paper have the function of insisting on his own perspective. He does not want the students to do the formula in one line, but to divide it "in smaller portions". Thus, he takes responsibility for the new path of investigation to be followed. This can be interpreted as an intervention in the student inquiry co-operation, but as the teacher said afterwards, he considered the students' attempt to write the formula in one line as just too difficult for them to handle. So it is the teacher's choice not to over-challenge the students which justifies his taking over. Over-challenging is risky, but so is laissez faire. The teacher runs the risk of destroying the students' learning process no matter which choice he makes. What actually comes to happen depends on the students' reaction and the quality of contact between the participants during the process.

The teacher then introduces a game, to illustrate the tax problem. This game serves as a vantage point to illustrate an overall idea. At the same time this illustration serves as a new turning point in their investigation. This includes Sophie (another student) to play the role of the tax minister, and the teacher directs the lines. By starting this game the teacher also brings an end to Mary and Adam's long walk.

Teacher: You are the bat dealer, right?
Adam: Yes.
Teacher: Then I say: Try telling me that you'd like to buy a bat.
Adam: I would like to buy a bat.
Teacher: It'll be 40 Kroner a bat, but...
Adam: Tips.
Teacher: [to Sophie] Would you like to be the tax minister?
Sophie: Mmm.
Teacher: Then you have to say to me: Remember the VAT
Sophie: Remember the VAT.
Teacher: Oh yes, I have to remember the VAT, did you say?

The teacher chooses a price of 40 Kroner, which makes it easier to calculate. By means of role play he makes the students reconstruct the following:

When we have a price, say 40 Kroner, and we want to add the VAT of 25%, then the result will be 50 Kroner, and this is the price including VAT. When we, however, know the price including VAT and want to subtract the VAT, then it does not make good sense just to subtract 25% of the 50 Kroner. The VAT is 25 % of the original price, 40 Kroner, and not 25% of the 50 Kroner. But how many percent, then, is the VAT of the 50 Kroner? The amount 10 Kroner represents 10/50 of the price including VAT, and this is 20%. In short, the new percentage is calculated as:

$$0.25/(1 + 0.25) = 25/125 = 20\%$$

In general, if the original percentage is x, then the percentage to be used in the inverse formula is: $x/(1 + x)$. Applied, for instance, to the duty the result will be $0.08/(1 + 0.08) = 8/108 = 0.074$. These ideas were illustrated by the role play. An alternative approach would have been to let Mary and Adam continue the construction of their spreadsheet. Then they might have *located* that their principles for calculation would not have worked.

It is rather difficult for the students to understand how 25% when added becomes 20% when subtracted. Given the explanation, it is not clear if Adam has understood the point of the teacher's explanation. In the first place Mary seems to understand: "Oh yes... then it's a fifth, yeah," but a little later she adds: "No, I really can't figure it out any more." So, in the following, the teacher mostly addresses Adam.

Teacher:	How many per cent is the VAT of the amount in total?
Adam:	I'm writing what it has to say here.
Sophie:	It's 20 per cent of...
Teacher:	It's 20%, right?
Mary:	Yes.
Teacher:	And 20% of 89 how much is that? Or whatever it's called in the spreadsheet?
Adam:	It's called... it's called 89 minus 89 divided by 20 er... 0.20 then you have taken away the VAT.
Teacher:	No, I'm just looking for the VAT... the way you have arranged it...
Adam:	Are we to add it to those 89, or what are you saying?
Teacher:	That's what you have to extract, right?
Adam:	Yes, that was actually what I was doing.
Teacher:	Then please extract it. [ic]
Adam:	I sa... I said 89.
Teacher:	Write that instead then, we're just looking for the VAT.
Adam:	Oh, then we'll just say 89 divided by 0.20.
Teacher:	You're not saying it right, try writing it.
Adam:	Times 0.20.
Teacher:	Yes, now you're saying it right, can you write it right too?
Adam:	Er... yes.
Teacher:	And where do we have the price in total? We're still talking boxes.
Adam:	Ah, delete.
Teacher:	No, just leave it. We might be able to handle it that way... I can't quite see where it may lead us.
Adam:	I'd rather start over, because this is too complicated. I'll just write here. Aha, then it'll be... 63.9. [The teacher is talking to some other students]
Mary:	I'm... now I simply cannot follow your line of thought at all.

Adam's responses to the teacher's quizzing questions look somewhat random, and combined with his tone of voice and the look at his face it seems like Adam does not take responsibility for his own contributions: "Are we to add it to those 89, or what are you saying?" which could be interpreted as: "You can get what *you* want." Later he regrets and changes his statement immediately: "Oh, then we'll just say 89 divided by 0.20" to "Times 0.20". It looks like the quizzing pattern of communication in this sequence, on the one hand, leads to arbitrary guessing, disclaiming of responsibility and to dropping out and, on the other hand, it represents a thinking aloud that later provides a glimpse of the hidden algorithm. But at the moment, it stays hidden: "now I simply cannot follow your line of thought at all," Mary claims. This might also be because she is not directly invited to participate in the quizzing game. One interesting question is whether Adam has now understood – if the "Aha!" really indicates a new understanding. However, guided here by the teacher they reach the formula: $C2 = C1 - 0.20C1$ (VAT subtracted).

We have been quite clever, don't you think?

They are now ready to start on a new track. They have got the first formula in the inverse spreadsheet. For the teacher the purpose is again to hand over the ownership of the process to the students.

Mary: Then we have to take away the profit, right?
Teacher: Yes.
Adam: Yes.
Mary: Then please write minus profit, no profit.
Teacher: Mmm.
Mary: And that will be… if it is 25%, right? Then I guess it is the same, isn't it, as the VAT? Where it has to be 20%, right?

They seem to get the formulae:

$C1$ (the maximum price)
$C2 = C1 - 0.20C1$
$C3 = C2 - 0.20C2$

They follow the new principles, and the teacher confirms their work without further interference, until they get to the calculation of duty. That is the big test. Mary is worried: "Oh no, isn't it difficult?" So the teacher helps them through by comparing it to what they did before: "The VAT was… 25% of the 125" and "Only it's not times 0.2 this time, now it is… what? Can't you do it… can't you fit in the problem here?"

Adam: This one 8%. That means it's 8% of the 100.
Mary: Yes.
Adam: 100 plus 8.
Mary: 100 plus 8 is 108, right?
Teacher: It's 8 out of 108.

The teacher leaves, and Adam and Mary are on their own before the problem of duty is solved.

Adam:	Er… what the hell, what now? Now I have to get rid of that stupid figure, er… then I have to write… duty.
Mary:	Total has to go. No, no, yes, yes then… it's then… total minus… no, total times 0.074, total times 0.074… point 07, yeah… mmm, right? Isn't it just that? It's duty that has to fit?
Adam:	What? Yes, yes.
Mary:	Could that be right?

They reach the formula $C4 = C3 - 0.074C3$ as they have calculated: 8/108 = 0.074. They are about to succeed:

$C1$ (the maximum price)
$C2 = C1 - 0.20C1$
$C3 = C2 - 0.20C2$
$C4 = C3 - 0.074C3$

Left alone they go into the same sort of inquiring questioning co-operation as they did in the beginning of the process. They have now *identified* a consistent approach. They *think aloud, reformulate* and *advocate.* Characteristic of their inquiring co-operation here is that they question their own proposals, jointly examine them and agree to accept or reject them. It is amazing that they are able to do so after being almost locked up with the inverse spreadsheet, and we interpret this as an indication that they have recaptured the ownership of the inquiry process.

They have subtracted the VAT, the profit and the duty, and now they face the problem with the exchange rate. Mary suggests that they can convert and Adam confirms: "We can figure it out." They encourage each other to continue as they both recognise a type of mathematical problem of which they both have some experience: "I have done some exercises on it…" and "Yes, me too."

The previous sequences indicate that for an inquiring dialogue to take place the teacher's challenge must be adjusted to the student's skills and experiences with the subject. A task may be too complicated or too easy. A mathematical algorithm may be too difficult for the students to handle. Being able to challenge not too much and not too little seems to be important for the facilitation of learning. Thus, when Mary and Adam recapture the ownership of the inquiry at this place, they both refer to their former experience with such a mathematical problem. They have been challenged in a proper way.

Mary seems to realise how to solve the problem with the exchange rate as she suddenly claps her hands, takes a piece of paper and claims: "Now I know."

Mary:	And then we multiply that figure up to 100.
Adam:	Divide it by 100.
Mary:	No, we want that figure to become 100. We also have to bring it down to 10, wouldn't that be easier?
Adam:	We'll say 1, oops.
Mary:	What will be times 8?
Adam:	One hundred... times... no, 100.
Mary:	No, you don't have to multiply it by 100, you have to say what multiplied... with 8... [ic] Is this that figure... it can't be.
	[The teacher informs the class. "I would like to thank you for a really fantastic effort. [...] We'll meet up in 20-25 minutes by the bus."]
Mary:	It can't be true that... [7 sec.] Well, should we give up this?
Adam:	Yes, no, we'll save it, won't we?
Mary:	Yes, it's actually very interesting, we have been quite clever, don't you think?

They have almost finished. At this moment the teacher ends the lesson by collectively praising the Danish division of 'Run for your life' for having done a very good job. At the same time he reminds the class of the time for the excursion. But, as we stressed at the very beginning, Mary and Adam want to complete their calculations. They tackle the problem of the last issue: insurance and freight, and they calculate $0.01.5/(1 + 0.015) = 0.0147783$. They have produced the following sequence of formulae:

$C1$ (the maximum price in Danish Kroner)
$C2 = C1 - 0.20C1$
$C3 = C2 - 0.20C2$
$C4 = C3 - 0.074C3$
$C5 = 1.23C4$[72]
$C6 = C5 - 0.0147783C5$

They have finished!!! Mary and Adam react almost like winners of a sports game, shouting with joy, as they have finished the spreadsheet. Mary cheers and claps Adam's hands. What an *evaluation*.

---

[72] They have had some difficulties with the exchange rate. However, they have calculated $1/0.8129$ and got 1.23.

Mary and Adam's inverse spreadsheet provides the following calculation:

$C1$ = 89.00 (maximum price in Danish Kroner)
$C2$ = 71.20 (VAT subtracted)
$C3$ = 56.96 (profit subtracted)
$C4$ = 52.74496 (duty subtracted)
$C5$ = 64.8849305 (price in Swedish Kroner)
$C6$ = 63.93112202 (insurance and freight subtracted)

So, 63.93 Swedish Kroner is what they can offer the Swedish supplier per table tennis bat, if they have to comply with VAT, duty, insurance, etc. still getting a profit of 25% and not exceed the price of 89 Danish Kroner as offered by Batman & Co. We can also observe that the price of 63.93 Swedish Kroner is pretty close to the figure 63.75 Swedish Kroner, which was already brought to their attention at the beginning of their long walk. But obviously they did not pay attention to this.

The headline of the spreadsheet that they give to the teacher says "Pure genius!" and Mary's evaluating comment also clearly expresses a strengthened self-esteem: "We have been quite clever, don't you think?" That day they really learnt something.

THE IC-MODEL RECONSIDERED

During the analysis of 'Batman & Co.' we have identified the communicative features of the IC-Model that we presented in Chapter 2: *Getting in contact, locating, identifying, advocating, thinking aloud, reformulating, challenging* and *evaluating*. These elements were present both in the student-student interaction and in the teacher-student interaction when the participants were in a process of inquiry co-operation. The elements did not occur in a regular linear order, but they could be observed repeatedly in different combinations. We consider these communicative features to be closely linked to a process of inquiry co-operation. Obviously these features have a great influence on the students' ability to make progress in work. When the elements from the IC-Model were temporarily absent and replaced by, for instance, quizzing and guessing or insisting on fixed perspectives, the students seemed to get stuck in their problems. In this respect, there was obviously no difference if the teacher participated or not. This indicates a more general scope of the IC-Model.

The analysis of 'Batman & Co.' revealed several new inquiring elements that seem to relate to the IC-elements. As we have stressed the notions of the IC-Model cannot be seen as isolated or well-defined units. They rather occur in different clusters and combinations. However, in order to be able to discuss related communicative features, we want to reconsider each one of the IC-Model notions separately.

Getting in contact in terms of tuning in on the co-participant and his or her perspectives is a precondition of being able to co-operate. We understand contact as *being present* and *paying attention* to each other and to the contributions of one another in a relation of *mutual respect, responsibility* and *confidence*.[73] We see the process of getting in contact both as a preparation for inquiry and as a mutual positive way of relating among the participants during their co-operation that makes them *open to inquiry*. Mary and Adam kept this contact during most of the session. It could especially be seen in their continual *inquiring questions, tag questions, mutual confirmation* and *support*. And not to forget the good *humour* and times of laughing together.

Sometimes, however, the contact faded out; for instance when one of them momentarily dropped out of the process and left the initiative to the other, or when they got technical problems and began to quarrel. The same features could be seen in the presence of the teacher, especially, in relation to Mary. He refrained from tuning in on their work when he first interfered, and this might have caused Mary to ignore his questions, interrupt him and oppose to his help. In other words, the loss of contact became a hindrance for the co-operation. Conversely, showing his own uncertainty ("I don't know myself either") became a turning point in the contact between them and an opening to inquiry.

Mutual respect, responsibility and confidence refer to emotive aspects of an inquiry co-operation. At the same time they relate to the element in the IC-Model which we have condensed as 'getting in contact'. We find that emotive aspects constitute an essential part of a learning process that brings certain qualities to learning.

Locating. To *locate* means finding out something that you did not know or was not aware of before. Teacher and students can try to locate existing or new perspectives by asking *inquiring questions,* meaning questions that express a wondering attitude, and questions to which there are no given answers beforehand. Locating in co-operation is a process of

---

[73] Such qualities in the relationship is also described by Rogers (1994).

expressing perspectives and making perspectives visible at the surface of communication. The process of locating is a process of *examining possibilities* and *trying* things out. Thus, *hypothetical questions* like *what-if questions* can also be understood in terms of openness and willingness to locate new possibilities. Locating means *zooming-in* and dwelling on a subject before rejecting it, for instance by questioning and examining an algorithm though it might turn out to be useless.

The hypothetical question can be an indicator of travelling in a landscape of investigation. The teacher can invite students into such a landscape by introducing some what-if questions. And when what-if questions are presented by the students, they can establish ownership of the process. Locating is closely related to the issue of ownership: Whose ideas are located? Can these ideas serve as *my* ideas? In the case of Mary and Adam, we observe different indicators of their ownership of the process. The teacher plays an active role in the process of handing over where he tries to make them re-establish their ownership.

Mary and Adam make great effort to locate the perspectives of the other. They ask a lot of questions that provoke *explanations, hypothetical questions, check-questions* and *confirmation*. They often question their own proposals, jointly examine them and agree to accept or reject them. So the process of locating activates other inquiring elements as well.

Hypothetical questions can have several other functions, as for instance being ironic or signalling distance or irrelevance. The function in use depends on the user's intentions and the communicative context. So, there has to be a wondering attitude and an openness in order to interpret hypothetical questions as constructive to the process of inquiry. This goes for other communicative acts as well. Thus, questions can also be interpreted as control, and they can be ironic. Reconsidering the first teacher interruption addressing "all those decimals," we can see that questions can also be experienced as pedantic and irrelevant. Such questions can be ignored, as Mary tried to do, so that the process of inquiry can continue. They could also be accepted, which could imply that the teacher would re-conquer the teacher authority and the communication turn into a bureaucratic teacher-student exchange of remarks.

Being involved in an open process also means running the risk of 'not being able to locate'. Maybe because one comes to ignore an interesting suggestion from another. Other obstacles occur when the students reject their own proposals before having examined them or object to each other without argumentation. The teacher being absent during most of the process is not able to catch all of the students' ideas, because he has simply not heard them. But when he co-operates with the students we see many examples of the teacher facilitating students' locating. For instance, he asks hypothetical questions that are followed up by the students' *widening, clarifying questions*. This mutual questioning seems to create new perspectives and elucidate others.

A set of slightly different formulae could have been used as a base for the original spreadsheet. VAT could be added to the price by multiplying the price by 1.25, etc. Or, more generally, equations of the form: $C5 = C4 + xC4 = (1+x)C4$, would have provided the following set of formulae:

> $C1$ (the original price)
> $C2 = 1.015C1$
> $C3 = 0.8129C2$
> $C4 = 1.08C3$
> $C5 = 1.25C4$
> $C6 = 1.25C5$

This would make clear that every cell is related to the previous one by a factor, and the first cell, *C1* is related to the last one, *C6,* by a factor which is the multiple of all the factors. Thus

$$C6 = 1.3923453C1$$

When the multiplier 1.3923453 relates *C1* with *C6*, then the divisor 1.3923453 will relate *C6* with *C1*. In particular, if the maximum price is 89.00 Kroner, then the price we could offer 'Batman & Co.' is 89.00/1.3923453 = 63.93112202.

Mary opened this line of thought. They could remove the VAT by dividing by 1.25 ("*divided* by 1.25, right?"). Thus, when a process of inquiry is in progress, there might be interesting and relevant perspectives which are ignored and left out. They are *not located*. It might be the case that the learners in the process are not able to catch the perspective of a certain suggestion, and that an 'authority' is needed in order to help underlining that certain ideas need particular attention. This need not be problematic. But it is important to realise that students taking part in a forceful process of inquiry are also is a situation where relevant ideas will be dropped and clues will be overlooked. Mary's idea about dividing by 1.25 was dropped. Adam was not getting its importance, and Mary could not explain it herself, and did not insist that there might be something in the idea. The teacher was not around and consequently he could not be aware that the idea had been presented.

Identifying. Examining perspectives and ideas in terms of locating makes *identifying* a perspective a possibility and makes it known to every participant in the inquiry. In that way it can be used as a resource for further inquiry. Sometimes the participants *reformulate* and change calculations in order to come to *identify* the nature of a mathematical problem. In other words, they try to *crystallise mathematical ideas,* meaning being able to identify a mathematical principle or algorithm that emerges from the mutual locating process. One overall idea of the project 'How much does a newspaper fill?' was to clarify the meaning of 'to fill', referring either to 'area' or to 'volume'. Such a crystallising of mathematical notions is necessary in order to give meaning to further activities and calculations.

A what-if question can naturally be followed by a *why question.* We relate the what-if question to locating, while, in many cases, why-questions can be related to the process of identifying (perspectives in general or mathematical ideas in particular). Thus the teacher helps Mary and Adam to identify the basic principle of constructing the inverse spreadsheet by the exemplification which includes Sophie as a tax minister. This story brings into focus an explanation why the percentage has to be changed when 'calculating backwards'. In order to grasp why-questions, it becomes important to crystallise mathematical ideas. We also need to demarcate the presented characteristic of why-questions from why-questions that are not inquiring and used in the traditional classroom to close or control student contributions.

Furthermore, we have to consider what can be called the dilemma of the 'quizzing' communication. In order to crystallise certain mathematical ideas a teacher can use a quizzing strategy. On the one hand, this may help to clarify particular issues. On the other hand, the students might step out of the inquiry process. Many quizzing strategies are in operation in the traditional mathematics classroom. It might be difficult for the students to distinguish one from the other, and they might feel insulted in any case. Thus, the teacher has to face this dilemma when he tries to identify the mathematical principles of the inverse spreadsheet. We characterised his question: "How do we get from $C6$ to $C5$?" in the section "Are you making it in only one line?" as a quizzing question, because the teacher knew the answer to his question himself. However, as we have seen, it served an important function in the inquiry process.

In the project 'What does the Danish Flag look like?' we also observed a sequence of quizzing questions (see the 'Intermezzo: Challenging or quizzing?'). Here the process led to the identification of a principle for determining the position of the white strips on the red paper. In 'Batman & Co.' the situation where Sophie served as tax-minister was also dominated by a quizzing strategy, but it served the purpose of identifying the principle of 'calculating backwards'. This last episode also shows the importance of humour as part of a process of inquiry. It was

possible for Mary and Adam to see the quizzing episode not as an interruption but as a support for the identification of an idea, which in fact
could be Mary and Adam's idea.

Why-questions lead to *justification*. In mathematics, justification has
taken a particular form, that of a proof. But many other forms of justification are possible. In the case of Mary and Adam it is not so clear that
justification becomes expressed in an explicit verbal form. That some
justification is related to a shared perception is indicated by the process
where Mary and Adam 'go backwards'. First, they do it their own way,
and their conversation makes clear that they are not too convinced about
the reliability of their method. It is not possible for them to identify a
confirming perception of what they are doing: Something is wrong. Their
long walk can be interpreted as a period, where they have not identified
any adequate perspective for a justification of what they are doing. They
probably experience what it could mean for students to operate in the risk
zone associated to a landscape of investigation. However, when, in the
second try they go backwards, their conversation clearly indicates that
they have grasped a shared perspective and identified a principle that
provides mathematical meaning to what they are doing.

From the dialogue we can read the principle: A statement must be
doubted if there is no (shared) confirming perception of its truth. This is a
radical principle, and it appears that Mary and Adam apply it strictly. For
instance, the principle is illustrated by the difference in their conversation
when they construct their first inverse spreadsheet and the joy they express when they grasp the idea of the inverse spreadsheet. The
construction of the 'wrong' spreadsheet is not accompanied by a justification in terms of shared perception.

In some sense the process of identifying is more clarifying than the
process of locating, as it includes a crystallising of mathematical ideas
and an opening for why-questions as a follow up of what-if questions.
Still we have to remember that not only mathematical ideas can be identified, but also perspectives in general which, naturally, also can be
explored in depth. Perspectives in general can be seen as sources for justification.

Advocating. Learning starts from somewhere. Something is already learnt
and known. When the learning subject is more than one individual then it
becomes essential to establish an inter-subjective sharing of what is
known. The way of establishing a shared platform of what is known
presupposes a sensitivity of the existence of different perspectives. It also
presupposes a shared understanding of perspectives as sources for
justification. Naturally, a way of considering a situation could establish

lines of justification, which, in the end, appear to be dubious or simply wrong. The way Mary and Adam originally considered the principle of calculating backwards would have led to inconsistent results. In order to illuminate a perspective it is important that lines of argumentation are tried out. This presupposes *advocating*.

Advocating can contribute to establishing a shared understanding of a perspective. Advocating means stating what you think and at the same time being willing to examine your understandings and pre-understandings. In that sense advocating involves stating or arguing with the purpose of mutual inquiry of a topic or a perspective in order to clarify what this perspective might involve. This is opposed to claiming, which means trying to convince the other that you are right without being involved in a process of justification. Advocating opens inquiry. In 'Batman & Co.' Adam's comment: "not as I understand it" as a reply to Mary's suggestion indicates an openness to inquiry. His doubt is put forward, not stated as an absolute refusal, but tentatively as something that can be examined. *Tag questions* like for instance "isn't it?", "don't you think?" or "I suppose?" can have the same invitational function.

Thus, another important implication of advocating is to keep the focus and dwell on a statement or suggestion and to examine it before it is accepted or rejected. We have seen a lot of examples of this throughout the work of Mary and Adam. However, we have also seen examples of the opposite, especially when Mary immediately rejects her own proposal, for example: "Of course, multiplied by that figure, right? No, well..." She does not advocate her own proposal but withdraws it in order to follow Adam's perspective. In the students' efforts to identify an algorithm to find the VAT, Mary's suggestion about dividing by 1.25 could have brought them to a new direction of inquiry. But she does not advocate her point of view, she regrets it immediately. Mary might be afraid of being mistaken. However, advocating does not mean arguing because it is a personal view, which should be maintained at any cost. Advocating means putting forward arguments for an idea, *as if* it for a while could be 'my' idea or 'our' idea. As part of an inquiry process it becomes relevant to advocate alternative ideas.

In terms of mathematics, advocating can be seen as a trying out of suggestions for proving. This means that proving becomes interpreted as a result of a collective process of inquiry. In this respect we find ourselves in accordance with the way Imre Lakatos (1976) presents the collectivity of proving. While Lakatos condenses a piece of the history of mathematics to take place in an imaginary classroom, inhabited by Alpha, Beta, Gamma and many other students, we consider real classrooms with students like Mary and Adam. However, we see the process of inquiry as similar, in particular the process of advocating.

Thinking aloud means expressing one's thoughts, ideas and feelings during the process of inquiry. Formulating what is inside makes perspectives visible and accessible to collective inquiry. Some *hypothetical questions* almost appear as thinking aloud, and serve as an invitation for further inquiry.

There is a beautiful example of thinking aloud in the section 'Yes, yes, you're right, no, it doesn't work'. Mary and Adam are not sure of anything, and they try to grasp the steps of the calculation by expressing them carefully. It may appear as a kind of trial and error, but, certainly, it is an example of thinking aloud: – How to subtract the VAT? – 0.25 can be subtracted. – No, it cannot be subtracted. – 25% can be subtracted. – Or devide by 0.25%. – 25% can also be added. – Or it is possible to divide by 1.25. This sequence appears as a long process of thinking aloud, where Mary and Adam are searching for a unifying principle. In the first part of the section 'We have been quite clever, don't you think?' there are also examples of thinking aloud. We have, however, only quoted a small bit of this conversation, but it has form as illustrated by their figuring out how to handle the 8% duty. Here their thinking aloud represents a 'triumph', it is a shared confirmation of the reliability of their calculations.

Students might learn through the process of expressing ideas and understandings in an inquiring dialogue with others. We suggest the term 'learning by talking' to describe a dialogic process, where the participants examine and develop their understandings and pre-understandings of the subject. Thus, 'talking' in that sense is not just any kind of talk, but a verbalised inquiry.

Thinking aloud can be understood as a particular form of *making thinking public*. For instance, diagrams have a role to play (not least in mathematics) as a way of communicating ideas. Diagrams can be interpreted in a much more general form as 'something to point at', as something that is visible. Thus, by means of a spreadsheet, 'public thinking' becomes accessible for experimenting. Generally speaking, thinking aloud refers to an important aspect of an inquiry process, namely making it public and thereby making it accessible for further examination. The use of computers has been interpreted as a tool in the process of learning. It can also be seen as a restructuring principle for the whole process.[74]

---

[74] For a presentation of computers as a restucturing principle, see Borba and Penteado (2001).

We agree with this latter perspective but here we only want to emphasise that a computer, and in this case in terms of a spreadsheet, provides a new form of thinking aloud. Mathematical procedures become visible, and the conversation includes literally much pointing at the screen. New ways of thinking aloud supports new ways of learning and of collectivity.

Reformulating means repeating what has just been said, maybe in slightly different words or tone of voice. Reformulating can mean *paraphrasing,* which focuses the attention of key terms or ideas simply by the process of saying things again. Paraphrasing can also be used to confirm that one participant has heard what the other said and as an invitation for further reflection. In that way the participants can confirm a mutual understanding or conversely, they can become aware of differences that need to be clarified.[75] Reformulating in that sense is an important element in a process of active listening, where the participants follow each other closely in order to come to understand the perspectives of one another.[76] This element is a predominant way in the inquiry co-operation of Mary and Adam.

A reformulation can be initiated by *check-questions* through which one can check up with the other whether you have understood him or her in the right way, or you can check whether things you imagine to being the case are really the case. Check-questions can serve as a tool for clarification that is important in any process of advocating as well as in an inquiry process in general. Closely related to the term of reformulating and of thinking aloud is the *completing of utterances.* We saw how Mary and Adam did this in their efforts to understand each other and we interpreted this as a common responsibility for the process.

Reformulating is important in order to specify what-if questions and why questions. In this way new precision in, for instance, advocating can

---

[75] Stewart and Logan (1999, 229) suggest 'paraphrase plus' which means adding ones own contribution to enlightening the paraphrase in order to promote the co-operative examination further.

[76] Rogers and Farson (1969) have introduced the notion of active listening in this sense. Davis uses the term 'hermeneutic listening' for a similar activity, which includes participation in the "unfolding of possibilities through collective action" (Davis, 1996, 53). Stewart and Logan (1999) distinguish between three different types of listening. Reflective, analytical listening where you reflect and try to understand what is said in relation to your own conceptions is one pole. This kind of listening is related to oneself. The other is emphatic listening, where you try understand the other and his way of seeing things. This kind of listening is related to the other. Dialogic listening focuses on both parties in a mutual proces. Dialogic listening means being more interested in creating meaning than in being right.

be developed. However, reformulating also has an important emotive element. It can be interpreted in terms of *staying in contact* during a process of inquiry. In this sense reformulating means a follow up of 'getting in contact', however, 'staying in contact' is related to the central part of an inquiry process. This aspect of reformulating is characteristic for the Mary-Adam dialogue.

Challenging means the attempt to push things in a new direction or to question already gained knowledge or fixed perspectives. An advocated proposal can be challenged for instance through *hypothetical questions* starting with a 'what if'. We have associated what-if questions with locating, and certainly locating an alternative perspective can mean a strong challenge. Challenging and hypothetical questions are related terms. They can both serve as an invitation for an *examination of new possibilities*. This is what happens when the teacher makes Mary follow his hypothesis and she gives in to her resistance against him.

Clarification of perspectives appears a precondition for challenging them. One reason for Mary's resistance to the teacher intervention could be that this precondition was not established. Maybe she did not feel that the teacher was aware of what they were doing and why, before he indicated the possibility of an alternative. So she rejected the challenge by interrupting the teacher and by defending her own position.

A challenge can occur through new advocacy or through *re-examination of perspectives* that are already taken for granted. Such a challenge can relate to the other's perspective as well as to one's own. A challenge becomes successful when somebody grasps it. We saw how the students were not likely to do so as the teacher first interfered. But we also saw how Mary and Adam realised that 'turning it upside down' could be a real challenge providing a new approach for their work. They took it on, and it became a *turning point of their investigation*. Other challenges might have been overlooked or ignored, like when Mary suggested the division operation to solve the problem with the inverse spreadsheet. Finally, we want to stress that challenging can be successful also when it is contradicted, for instance by elaborated advocating.

Evaluating. An *evaluation* can take many forms. Correction of mistakes, negative critique, constructive critique, advice, unconditional support, praise or new examination – the list is incomplete. Evaluation can be made by others and by oneself. In the analysed course of 'Batman & Co.' we can observe two kinds of teacher evaluation. One is the continuous attention to what the students are doing. Another is the final evaluation where he gives unconditional support and praises their work. Mary and

Adam also evaluate their own work. "We have been quite clever" is one example, and their non-verbal reaction after they have finished leaves no doubt about the nature of their self-evaluation.

In the evaluation the emotional and epistemic part of an inquiry process are brought together.

In this chapter we have tried to specify the elements of the IC-Model by considering related terms that emerged from our analysis. Thus, *getting in contact* involves inquiring questions, paying attention, tag questions, mutual confirmation, support and humour. *Locating* has been specified with the clues of inquiring, wondering, widening and clarifying questions, zooming in, check-questions, examining possibilities and hypothetical questions. *Identifying* involves questions of explanation and justification and crystallising mathematical ideas. *Advocating* is crucial to the particular trying out of possible justifications, and it is closely related to arguing and considering. *Thinking aloud* often occurs as hypothetical questions and expression of thoughts and feelings. *Reformulating* can occur as paraphrasing, completing of utterances and staying in contact. *Challenging* can be made through hypothetical questions, examining new possibilities, clarifying perspectives, and it can be a turning point of investigation. *Evaluating* implies constructive feedback, support and critique.

The development of the IC-Model helps us to concretise important communicative features of an inquiry process of learning, where the examination of perspectives and the ability to reflect different perspectives is a crucial aim. As we have seen this implies a curiosity to examining ideas and suggestions in an open and unprejudiced way and a flexibility to change direction when a new perspective is located or an established perspective is challenged. We have also pointed out the importance of a teacher challenge being adjusted to the students' competencies and abilities in order to be accepted as a challenge.

The IC-Model refers to a cluster of communicative elements, which may occur in different forms and order. Sometimes a communicative flow may be interrupted by other patterns of communication, maybe by some degenerated elements of the IC-Model, like a challenging turning into a quizzing. We are interested in this cluster of elements as we find that the IC-Model represents certain qualities of communication, which can turn into certain qualities of learning. Although we have presented the elements of the IC-Model somehow separately, they represent aspects of the same unified process of inquiry. The separation only serves as an analytic device to provide a more detailed presentation.

Before getting into a discussion of 'qualities of learning', we need to clarify further what we have in mind when talking about 'qualities of communication'. Some of these qualities we will express in terms of 'dialogue'. We have already used this word several times, but in the following Chapter 4 we shall try to specify our use of 'dialogue'. With this clarification in hand, we shall develop further the link between qualities of communication and qualities of learning. In Chapters 5 and 6 we shall, by means of an analysis of new empirical observations, suggest the notions of intention and reflection as essential for clarifying how dialogue becomes a source for learning with certain qualities – qualities which we will come to refer to as critical learning. However, first we need to take a closer look at the concept of 'dialogue'.

CHAPTER 4

DIALOGUE AND LEARNING

The analyses in the previous chapters have focused our attention on qualities of communication in learning processes. In Chapter 1 we considered a quizzing and guessing communication as an overall pattern in classroom absolutism, where mistakes and correcting of mistakes play a predominant role. We referred to the exercise paradigm where bureaucratic absolutism was often present. In Chapter 2 and 3 we challenged this paradigm by introducing landscapes of investigation, looking at, for instance, students' perspectives as a resource for learning, and we developed a communication model for inquiry co-operation, the IC-Model.

In this chapter we want to discuss the IC-Model with a theoretical reference to other concepts. In particular, we want to take a look at the notion of dialogue as it is closely related to a communicative interpretation of inquiry. We see a dialogue as a learning oriented conversation. This indicates an interpretation of dialogue as being not just any conversation but a conversation with certain qualities: "Dialogue implies more than a simple back-and-forthness of messages in interaction; it points to a particular process and quality of communication in which the participants 'meet', which allows for changing and being changed." (Cissna and Anderson, 1994, 10) We shall discuss such qualities with a special reference to their learning potential.

The elements of the IC-Model emerged through observations in the mathematics classroom. The notion of dialogue that we are going to present in this chapter is developed through a theoretical clarification that includes ideal elements, and certainly the notion is not restricted to the mathematics classroom. This means that dialogue becomes an ideal concept, referring to certain qualities. We are interested in the particular nature of these qualities, and we will consider how they relate to the elements of the IC-Model and to qualities of learning.

THE SOCRATIC DIALOGUE

Dialogue and learning have been related terms since the ancients and the Socratic dialogues. In one of these dialogues, *Menon*, Plato describes how Socrates teaches the slave, Menon, geometry.

Plato wants to show that knowledge resembles memory. In the dialogue Socrates does not inform Menon about any geometric facts. Socrates only asks questions, and thereby he does not exactly pass information to Menon. Nevertheless, Menon recognises that when the sides of the square are doubled, then the area becomes quadrupled. Later, Menon is able to state that in order to double the area of a square the diagonal of the original square should be used as sides of the new square. (Or in other words: the sides of the original square have to be multiplied by $\sqrt{2}$ in order to get the length of the sides in the new square.)

This presentation of the Menon-dialogue indicates that knowledge is not passed from one person to another. At this point, Plato is in accordance with modern educational theory as, for example, radical constructivism (see, for instance, Glasersfeld, 1995), which also claims that knowledge cannot be transferred from one person to another. According to Plato, and this is different from radical constructivism, knowledge already exists within the person, but knowledge is 'slumbering'. Plato claims that all kinds of knowledge exist beforehand within the person, but that the person has forgotten what he or she somehow already knows. The right method of teaching is, consequently, to bring the person to remember what he or she already knows. When the proper way of teaching is to help the learners to remember, nothing seems more natural than asking.

This is the main inspiration from the Socratic dialogue: the teacher's task is not to tell something to students or to provide information, but to ask questions. However, these questions do not have the function of 'checking' the students but to bring back their memory or, using the terminology of constructivism, to support the students in their knowledge construction. Plato considered learning as recognition and the teacher as a midwife helping through questioning with the delivery of the (reborn) knowledge.

The whole idea of a teacher-questioning attitude in facilitating the learning process refers to the Socratic dialogue. A closer look at the Menon dialogue, however, reveals that the 'dialogue' is not a dialogue in our use of the term.[77] The conversation is lead by Socrates who asks

---

[77] See Struve and Voigt (1988) for a discussion and critique of the Menon dialogue.

questions of the mathematical subject. In that process the 'teacher inter-pretation' of the topic structures the main part of the conversation. Socrates presents and discusses the topic, and he refutes false assump-tions by argumentation that results in Menon's agreement. Menon's contribution to the conversation is 'yes' or 'no', once in a while as very short confirming answers to Socrates' rhetorical questions. This is cer-tainly minimal response to the teacher questions (see Chapter 1). So, from our perspective this conversation looks more like a quiz than like a dialogue. Socrates appears like a teacher that has the answers to his ques-tions beforehand, and the purpose is to make Menon follow his track by making him confirm the arguments step by step. Nowhere in the conver-sation does Menon take the initiative by asking new questions, suggesting other perspectives or making his own statements. The Socratic method, unfolded in the conversation with Menon, is very much like the step by step communication pattern we find in the traditional classroom, and it could easily remind us of the quizzing intermezzo, which we described in the previous chapters.

By these critical comments we do not in any way pretend to provide an analysis of the original Platonic dialogue. However, we want to draw attention to the problematic references found in much recent educational literature to the Socratic method, indicating that a certain pattern for edu-cational practice is already available. The situation is much more complex, and in what follows we want to reconsider the role of dialogue in the facilitation of learning by the inspiration of different theoretical concepts of dialogue.

DIALOGIC QUALITIES

A dialogue can take place among two or more participants. The crucial point is not the number of participants but the nature of the conversation and the relationship between the participants. Dialogues take place through verbal and non-verbal interaction.

Ethymologically the word 'dialogue' stems from the Greek 'dia' which means 'through' and 'logos' that can be translated by 'meaning' (Bohm, 1996, 6). Such ethymologic references can be used as inspiration for further clarification. For instance, John Stewart concludes: "So dia-logue in this sense means 'meaning through', or the process of helping meaning flow through the people involved in co-constructing it." (Stew-art, 1999, 56) And William Isaacs states: "During the dialogue process, people learn how to think together – not just in the sense of analysing a shared problem of creating new pieces of shared knowledge, but in the sense of occupying a collective sensibility, in which the thoughts, emotions, and resulting actions belong not to one individual, but to all of them together." (Isaacs, 1994, 358) Dialogue in this sense differs from a discussion, which in Latin means 'smash to pieces'. (Isaacs, 1999b, 58) A dialogue aims at the opposite, namely at constructing new meaning in a collaborative process of inquiry.

In the Introduction and with reference to Freire (1972), we characterised a dialogue as related to emancipation. Dialogue in this respect is a humble and respectful way of co-operating with the other in an equal relationship of mutual confidence. According to Rogers (1962), a facilitating relationship is created through certain qualities in the contact between the participants.[78] David Bohm emphasises that in a dialogue participants "are making something in common, i.e., creating something new together" (Bohm, 1996, 2). Judith Lindfors states that "dialogues that are truly dialogic [are] interactions that are 'exploratory, tentative and invitational.'" (Lindfors, 1999, 243)

The list of such clarifying interpretations can be extended quite substantially. However, we will take a look at one of these claims. Lindfors' statement, "dialogues that are truly dialogic," includes the notion of 'dialogue' twice. The first occurrence of 'dialogue' may be interpreted as descriptive of conversations which we, in everyday language, describe as dialogues. The second expression, 'truly dialogic', refers to a more ideal concept of dialogue. Not everything we normally describe as a dialogue can be expected to be truly dialogic. Some conditions need to be fulfilled. Lindfors suggests that a true dialogue is exploratory, tentative and invitational. This seems reasonable, but how can such clues be justified? We see the nature of this justification as conceptual. It has to do with a specification of the way we choose to use the notion of dialogue. And in what follows, we also choose to provide the notion of dialogue with some 'ideal' qualities.[79]

---

[78] Rogers does not use the notion of dialogue, but his work on facilitating relationships has been interpreted in this way, see, for instance, Cissna and Anderson (1994) and Kristiansen and Bloch-Poulsen (2000).

[79] Only based on such an idealisation does it make sense to question whether the Socratic dialogue in fact is a dialogue. With ideas from Bohm (1996), Isaacs refers to four ideal principles of dialogue: participation, coherence, awareness and unfoldment that lie beneath the communicative practice of listening, respecting, suspending and voicing. (See Isaacs, 1999a, 81f.).

With reference to different theories, Kenneth Cissna and Rob Anderson (1994, 13f.) emphasise the following qualities of a dialogue:[80] Immediacy of presence, which means the here-and-now of interpersonal communication; Emergent unanticipated consequences, as a dialogue cannot fully be predicted; Recognition of 'strange otherness', which means being curious and flexible towards the perspectives of the other; Collaborative orientation, which includes the joint project of sense-making, rather than focus on winning and losing; Vulnerability, as dialogue involves risk; Mutual implication, as dialogue is a process in which speaker and listener interdepend, each constructing self, other, and their talk simultaneously. Dialogue represents a temporal flow and a historical continuity, as it emerges from the past, fills the immediate present and anticipates and prefigures an open future. Finally, dialogue means genuineness and authenticity, in other words being honest and transparent. This suggestion for an understanding of dialogue also contains ideal elements.

The notion of dialogue is part of the vocabulary of quite different traditions in philosophy, epistemology, anthropology and communication theory.[81] Thus, dialogue can be interpreted as a 'meeting' as in Martin Buber's (1957) philosophic anthropology, where the meeting between people is the basic existential category. Freire's emphasis on dialogue can also be read along these lines. His description of dialogue appears as a basic human and political category, which at the same time is essential for learning. Dialogue can also be described in terms of qualities in the interpersonal relationship as in Rogers' (1958, 1961, 1962, 1994) humanistic psychology. Here the qualities of dialogue can support the successful outcome of a therapeutic process, as well as they can support a person-centred approach in education (as mentioned in the Introduction). Following Bohm (1996), dialogue provides a holistic epistemological perspective, and with reference to Isaacs (1994, 1999a) as his follower, dialogue refers to a collective inquiry of basic assumptions that can be carried out in organisational contexts and be interpreted with reference to organisational learning.[82]

Dialogue can be considered in terms of construction, not only as a construction of knowledge, but as construction of relations, as in Ger-

---

[80] This paragraph is a summmary of Cissna and Anderson's (1994) description using their words and concepts.

[81] This summary of different traditions in the discussion of dialogue is based on Kristiansen and Bloch-Poulsen (2000, 191f.).

[82] See, for instance, Senge (1990).

gen's (1973, 1997) social constructionism. Dialogue as construction can also be read into Mikhail Bakhtin's (1990, 1995) theory of language and of literature.[83] With reference to the philosophical hermeneutic tradition, dialogue comes to refer to the 'melting together' of the horizon of the interpreter and the interpreted (Gadamer, 1989). In fact, fundamental discussions in philosophy do help to clarify aspects of dialogue, possibly first of all from an epistemological point of view. We can also think of Jürgen Habermas' (1984, 1987) discussion of communicative action and of a discourse ethics, and of John Rawl's (1971) discussion of a theory of justice. Lakatos' (1976) philosophy of mathematics, focussing on the interplay between proofs and refutations, can be interpreted in terms of dialogue, as he certainly indicated by presenting his exposition in the form of a dialogue. The list of interpretations is not complete, but it should not be forgotten that in everyday language dialogue is used as synonymous with conversation and communication. (Markova and Foppa (eds.), 1990, 1991)

The theoretical manifold nature of the concept of dialogue makes it necessary to explicate the use of the term when relating dialogue to learning. We shall try to condense our first characteristic of dialogue including ideal elements. We concentrate on three aspects of dialogue: (1) making an inquiry; (2) running a risk; and (3) maintaining equality.

Emphasising these aspects of dialogue helps us to focus our interpretation of dialogue and learning. Although we could maintain that 'making an inquiry' is also part of a dialogue being part of a therapeutic process or apolitical negotiation, we find that this aspect will help us in our epistemological interpretation of dialogue. 'Running a risk' is a way of expressing the basic unpredictability of the directions and the outcome of a dialogue. 'Maintaining equality' refers to an interpersonal relationship essential for the characteristic of dialogue.[84]

Making an inquiry means moving from certainty to curiosity. Isaacs describes a dialogue as "a sustained collective inquiry into every day experience and what we take for granted" (Isaacs, 1994, 253-254). We also want to highlight that a dialogue is a conversation of *inquiry*. The participants want to find out about something – they want to gain knowledge and new experience. The process of dialogue encourages

---

[83] Høines (2002) refers to the Bakhtinian concept of dialogue in her dissertation about dialogue in the mathematics classroom.

[84] In many cases the notion of equity has been used instead of equality. However, we will use the notion of equality with its roots in philosophy.

people to develop a shared intention for inquiry. Decision-making is not an intrinsic part of dialogue: "'Inquiry' comes from the Latin 'inquaerere', to seek within. [...] The word decision, from the Latin 'decidere', literally means to 'murder alternatives'. It is best to approach dialogue with no result in mind, but with the intention of developing deeper inquiry, wherever it leads you." (Isaacs, 1994, 375) A process of inquiry is open-ended.

Lindfors who is concerned with learning in education characterises inquiry as an activity of open-minded and curious 'stance': "The inquirer expresses an orientation toward partner and topic that is uncertain and invitational." (Lindfors, 1999, 106) It is this stance of uncertainty and of invitation towards the other that guides the inquirer in the new land and in his or her seeking for help and assistance.

Lindfors puts forward the term of 'collaborative inquiry' (Lindfors, 1999, 157f.) meaning "engaging in reflection together" where the partners through a common probing process try to reach new understandings.[85] Some acts of inquiry are identified: explain, elaborate, suggest, support, consider consequences. They are identified as inquiry acts because they are attempts to go beyond, and help others to go beyond their present thinking. In this sense inquiry operates in the field between the already known and what is not yet known – or with Lev Vygotsky's expression in the Zone of Proximal Development (Vygotsky, 1978, 84f.). More generally, our notion of inquiry includes collectivity and collaboration. Naturally, the notion of inquiry could also be developed in individual terms, clarifying how the individual would carry out a process of inquiry. But this is not the approach we will elaborate on.

Entering an inquiry means taking control of the activity in terms of ownership. The inquiry participants own their activity and they are responsible for the way it develops and what they can learn from it. The elements of shared ownership distinguish a dialogue as an inquiry from many other forms of inquiry where, for instance, an authority sets the agenda for the investigation and the conversation. We observed examples of this in the quizzing pattern of communication which, somehow, represents an inquiry, but which does not represent a dialogue.

Isaacs refers to Argyris (1988) when pointing to a combination of inquiry and advocacy in dialogue:[86] "Advocacy means speaking what you

---

[85] This formulation resonates with the discussion of democracy as characterised by collectivity, transformation, deliberation and coflection (see Valero, 1998a; and Skovsmose and Valero, 2001).

[86] Isaacs' (1999a) own term of 'voicing' seems closely related to advocacy.

think, speaking from a point of view. Inquiry means looking into what you do not yet know, what you do not yet understand, or seeking to discover what others see and understand that may differ from your point of view. It is the art of asking genuine questions, ones that seek to understand the rules that govern why people do what they do as much as to challenge what they do [...] balancing advocacy and inquiry means stating clearly and confidently what one thinks and why one thinks it, while at the same time being open to being wrong." (Isaacs, 1999a, 188) Expressing one's perspective as is the meaning of 'advocacy' is part of our understanding of inquiry. It is a condition for a mutual inquiry that the participants speak what they think. This emphasises that in a dialogue the resources for the inquiry are also to be found in the participants and in their perspectives. It is possible to advocate a perspective but also to advocate a certain point by means of a perspective.[87]

The notion of inquiry can be related to research and to learning in general. It is possible to make an inquiry of all kinds of subjects with the purpose of getting to know. Thus, focusing on dialogue means considering a certain kind of inquiry and this inquiry has very much to do with the participants' thoughts and feelings, understandings and pre-understandings of things, ideas and possibilities. In dialogue it becomes important to explore participant perspectives as resources for inquiry. It also becomes important to be willing to suspend one's perspectives and to be able to construct new perspectives. We will comment on these three aspects of 'making an inquiry' and how they relate to the notion of perspective.

Exploring participant perspectives cannot take place as a process of transmission. The participants of a dialogue go through a collaborative process of perspective inquiry. In this process perspectives must be expressed in words in order to become accessible on the surface of communication. The process of making perspectives explicit can be an entrance to hidden perspectives that makes it possible to use them as resources for further inquiry. Further, each of the participants can gain new insight through the other by coming to see a problem or a solution from new perspectives. In a classroom dialogue, the teacher's exploration of students' perspectives can be seen as a way of helping the students to express their tacit knowledge.[88]

---

[87] The notion of advocacy also makes sense in the philosophy of mathematics as illustrated by Lakatos (1976), where the participants in the dialogue advocate different theses about the nature of mathematical truth and proof.

[88] This term refers to Polanyi (1966). Talking about mathematics education this means that the insight produced by the process of inquiry is in focus and not whether a result

A dialogue also means *willingness to suspend one's perspectives* – at least for a moment. Bohm (1996, 20f.) uses a similar term 'suspending assumptions' that means neither to carry out one's pre-understandings nor to suppress them. The point is to keep them at a level where the opinions come out, but where you can look at them and explore them: "Suspension requires that we relax our grip on certainty." (Isaacs, 1999a, 147) Suspending assumptions or suspending perspectives means becoming aware of them in the first place. Expressing them is a condition for a common inquiry, but maintaining the assumptions as a given means an obstruction to dialogue. Suspending assumptions means a willingness to consider what it would mean *if* the assumptions were not maintained, but the suspension does not mean quitting the assumption for good.

In that sense suspending assumptions is closely related to 'advocacy', when you speak what you think not as the absolute truth but as something that can be examined: "It means exploring your assumptions from new angles: bringing them forward, making them explicit, giving them considerable weight, and trying to understand where they came from." (Isaacs 1994, 378) For a teacher to enter a classroom dialogue this means not having fixed answers to given problems; being curious about what the students might do, and being willing to reconsider his or her own understandings and pre-understandings. The teacher's vital gain is that by observing, reflecting and expressing his or her understandings in a cooperative process, he or she may be able to change and get to know things in a new way. For the students this means being ready to let their understandings be explored, to enter a process of momentary uncertainty, and to accept that there are no fixed authoritative answers to their questions.

Exploring perspectives need not only mean considering already existing perspectives, i.e. perspectives that implicitly or explicitly are represented by the participants of the dialogue. An exploration can also take a more radical form. It can mean *constructing new perspectives*. We find that this constructing element is essential to any dialogue. If we think of dialogue where, say, a kind of compromise has to be located, then it could make sense to think of exploration of perspectives as an exploration of already established perspectives. But when we think of dialogue as a process of finding out and of learning, then an essential aspect becomes to see things in a new way. Dialogically constructed perspectives need not be a manifestation of any pre-existing perspective. Although the

---

is right or wrong. However, it does not mean that nothing is right or wrong, but the focus of exploring perspectives is placed elsewhere.

students' perspectives are a resource for the inquiry process, the dialogue can bring about something radically new. The teacher may realise new things as well. In this sense we see dialogue as a process of collaborative perspective construction.

The nature of the inquiry process we have in mind is, however, absolutely different from the constructive steps suggested by radical constructivism. Here the constructions are carried out by the individual, while we see the constructions carried out in a co-operation as also suggested by social constructivism. This is the reason why we emphasise the notion of inquiry co-operation.

Running a risk. Entering an inquiry of suspended pre-understandings means having confidence that something unforeseen can happen. Previous beliefs and understandings might change and develop as they are challenged through inquiry. A dialogue is unpredictable. There are no given answers to questions beforehand. They emerge through a common process of curious investigation and collective reflection with the purpose of getting to know. Unpredictability means the challenge of trying new possibilities, as we saw for instance in Chapter 3 when Mary and Adam started out with the inverse spreadsheet, and it also means taking risks when probing or trying things out.

Dialogue includes risk-taking both in an epistemological and an emotional sense. These two aspects, however, occur in a mix, and they can only be seperated analytically. In a dialogue the participants share thoughts and feelings – they invest part of themselves: "The process [of dialogue] involves people thinking together, so it requires commitment, focus, attention, and the willingness to risk your ideas as you explain and describe what you believe." (Stewart, 1999, 56) This makes the participants open to inquiry and learning but openness also makes them vulnerable.

Risk could be seen as a negative concept, say referring primarily to non-pleasant feelings emerging when one's suggestions are refuted or one's opinions questioned. But risk also includes the possible excitement experienced when, for instance, one's suggestions find their way into a bigger picture, and it becomes revealed that the suggestions, which originally from one's own perspective might have appeared a mere detail, come to play a significant role in the further inquiry process. A dialogue is risky, in the sense that it can stir up emotional problems as well as cause enjoyment. This becomes obvious when we consider the Mary-Adam dialogue in its total. It appears unpredictable in what direction the emotions may turn.

A dialogue is also risky in terms of epistemic content. Or as we have already put it, in a profound way a dialogue is unpredictable. Thus it becomes important to relate the discussion of scientific methodology to the concept of dialogue. Methodology can refer to scientific processes and condense the idea that it is possible to specify a way of getting to know (about nature for instance). Thus Dewey was keen to clarify scientific methodology, as he saw this methodology as significant not only for making scientific progress but also as significant for any kind of process of getting to know, including learning processes taking place in school. We do not share this hope about the existence of any overall methodology of getting to know. We find ourselves more in accordance with *Against Method*, where Paul Feyerabend (1975) emphasises that there is no simple pattern in scientific methodology. Similarly, we do not find any simple pattern in dialogic processes. They are unpredictable and they are combined with taking risks.

In a classroom students may be on the track of progression, but sometimes they are just on a blind track. In the latter case an inquiry can make them feel uncomfortable. For a dialogue to take place in an educational situation it is important that feeling uncomfortable is not getting too uncomfortable. Too much out of balance might make the students so frustrated that they will give up. The point is not to remove the risk phenomenon, but to establish a comfortable and respectful learning environment and an atmosphere of mutual confidence where it is possible to contain momentary uncertainty (Alrø and Kristiansen, 1998, 170). One essential question is how, in such a situation, a teacher can function as a supervisor, not letting the students be lost when they experience the risk, and not saving the students by eliminating the risks. Isaacs has used the term 'container' or 'field of inquiry' for such environments that emerge as a group moves through a dialogic process: "A container can be understood as the sum of the collective assumptions, shared intentions, and beliefs of a group. As they move through the dialogue progression, participants perceive that the 'climate' or 'atmosphere' of the group is changing, and gradually see that their collective understanding is changing it." (Isaacs, 1994, 360) A classroom dialogue cannot take place in any sort of fear or force. There has to be a climate of mutual trust and confidence. There has to be a careful container.[89]

---

[89] Kristiansen and Bloch-Poulsen (2000, 142f.) have developed the notion of 'careful container' to describe their model of dialogue in an organisational context.

The notion of risk zone has been developed by Miriam Godoy Penteado (2001) with respect to the introduction of computers in learning environments, which can be characterised as landscapes of investigation.[90] The point is that moving from an exercise paradigm to a landscape of investigation also means moving from a comfort zone to a risk zone. What is going to happen in the classroom appears unpredictable. The point, however, is not to return to the comfort zone provided by the exercise paradigm, but to use the potentials for learning, which become available in the risk zone accompanying landscapes of investigation. These considerations are in accordance with our interpretation of dialogue. We find that landscapes of investigation invite inquiry cooperation and communicative patterns, which can be characterised as dialogue. Risks are an integral part of a dialogue. And risks include both positive and negative possibilities.

Maintaining equality. A dialogue is based on the principle of equality. In a dialogue there is no demonstration of power, and "nobody is trying to win" (Bohm, 1996, 7). One participant cannot be superior to the other. A dialogue progresses according to the force of the inquiry, and is not modulated by considerations of, say, the effects of making some particular conclusions. This aspect of dialogue can be further clarified in terms of Habermas' analysis of communication. A dialogue cannot be modulated by the roles (and the power associated with these roles) of the persons participating in the dialogue. But how does this come to correspond with a classroom, where the processes of teaching and learning are closely related to teacher and student roles in an asymmetrical relationship? Teacher and students certainly are professionally unequal, otherwise there would be no purpose in teaching. Nevertheless they can maintain equality at an interpersonal level of communication and relationship.

It is important to make a distinction between equality and sameness. Thus, Jill Adler (2001a, 187) uses the term equity "to engage diversity and difference not through sameness but through fairness." We use the term equality as Adler uses equity. As a consequence, maintaining equality does not mean that diversity and differences are negated. Maintaining equality refers to ways of dealing with diversity and difference, and the principal concept is fairness. Fairness does not only refer to emotional aspects, it also refers to the way the content matter of the dialogue is dealt with. Thus, maintaining equality in a dialogue

---

[90] See also Borba and Penteado (2001).

between teacher and students includes dealing with diversity and differences.

Entering a dialogue cannot be forced upon anybody. In a classroom this means that the teacher can invite the students into an inquiring dialogue, but students have to accept the invitation for the dialogue to take place. In Chapter 2 we suggested that landscapes of investigation could provide such an invitation, and in Chapter 3 we have witnessed students accepting the invitation and entering a proper dialogue. In Chapter 5 we shall see what happens when students refuse to accept the teacher's invitation. The notion of invitation reflects the notion of equality. If, say, the students are forced to do something, then the principle of equality is lost.

With reference to learning mathematics Stieg Mellin-Olsen describes a dialogue as "a method of confrontation and exploration of disagreement [...] in a friendly and co-operative setting". (Mellin-Olsen, 1993, 246) It is important to observe that 'maintaining equality' does not mean 'maintaining agreement'. The purpose of dialogue is epistemic development not in terms of consensus but as a "search of deeper insight with the partners of the dialogue" (Mellin-Olsen, 1993, 247).

Particular qualities of contact are important in order to maintain equality in an asymmetrical relationship. Rogers focuses on three essential qualities for a person who wants to facilitate another person's learning: congruence, empathy and positive regard. Being congruent means being genuine without any front or facade. The facilitator's thoughts and feelings should be consistent with his way of acting, and this should be obvious to him- or herself and to the other person. Congruence stands for transparency and genuineness. (Rogers, 1962, 1994) In a dialogue congruence can be shown explicitly through meta-communication and through advocacy. In Chapter 3 the teacher comment: "I don't know either" is an example of teacher congruence that seems to establish a contact and an equality that makes the participants open to inquiry. Empathy means that the facilitator tries to understand the other person's world as if it were his or her own. The facilitator should resonate the expressions of the other person in order to help him clarify his perspective. It is important to maintain the 'as if' quality of empathic behavior. This means that the facilitator should not lose his awareness of his own perspective, while on the other hand the facilitator runs a risk of changing this perspective. Thus, the process of emphatic behavior may lead to a clarity of shared perspectives or an awareness of different perspectives. The third condition is positive regard. In order to be able to help another person you have to accept and to respect him or her and as a(nother) person. This implies respecting the otherness of the other without intending to change him or her as a person. It is important to the relationship that these facilitating conditions are also experienced by the other. In that way, congruence, empathy and positive regard can provide preconditions for maintaining equality even in an asymmetrical relationship, where the quality of contact and communication can facilitate the process of learning.

No authority can decide to have a dialogue in any a priori way. A dialogue can only proceed by its own dynamic sources, by the perspectives, the emotions, the intentions, the reflections and actions of participating equal partners. This principle of equality has been a defining element in Freire's pedagogy, and also in educational studies of classroom discourse which are inspired by Habermas (e.g. Young, 1992).

HOW TO DO THINGS WITH DIALOGUE

'How to do things with words' is the title of Austin's (1962) famous lectures on speech act theory. This theory emphasises that many different things can be done by means of language.[91] When we use a similar expression: 'How to do things with dialogue' as headline of this section, our purpose is to emphasise that participating in a dialogue is also a process of acting and of meaning production through the use of language. Dialogue means acting in co-operation.

Austin was inspired by Wittgenstein (1953) who related the concept of meaning to the notion of 'use'. In order to find what can be the meaning of a concept, Wittgenstein suggested studying what can be done by means of the concept. In a similar way the meaning of an utterance becomes a study of what the speaker does by means of this utterance. This opens for a pragmatic interpretation of the role of language. The notions suggested by Austin and further elaborated by Searle (1969) are fundamentals of the philosophy of speech acts. The basic assumption is that speech includes act. We not only speak by means of words and sentences, we act as well. One single speech act has a locutionary content (utterance and predication), an illocutionary force (meaning in context) and a perlocutionary effect (intended effect on hearer). The illocutionary level of communication is central to speech act theory, because this refers to the speaker's intended meaning of the utterance towards a hearer in a certain context.

---

[91] See also Austin (1970).

The notion of speech acts is opposed to the structuralist approach and the focus on language as a system of underlying structures. According to speech act theory the function of language cannot be understood in terms of providing a description of some state of affairs or of some imagined situation. Nor can the quality of such a description be discussed in terms of the descriptive qualities of language. Speech act theory focuses on the use of language in context. And the use of language means acting through language. In order to look at the dialogic aspects of communication we shall try to develop further the notion of speech acts.

It is important to realise that a dialogue cannot consist of just any kind of speech acts. Speech act theory was introduced with a particular aim: to emphasise that much more can be performed by language than just 'making descriptions'. We definitely agree with this interpretation, but our aim here is to locate a certain group of communicative acts, namely *dialogic acts*. Some acts can express power, control or in other ways one part being superior to the other, and so can speech acts, but such acts are not dialogic acts. The priest's: 'I baptise you Mary' can hardly exemplify a dialogic act, although the name Mary may have been decided upon in a most complicated dialogue in the family. The judge's statement: 'I sentence you to two years in jail', would serve as a straightforward example of a speech act, not open to question and as a consequence not a dialogic act. In mathematics education questions to which it is assumed as a given that there is one and only one correct answer are non-dialogic speech acts. In Chapter 1 we gave such examples to illustrate classroom absolutism, e.g.: "If they [the authors of the textbook] made the exercise, they are the ones to decide whether it is right, aren't they?" Some questions are not even supposed to be understood as questions but as other kinds of speech acts as, for instance examination, correction or control.[92] Thus, *dialogic acts are speech acts with certain qualities.*

Speech acts are more than words. The intended meaning to the words is often indicated by non-verbal communication features such as: facial expressions, gesture, intonation, volume, pauses, word-order and other contextual elements that have to be interpreted in the situation in order to understand the inquirer's stance. And as mentioned, in mathematics education diagrams and written expressions are an essential part of the meaning-producing context. Thus, in accordance with speech act theory we use a broad definition of language that includes both verbal and non-verbal elements.

---

[92] See Streeck (1979) and Herrlitz (1987).

Dialogic acts and dialogic interaction involve at least two persons in an equal relationship. It is possible to do something together by means of dialogue. In fact, we can jump directly to making our first characteristic of dialogue by summarising what we, in the previous section, have said about dialogic qualities. *Dialogue involves making inquiry, running risk and maintaining equality.* These characteristics of dialogue show some ideally identified qualities.

DIALOGIC ACTS – THE IC-MODEL RECONSIDERED

We can develop the notion of dialogue further, by being more specific about the notion of dialogic acts. It becomes important to provide some further exemplification, and in particular to consider if the ideal conception of dialogue makes sense when we face real life communication, for instance in the classroom.

The IC-Model is constituted by certain elements, and Chapter 3 finished with a further elaboration of these elements. We find that the elements of the IC-Model all exemplify dialogic acts. And, as a consequence, they all involve making an inquiry, running a risk and maintaining equality. Dialogic acts gain their significance by being part of a dialogic process. We do not suggest a reductionist theory of dialogue stating that a dialogue is made up of particular elements, like the elements of the IC-Model. A dialogue is a process of inter-acting, and we see dialogic acts as special events in this process. Such acts are represented by (verbal and non-verbal) language in dialogue, and these acts also help to stabilise, to maintain and to develop the dialogue. We find that dialogic acts express particular 'events' in a dialogic process. We have characterised eight such events. We do not make any claim that these are the only possible dialogic acts. We can easily imagine an extended list of such acts. This said, we come to our second characteristic of *a dialogue as a process involving acts of getting in contact, locating, identifying, advocating, thinking aloud, reformulating, challenging and evaluating.* While our first characteristic of dialogue referred to aspects that have been presented in literature, this second characteristic can be seen as a further specification particularly related to empirical observations.[93]

---

[93] Some of the theoretical concepts of dialogue that we refer to are also empirically based, see Lindfors (1999); Rogers (1962, 1994); Isaacs (1999a) and Kristiansen and Bloch-Poulsen (2000).

When we observe a process of learning where dialogic acts are a main feature we will talk about a *dialogic learning process* (as when Alice and Deborah in co-operation with the teacher constructed the Danish flag, and when Mary and Adam in co-operation with the teacher constructed the spreadsheet). Naturally, we will use the expression *inquiry co-operation* as well, which by now has been broadened in meaning, as the elements of the IC-Model are seen as dialogic acts. In his book *Dialogic Inquiry*, Gordon Wells makes the following claim: "Briefly, I shall propose that classrooms should become communities of inquiry, in which the curriculum is seen as being created emergently in the many modes of conversation through which teacher and students dialogically make sense of topics of individual and social significance, through action, knowledge building and reflection." (Wells, 1999, 98) Having mathematics education in mind, this formulation includes a suggestion for moving from the exercise paradigm to landscapes of investigation. Such landscapes welcome 'communities of inquiry' where dialogue becomes a constituent aspect of the learning process.

Processes of learning cannot be observed directly, but the verbalised inquiry among learners can. Their expression of reflections and actions gives us a glimpse into their learning process: "It is an imperfect murky window to be sure, but it's the best we've got." (Lindfors 1999, 16) We have to be aware that the status of our first characteristic of dialogue (in terms of inquiry, risk and equality) is different from the status of our second characteristic (in terms of the elements of the IC-Model). Thus, the IC-Model is based on an analysis of a process of communication; it represents a condensed observation.[94] By studying what was happening during mathematics lessons some episodes appeared as 'outstanding'. This drew our attention to what was happening during these episodes, and the elements of the IC-Model were identified. Contrary to this, our first characteristic of dialogue is based on an idealised notion of dialogue. By relating these idealisations with the outstanding episodes, the IC-Model becomes an empirical indicator of dialogic learning taking place.

The clarification of dialogic learning is certainly not limited to a school context. It can take place in formal and non-formal settings, in

---

[94] It is possible to observe different IC-Model variants. The IC-Model is based on situations in which teacher and students communicate explicitly; other possibilities for inter-action do exist. We can for example imagine that a teacher and an 'apprentice' are co-working. Maybe the verbal communication is kept to a minimum, but still we conceive it a possibility to observe (a variant of) an IC-Model, however not by means of focussing on the verbal dialogue between teacher and apprentice, but by studying the non-verbal interaction.

companies and organisations.[95] Furthermore, clarifications made with respect to mathematical learning may be useful with respect to many other and very different forms of learning.

In Chapter 1, we talked about learning as action, and now we have specified this term as *learning as dialogic action*. Naturally, some learning can hardly be characterised as dialogic action (seen from the student perspective), for instance the learning that takes place through drill training. Drill and practice can bring about learning, but this is not the kind of learning we have in mind. What becomes of particular interest is the qualities of learning that are emphasised when learning is realised as dialogic action. Such qualities need to be discussed further.

As dialogic acts certainly can include the teacher, it makes sense to talk about *dialogic teaching* as well. In this case the teacher mode of communication acknowledges elements of the IC-Model. In fact the qualities of dialogue tend to eliminate any sharp distinction between teaching and learning processes. However, before we say more about the significance of dialogic teaching and learning, we must be aware of its fragility.

DIALOGIC TEACHING AND LEARNING – AND ITS FRAGILITY

Dialogic learning processes take place when we can observe a richness of dialogic acts. However, dialogic acts are fragile. We can easily observe that such acts switch into other patterns of communication that can hardly be labelled dialogic. The quizzing pattern is one example. As we described in both Chapters 2 and 3, this pattern emerged as an intermezzo in the middle of a sequence of dialogic acts. It is very common to observe obstructions of dialogic acts, and this makes us emphasise that a dialogue is seldom a whole conversation, it is rather moments or sequences of a conversation.[96] Sometimes dialogic sequences are so small that they even themselves appear as intermezzos – but certainly as intermezzos with qualities that can bring about dialogic learning.

We also have to be aware that, in a school context, many reasons exist for a teacher as well as for students to turn away from dialogue and not to act dialogically. A teacher is responsible for managing the class, and situations do emerge where it becomes essential for a teacher to carry out

---

[95] See, for instance, Isaacs (1994, 1999a); Alrø and Kristiansen (1998) and Kristiansen and Bloch-Poulsen (2000).

[96] See also Kristiansen and Bloch-Poulsen (2000, 15).

a prompt decision. Further, the school context in general does not provide a convenient background for acting dialogically. One of the reasons for us to introduce landscapes of investigation is to support different ways of making inquiries. Landscapes of investigation could help to minimise certain school routines and facilitate processes of inquiry and dialogue. Still, we do not consider a dialogue as a universal solution to every educational problem. It might for instance be difficult to establish a dialogue if one participant does not have any idea of the topic, or if the purpose of the conversation is to test or evaluate some specific understanding of a problem. We can think of many such situations in education.

Jeppe Skott (2000) has identified what he calls 'critical incidents of practice' where particular circumstances make declared and dedicated progressive teachers act in a way, which cannot be explained with reference to their beliefs in a 'progressive' classroom. Nevertheless, teacher actions can be seen as adequate in these particular incidents of practice, although the acts can no way be called dialogic. When 'Batman & Co.' came to an end, with Mary an Adam still grappling with completing the inverse spreadsheet, we hear the teacher voice: "I would like to thank you for a really fantastic effort... We'll meet up in 20-25 minutes by the bus." The inquiry process has come to an end. The dialogue, too. The teacher is exercising quite a different role, being the responsible organiser. In all teaching practices the teacher has different roles; being a participant in an inquiry process is only one of them. All this said we continue to pay special attention to dialogic learning, and thus we try to be aware of how, in a school context, dialogic acts can easily collapse or change into other forms of interaction.

If dialogue is based on a principle of equality, how, then, can one talk about dialogue in an asymmetrical relationship as that between teacher and students? The teacher has a fundamental responsibility for the educational setting, as he is the person in charge. Further, he is supposed to be better educated and more experienced in the matter taught. However, equality not only refers to professional competence, it must also be understood in terms of treating each other respectfully as partners of inquiry. As already said, maintaining equality does not mean negating the existence of differences. Nevertheless, in a school context the formal asymmetrical relationship between teacher and students (in terms of organisational responsibility of knowledge, for instance) often makes it difficult to maintain equality.

An inquiry co-operation between teacher and students has to distinguish between 'teacher-as-questioner' and 'teacher-as-inquirer' (Lindfors, 1999, 112). An inquiring stance is often understood in terms of a questioning attitude. But as stressed by Lindfors (1999) inquiry and interrogative are not necessarily the same thing. Not every question is inquiring and inquiry is often expressed in other ways, for instance as wondering.[97] Some questions – as in the quizzing pattern of communication – often lead to mechanical or reproductive answers that do not necessarily involve reflection on the content of the question. As we have shown, teacher-as-questioner is found in the traditional classroom where the students are supposed to follow the teacher perspective answering the questions to which the teacher already knows the answer. In a dialogue the inquiring teacher has a wondering and curious attitude to what is going on in classroom interaction, and an attention to questions to which he does not necessarily have the right answer.[98] However, in many cases the teacher does in fact already know, or he or she may almost know. Still, dialogic teaching and learning can be maintained, although it is certainly a fragile process.

DIALOGIC TEACHING AND LEARNING – AND ITS SIGNIFICANCE

Dialogic teaching and learning is a fragile process. But why worry about this fragility? Because dialogic teaching and learning also has potential. In the Introduction we referred to the work of Freire. He finds that learning based on dialogue has certain qualities, which he sees in political terms. Others have emphasised more personal and relational qualities. Thus, Rogers finds that 'significant learning' can be supported by

---

[97] Questioning and answering is a characteristic pattern of any classroom communication. Some would argue that questions in general stimulate the students' learning process, because questions require reflection. So do for instance Sigel and Kelley (1988) who suggest the term of 'distancing strategies' referring to a teacher questioning strategy that copes with discrepancies between events. While confronted with an inconsistency between for instance internal and external events, the student tries to (re-)establish balance or harmony. The term 'internal events' refers to thoughts and feelings within a person, whereas 'external events' refers to circumstances in the environment of the individual. This process needs reflection, which will lead to learning.

[98] Lemke (1990, 52) uses the term 'true dialogue' for a teacher questioning attitude, where the teacher does not know the answer to the question beforehand. Dysthe (1997, 62) uses the term 'authentic' for this attitude.

'helping relationships'. Again the idea is that qualities of communication influence qualities of learning.[99]

Let us take a further look at how Rogers see this relationship between interaction and learning. Rogers describes the aim of education as the "facilitation of change and learning". (1994, 151 f.) Knowledge is dynamic as it changes over time. What is true today has perhaps changed tomorrow.[100] Consequently, instead of learning how things are (at a certain time) it becomes more important to learn the process of gaining knowledge – to learn how to learn. So, according to Rogers the challenge for education is to encourage 'true learners' and to arrange learning environments that facilitate the processes of learning, being curious, inquiring, exploring processes of getting to know. A facilitation that provides the 'freedom to learn.' Rogers distinguishes between the learning of facts and 'significant learning': "By significant learning I mean learning which is more than accumulation of facts. It is learning which makes a difference – in the individual's behaviour, in the course of action he chooses in the future, in his attitudes and in his personality. It is pervasive learning which is not just an accretion of knowledge, but which interpenetrates with every portion of his existence." (Rogers, 1994, 280)[101]

Significant learning can be facilitated in a helping relationship. Rogers (1958, 269) defines such a relationship "as one in which one of the participants intends that there should come about, in one or both parties, more appreciation of, more expression of, more functional use of the latent inner resources of the individual". Rogers uses the term to describe

---

[99] Davis (1996) presents a careful analysis of the importance of 'listening', and of 'hermeneutic listening' in particular, for providing a sound alternative to the school mathematics tradition and to the patterns of communication that dominate this tradition. Although Davis does not use the notion of dialogue as a main construct of his conceptual framework we see his work very much in line with the idea that qualities of communication influence qualities of learning.

[100] Rogers has a total focus on the process of learning in education whereas he often claims a provocative view on the role of teaching: "Teaching is, for me, a relatively unimportant and vastly overvalued activity." (Rogers, 1994, 151)

[101] Significant learning seems to correspond with the term of another existentialist, Poul Colaizzi: 'genuine learning'. Genuine learning means having integrated the subject matter in ones person (body and mind). Significant or genuine learning can never be forced upon anybody. This kind of learning always occurs in relation to others, and it changes the learner in a radical way that cannot be predicted. In that sense learning is also connected with taking risks. (Colaizzi in Hermansen, 1998, 200f.) These qualities of significant learning correspond with our description of dialogic qualities in this chapter. The concept of 'learning of facts' is similar to Mellin-Olsen's (1977, 1981) 'instrumental learning'.

both a therapist-client relationship and a teacher-student relationship. In this sense we could also consider the helper (the teacher) as a supervisor.

Like Freire and Rogers, we also find that qualities of communication influence qualities of learning. In particular we want to consider in what sense dialogue may support critical qualities of learning. On the one hand, learning can mean learning for a particular socio-economic purpose, and the content of what has to be learnt can be defined in terms of topics and competencies that seem to serve 'productivity' the best. In this way, economic perspectives can come to set the agenda for how to measure school productivity. On the other hand, learning can mean learning for citizenship; and citizenship refers to competencies that are important for a person to participate in the democratic life and for developing a *Mündigkeit*.[102] In Skovsmose and Valero (2001), three possible relationships between mathematics education and democracy were presented. Much literature emphasises that mathematics education, because of the very nature of mathematics, maintains an intrinsic resonance with democratic ideals.[103] Because of its logical structure, mathematics becomes a clearly argumentative enterprise, where dogmatism has no role to play. Mathematics is a topic where only sound arguments can survive, and in this way mathematical thinking becomes an excellent preparation for the type of reasoning and dialogue which ought to characterise a democracy. This thesis of a harmony between scientific thinking and a democratic way of life has been supported strongly by Dewey and repeated by many others.[104]

Contrary to this, it has been emphasised that mathematics education, in particular as it is carried out by the school mathematics tradition, demonstrates basic undemocratic features. This reality of mathematics education contradicts democratic ideals. Support for this statement is found in statistics showing how mathematics education differentiates according to gender, race and class, and how mathematics education could serve as a new form of cultural suppression.[105] Our interpretation of bureaucratic absolutism can also support this claim. In Borba and Skovsmose (1997) it is suggested that the ideology of certainty is supported by bureaucratic absolutism. This ideology refers to the

---

[102] The German concept *Mündigkeit* has been discussed with reference to critical mathematics education (see Skovsmose, 1994).

[103] See, for instance, Hannaford (1998).

[104] See the introduction in Archambault (ed.) (1964).

[105] See, for instance, Boaler (1997); Frankenstein (1995); Volmink (1994) and Zevenbergen (2001).

conviction that questions formulated in mathematical terms have one and only one solution, and that it is possible to identify this solution by an adequate mathematical algorithm. This ideology fits nicely into the exercise paradigm of the school mathematics tradition. However, the ideology becomes highly problematic when it is removed from this special, almost pathological context to real-life applications of mathematics. The ideology of certainty turns into a blind belief in number-based statements. Thus, 'trust in numbers' becomes an ideology and a threat to the development of citizenship, not least in the information age.[106] Finally, following Bourdieu (1996), it can be claimed that mathematics education exercises a kind of 'state magic' by means of which the 'state nobility' obtains an authority, which, as it is based on formal mathematical skills, is illegitimate. Thus, a very negative picture of the actual functions of mathematics education can be presented.

A third possibility is to realise that the relationship between mathematics education and democracy is critical in the sense that it can go both ways. It is simply an open question what kinds of interest mathematics education can come to serve. There is no 'essence' in mathematics education that guarantees central attractive functions as a given. Nor are there in mathematics education any built-in features which make it a lost case. It remains an open question what way mathematics education might turn and to what extent it might come to support democratic endeavours. Facing this third possibility is a characteristic of critical mathematics education.

In this study we acknowledge that the relationship between mathematics education and democracy is critical. And if mathematics education is to be organised in support of democratic ideals, then it becomes essential to reconsider and rework all aspects of mathematics education. In particular, it becomes essential to study what is going on in the classroom, as the classroom represents a micro-society, and we cannot imagine learning for democracy to take place without the classroom representing basic democratic values. This means that we must also consider particular relationships between teacher and students, as well as the nature of their inquiry process.[107]

We find that if learning is to support the development of citizenship, then dialogue must play a basic role in the classroom. Thus, a critical theory of learning comes to contain dialogue as a defining concept. Throughout this study we try to explore what this could mean. We find

---

[106] See Porter (1995).

[107] See Skovsmose (1998c); Valero (1998a) and Vithal (1998b).

that the significance of dialogic teaching and learning in mathematics has to do with the critical relationship between mathematics education and democracy. *Dialogic teaching and learning is significant for classroom practice that supports a mathematics education for democracy.* We find that the qualities of communication, associated with dialogue, create a resource for learning with certain qualities, and this learning we refer to as critical learning of mathematics.

In the Introduction we talked about *mathemacy* as a competence with a meaning parallel to 'literacy' (in the Freire-interpretation). We let mathemacy designate a not-very-well specified competence which includes the 'critical reading' of a socio-political context. As described by Skovsmose (1994), mathemacy includes more than an understanding of numbers and figures, also more than an ability to apply numbers and figures to a variety of situations. It includes as well a competence in reflecting and reconsidering the reliability of the applications. Mathemacy represents *Mündigkeit*. As Rogers finds that significant learning, and Freire that political learning, are supported by dialogue, so we hope to find resources for the development of mathemacy in the dialogue which accompanies inquiry co-operation. In the following chapters we try to be more specific about what this hope could mean.[108]

We are going to include new empirical studies, in particular with reference to the notions of intention (Chapter 5), reflection (Chapter 6), and critique (Chapter 7). We hope that a better understanding of how learning may include intention, reflection, and critique will illuminate the qualities that dialogue could bring to learning. In this way we try to provide more meaning to the notions of 'critical learning of mathematics' and 'mathemacy'.

---

[108] Let it be added immediately that there could be many other reasons for considering dialogue as part of the theory of learning. Thus, Rogers' idea of significant learning does not point directly towards the development of critical citizenship.

CHAPTER 5

INTENTION AND LEARNING

Most teachers have experienced the following: The class is split up into groups, a specific task is presented, but members in one of the groups do not engage themselves in the work. Instead, they pre-occupy themselves with all other kinds of activities. And, certainly, they do disturb the whole class a lot. When such a group makes itself known in a classroom, the teacher has to divide his attention between keeping this group in as much control as possible and supporting the other groups in their work.

Most learning theories build upon situations where the students are well adjusted to the learning environment and where they accept the tasks presented to them. In fact, we are not aware of any learning theory that includes, in its construction, empirical observations of students strongly resisting a learning situation. However, in order to develop a theoretical understanding of learning mathematics, we find it important also to consider problematic classroom experiences and to pay attention to non-accommodating students.

In Chapter 2 and Chapter 3 we have seen examples of mathematics education where the teacher has invited students into landscapes of investigation, and we have seen an inquiry co-operation emerge when the students accepted the teacher's invitation. In this chapter we will pay attention to what happens in a situation where the students do not accept the teacher's invitation into a learning environment. We meet a group with a strong resistance to it, whose communication is far from being dialogic.

In the previous chapters we have emphasised that dialogic communication is fragile. There is always an imminent risk that it may break down. We have observed many classroom intermezzos where the teacher seems to break away from dialogue. Also students can refuse to engage in dialogue and in the official classroom activities, and they may have good reasons for doing so. As dialogue is action, it can only be carried out if people have real intentions of participating in the dialogue.

In this chapter we will refer to the 'Travel agency' project, where the teacher invites the students into a landscape of investigation. Observations related to this project call for further discussion of *intentions-in-learning* as being important for an interpretation of the process of interaction. In this and in the following two chapters we will try to establish conceptual connections between 'qualities of communication' and 'qualities of learning'. Dialogue represents certain qualities of communication that are of particular interest to us. In Chapter 7 we will use the notion of critique to characterise certain qualities of learning, and we will talk about 'critical learning of mathematics' and consider what the competence of mathemacy could include. In Chapter 5 and Chapter 6 we will outline two fundamental conceptual links between dialogue and critique, namely intention and reflection. While intention refers to the involvement of persons, reflection refers to considerations carried out by persons. We try to clarify the dialogic basis for critical learning (of mathematics) in terms of intention and reflection.

'TRAVEL AGENCY'

We are in a 7th grade mathematics class with sixteen 13-14 year olds. The class is rather lively, especially the boys, and there is a lot of talking, shouting, teasing and laughing. This morning the class is going to have four lessons of mathematics. This arrangement differs from their normal schedule, partly because of our observation. The students know in advance what is going to happen, they are familiar with the type of activities they are going to be involved in, and they have agreed to participate. As it is Monday the teacher gives the students about 10 minutes' time to discuss their weekend experiences among themselves before they start the mathematics course.

The teacher sets the scene: The groups are supposed to imagine being travel agencies, and they are going to advise a family: "The family would like to rent a summer cottage or camp in Denmark. They would also be interested in going abroad. They think they prefer going by bus, train or airplane. Would you please help the family find out what the possibilities are? What would they need to know before leaving? What would they need to do?" A piece of paper with these and other questions is handed out to the groups. The teacher emphasises that it could be helpful to use the first ten minutes inventing a family and deciding upon family members, names, age, residence, interests and occupation.

There are no exercises included in the teacher introduction. Of course he has thought of different possible problems with mathematical content to be examined: travel charges and the estimation of costs, which could be part of a budget planning, maybe using a spreadsheet; distances (scales) and the reading of maps, which would be a natural part of the overall planning of the trip as well as of the choice of the particular routes to be taken; transport time and speed, which have implications for where to book places overnight during the trip; weather conditions (statistics), which may be relevant for a decision about the destination; currency and exchange rates come almost as a given. However, the groups are going to decide upon their own tasks and do their own problem posing and solving. There are magazines, statistical outlines, atlas, newspapers, material from travel agencies, and other kinds of material available. The students are also able to search for information on the internet.

As the planning of holidays in fact occupies some of the students and their families at the present time, it could be expected that holiday planning could become both relevant and realistic. There seems to be no restriction in the possibilities of real-life references to the proposed classroom activities. And mathematical challenges are just waiting for the students, who engage themselves in the investigation.

Besides the students, divided into four groups, the teacher and the observer are present. The observer is not supposed to participate directly in the classroom activities, but to keep the position of a 'fly on the wall'. The group we concentrate on consists of Linda, Brian, Robert and Martin. Initially, Linda was a member of another group but, as a couple of students are missing this day, the teacher decides to reorganise the groupings. The group is sitting around a table, Brian and Martin on one side, Linda and Robert on the other. Martin has a bunch of keys in his hand that he swings around. The continuous clack-clack-clack of the keys against the top of the table provides the background rhythm for the following. Brian leans over the table and faces the camera.

Brian: Are you saying that I look good on pictures?
Observer: You look smashing.
Brian: Look, I can make faces.

Quite right, Brian can make faces. He sticks both his forefingers into his nostrils. Robert also tunes in on the camera and makes faces. The boys are not only paying attention to the camera, they also comment on Linda: "Take a look at her. Pimples on her forehead!" And they imitate the way she sits at the table. Martin continues to swing his bunch of keys. The observer places the tape recorder in the middle of the table. Brian waves a sheet of paper in front of the microphone making a deafening rattling on the recording:

Brian:	Bah! I'm not so happy about that. [the tape recorder]
Robert:	Well now I won't say something strange. [laughs]
Martin:	Just try shoving it down.
Brian:	If you come over here then you'll put it next to me.
Observer:	Well if you move this cap here.
Robert:	What happens if you accidentally push stop or off? [addressed to the observer]
Observer:	You won't accidentally do that. [smiles and puts down the tape recorder]
Robert:	I won't?
Brian:	I did it last time.

As we shall see, paying attention to what is not supposed to be paid attention to is basic behaviour of the *resistance group*.[109]

A little later Robert lifts up the tape recorder, examines it, and says into the microphone with a mocking voice: "How do you turn this thing off?" It makes a rattle. Then Brian tampers with the tape recorder, while Alex (a boy from another group) asks what they are going to do? Martin shortly states: "A family, Alex," and swings his bunch of keys. Then he makes a face at the camera and a thumbs-up sign. The tape recorder gets put back on the table.

The teacher is around, and the first task is repeated to the group: they have to make up a family. The boys, however, make some comments about the reorganisation: Why is Linda becoming a member? "Is it because we can't be serious?" Brian asks. He obviously refers to Robert, Martin and himself. They keep a distance from the teacher's pragmatic answer: "No, no, we only wanted to settle on four groups" by patting him on the shoulder in a friendly manner: "All right, Henning," "Henning that's fair enough" and "Come again, Henning".

We are a family of four

The reorganised group seems to maintain a certain distribution of roles. While the three boys provide the main strategies for resistance, Linda

---

[109] By labeling this group of students with a metaphor from World War II we want to emphasise not only their explicit resistance but also their status as 'heroes' opposing any school authority. For instance they are so proud of their behaviour in this course that they wanted to have their real names in the present book and a special thanks in the acknowledgements.

tries to keep a focus on the task. The first is to set up a family, and why not consider the group itself as such a family? Brian tosses his pen in the air, while Martin swings his bunch of keys:

Linda:	Hey, we are getting started here.
Robert:	Yeah, we are starting.
Martin:	Linda, it's going to be, OK we are a family of four, then I'm the dad, and then you're the mum [Brian laughs], and then Robert can be…
Brian:	[laughing] You might as well forget it. Then I want to be the bath attendant or something like that.
Martin:	Bath attendant?
Brian:	That's the one who's in the water world when somebody is having a bath.
Martin:	No, you can be in a swimming pool. I'm the dad, and you're the mum, Linda, right? [...]
Martin:	[swings his keys] Yes, you're the mum, and I'm the dad.
Linda:	No.
Martin:	[swings his keys] And Robert, he is…
Brian:	He's an uncle.
Martin:	He's the little brother, and you're the big brother.
Brian:	Hi, little brother. [in a mocking voice]
Martin:	Right? No, you are twins.

Martin then rests his head on his arm, drops his bunch of keys on the table and laughs. Brian joins in, and Martin pokes Brian in the side, making him jump. Linda starts writing. The mother needs a name.

Martin:	OK, we need a… she's called Marie. Marie Biscuit.
Brian:	No, you can forget about it.
Martin:	She is called Marie.
Brian:	Marie.
Martin:	Marie.
Brian:	Oh, yes.
Martin:	It is the mum, she's called Marie. And the dad, he is called Torben, right? No, Torben, we don't want that.
Brian:	No, it's gross.
Linda:	Do I write the mum?

Somehow the group occupy themselves in the project, but with some basic exceptions. Constituting themselves as the family is a sidetrack which, however, opens up a rich variety of bizarre complications: Martin becomes the father, Linda the mother, and Brian wants to be a bath attendant. One could be the big brother, another a little brother. But why not let them be twins? The sidetracking clearly emphasises that the group does not accept the proposed task as serious enough for them to be occupied with. Furthermore, the group provides a general noise level that disturbs the classroom activities a lot. Their shouting voices and the clack-clack-clack from the keys is an almost permanent part of the sound track.

Nevertheless, from their free associations they return to the task, and now they have to find out about the members of the family. Linda is going to write down the name of the mother:

Martin:	[swings his bunch of keys] The mum, the mum is called…
Robert:	Why do you call yourself Helle?
Linda:	But I don't.
Martin:	Elisabeth, she's called Elisabeth.
Robert:	Why are you crying out for your mum?
Martin:	[swings his bunch of keys around]
Linda:	Elisabeth
Martin:	[ic] Iiiiiihaaaaa.
Linda:	E-l-a-e-s-a-b-e-t, no, I don't want to. She's not going to be called Elisabeth, I don't know how to spell it.
Brian:	E-l-i-s-a-b-e-t-h.
Martin:	OK, you're called Marie.
Brian:	That is sure hard to spell.
Robert:	Elisabeth, or what was it? [laughs]
Brian:	E-a-l-i-s…
Martin:	[laughing] Elisabeth.
Robert:	E-l-i-b-z-a or something like that. [laughs]
Brian:	E-l-i-s-a-b-e-t-h.
Martin:	Elibsabeth, Elibsabeth.
Linda:	Marie, and is how many… old?

So, the name of the mother is Marie (Elisabeth and Helle are dropped for different reasons), and they decide her age to be 48. Linda writes the age next to her name. Robert comments about the writing:

Robert:	Wow, an eight. Only it looks like a seven.
Linda:	I'll just write 48.

Martin, maintaining the position of the father, declares that he wants to be a pimp and to be called Poul, but then he changes his mind:

Martin:	He is called Ole, yeah. He is a builder, that's so Ole, that is really such… a builder.
Brian:	That is you, that is Ole Thomsen.
Linda:	And he is 50.

Martin:	No, he's not.
Linda:	Yes!
Robert:	He is 45.
Martin:	He is 39.
Linda:	No, when I'm going to be 48, right?
Martin:	Well, so?
Brian:	Well, you just fancy kids, you like kids.
Linda:	Then I'll be 38.
Martin:	No, the man he's younger.
Brian:	Paedophile.
Linda:	No, it's gross.
Martin:	Yes. It's not you, silly.
Linda:	3-8.
Robert:	Then he's 40.
Martin:	No, he's not, he's got to be younger.
Linda:	No!

It seems reasonable to give the mother as well as the father a name and to decide upon their ages, but this simple job has developed into a new tangent-activity.

Are the students involved in a dialogue? There appears to be no lack of thinking aloud. We can observe lots of getting in contact, reformulating, challenging, evaluating, etc. And the unpredictability of the direction of the conversation is at its maximum. Still there seems to be something completely divergent. Although we might locate seemingly dialogic acts, it seems impossible to characterise the conversation as a dialogue. Something is missing.

A communicative process that originates from the main task but takes a disproportionate form, we will call *zooming-out*. We have already seen several examples of zooming-outs. Robert provides a zooming-out when he asks Linda why she gives the mother the name of the observer: "Why do you call yourself Helle?" and when he pays special attention to the shape of the numbers: "Wow, an eight. Only it looks like a seven." In the conversation Linda responds to this by a back-to-the-task comment, which can be understood as a *zooming-in* on the task. But such a zooming-in seems only to provide an excellent starting point for new zooming-outs, which appears to be a principal part of the resistance strategy. Thus, the point is not to stay away from the task, but to be involved, somehow, and then to provide remarkable 'tangents'.

Martin:	Linda, you cannot be a part of this group if you don't want to be the woman.
Linda:	Yes.
Martin:	No, you can just sod off.

Linda:	Shut up!
Martin:	You can just beat it.
Brian:	Take your fat…
Linda:	OK, and what do they do for a living?
Brian:	[whispers to Linda] Take your fat tits with you. [rests his chin on the pencil case]
Linda:	Shut up!

This "shut up!" apparently brings the group back to the task for a short while.

Robert:	The mum, she's an air-hostess on a plane. She's a stewardess.
Martin:	No, she just crashed with a plane, so she's not there anymore.
Brian:	She's dead.
Martin:	That's why we're going on a plane, to show you where the mum died.
Brian:	So are we going to see where she crashed or what? [makes a crash sound]
Martin:	Because the dad was a pilot, and he was drunk as a skunk.
Linda:	No, come on damn you.
Brian:	[ic]
Martin:	The dad, he's a builder.
Robert:	Just write bricklayer.
Brian:	It's good we can be so serious.

We see some characteristic aspects of the zooming-out. It must be *surprising, humorous, sexual, bizarre* or *amoral*. Surprisingly: the mother becomes an air-hostess. Humorously, including a heavy piece of self-irony: "It's good we can be so serious." Sexually or rather sexist: Linda "cannot be a part of this group…" She "can just beat it" and take her "fat tits" with her. Bizarre and amoral: the mother has just crashed with a flight, and why not go and take a look at the spot? And Linda has provided the necessary zooming-in: "OK, and what do they do for a living?"

A successful stand up comedian will master this process of making surprising, humorous, sexual, bizarre and amoral associations in a complete unpredictable combination. The teacher, however, comes over and pokes Martin on the arm: "I think you should be a little more serious." (And so does the observer: When is something of relevance for the study of learning mathematics going to happen?) Martin keeps swinging his bunch of keys. Linda concentrates on the task, and she provides hope for the ongoing data-collection.

| Linda: | What's the child's name? |
| Martin: | [swings his keys] The child! |

Robert:	Viggo!
Martin:	It is Viggo Poul. [laughs]
Brian:	Pimp.
Martin:	No, it has to be so he'll get picked on for real, he's called Pimp.

And what can be the name of the girl?

Martin:	Lolita. Lolita, that is a lady's name, OK, the girl is called Lolita.
Robert:	No, Benitta, Benitta.
Martin:	No, Lolita.
Brian:	Lolita.
Robert:	No, Benito or something.
Martin:	Lolita.
Brian:	Lolita, we have got that.
Robert:	Lolito.
Brian:	Lolita.
Linda:	What?
Martin:	Lolita. [gets up and leans over the table]
Brian:	L-...
Martin:	Lolita.
Brian:	...o-l-i-t-t-a.
	[...]
Linda:	OK, and how old are they going to be?
Martin:	Yes, 14 and 18.
Robert:	No, 14 and 15.
Martin:	14 and 16.
Robert:	14, and then she's going to be 16. Hey, Martin, She's going to be 16, because then she's a trouser-virgin. [laughs]

Well, if the father cannot be a pimp, then the name of the son can be Pimp. This kind of logic-by-association fits perfectly well the zooming-outs of the present sit-down comedians. The quality of being *amoral* is maintained. Thus, they did choose the name Pimp for the boy, because, as presented by Martin, in this way they make sure that he would become teased: "...it has to be so he'll get picked on for real." An argument that is accepted immediately.

The discussion continues. What could be the job of the mother? A cashier? A nursery teacher? At a certain point Robert states with a smile: "We're just the most provocative group." His meta-statement shows a consciousness of what is going on, but his smile and tone of voice does not disclose any regret or shame. The group tries to get into contact with the teacher, and he is occupied elsewhere, so the group continues to figure out where the family might be living. Different cities are suggested. It is not clear whether or not they come to any agreement. Apparently, Linda has had enough. She leaves the group to find the teacher who arrives at their table.

Teacher:	Right, can I hear your family?
Brian:	No.
Linda:	OK.

Robert takes the tape-recorder to his mouth, then he sticks the tape recorder up to Linda's mouth:

Linda:	The mum of the family is called Marie, she is 48... no, 38 years...
Teacher:	[pokes Robert on his arm and pokes the table to make him put the tape recorder back]
Linda:	...and she's a Sonofon girl. The dad is called Ole, he is 40 years old and a bricklayer. The first child is called Pimp and is 14 and a paperboy. And the other child is called Loritta.
Robert:	Lolita.
Linda:	Lolita.
Teacher:	Mmhm.
Linda:	...and is 16 and works in a 24-hour kiosk. And they live in Sønderup Syldrup.
Robert:	Sønderup Suldrup.

The group presents the whole family: The mother, Marie (38), is a Sonofon girl, the father, Ole (40), is a brick-builder, Pimp (14) is a paperboy and Lolita (16) works in a 24-hours kiosk. By means of a considerable number of zooming-ins from Linda the group has completed the first task. The family is ready to go on holiday, and more specific planning of the trip would open up issues and questions, which could bring the group to face some of the mathematical tasks considered by the teacher.

Shooting Indians or what?

"Then you should be able to get going," the teacher comments (with some hope in his voice). He reminds the group that being employed by a travel agency, they have to advise the family who would be interested in renting a summer cottage. The family would also be interested in going abroad. Robert sighs: "Gee, how boring."

Linda reads aloud from the worksheet handed out by the teacher. However, Brian accuses her of being unable to spell, and in order to prove his prejudice he takes over and reads the text aloud himself, and he teasingly offers to help her: "Should I help you with the spelling, dear?" The others interrupt or comment on the text during her reading. It is difficult for Linda to keep face and her concentration. Robert states with a laugh: "I didn't even hear what you said." He also indicates that the observer might react to his repeated rattling of paper close to the microphone: "Now she'll get cross in a minute." As this has happened before and happens again in the next excerpts, too, it might indicate another aspect of zooming-out: the importance of being able to tease or challenge somebody – especially the classroom authorities.

Linda once again focuses on the task: "We're helping them by describing those holiday destinations." While the boys, for no obvious reasons, stick to places in Denmark close to Sønderup Suldrup, Linda goes to get a travel catalogue with interesting destinations abroad. She shows them the place she is going to visit soon. Apparently this makes the boys interested, and for a while they talk about where to go. They, especially, pay attention to places they have been to or are going to visit themselves. They suggest places like: Fuerte Ventura, Gran Canaria, Costa del Sol. There is not much coherence or advocating, just isolated statements. Anyway, they seem to be on their way.

Brian and Martin suddenly claim that Linda does not participate in the group work, and they take the opportunity to tell on her, but the teacher has his attention somewhere else. A little later, as the boys do not react to her back-to-the-task question, Linda calls for the teacher in a complaining tone of voice: "Henning! Why did you put me in this group?" The teacher returns to the group and leans over the table.

Teacher:	Are you getting into the situation?
Robert:	Yes, very. We're going to Tenerife, and we're going to find out what is best and what is worst.
Linda:	I think we should go to Gran Canaria to Koala Garden because that's where I'm going the 18th.
Robert:	Linda she is tough, she's going to Koala Garden.
Brian:	Ooh, that's where I'm going the 18th. [distorted tone of voice]
Martin:	We're going to Mexico.

As a response to the teacher question, Robert simply states: "We are going to Tenerife," not that Tenerife has been considered before. It turns out that Linda has a special interest in deciding upon the destination. She is in fact going on holiday on the 18th, to Koala Garden on Gran Canaria. Robert's next comment is: "Linda she is tough, she's going to Koala Garden." And Brian raises his tone of voice to imitate Linda: "Ooh, that's where I'm going the 18th." Then Martin obviously out of nowhere states a conclusion: "We're going to Mexico."

> Robert: Where is Koala Garden?
> Linda: That's where I'm going soon.
> Martin: Gran Canaria.
> Robert: Gran Canaria, where is Gran Canaria?
> Martin: We're going to Mexico!

Robert at least pretends an interest towards Linda: "Where is Koala Garden?" They are looking for the map to find out. It seems difficult to find a map, and when found it seems difficult to find Gran Canaria. Martin, maybe still maintaining the authority of the father, repeats his statement about going to Mexico.

When Robert and Linda seem to ignore him and continue their search on the map he insists by putting his idea forward for the third time: "Hey, we're going to Mexico!" He almost shouts it out, but a fourth time is needed to make the others listen.

> Martin: Listen, we're going to Mexico.
> Linda: Gran Canaria.
> Martin and
> Brian: Mexico!
> Martin: Don't you vote for that too, Robert?
> Robert: Yes, yes that'll be all right. [leafs through the atlas]
> Martin: There are both [ic] and…
> Brian: We're going to Mexico.
> Martin: …iguana and everything, and turtles and fish.
> Linda: OK, we're going to Mexico. [writes on her piece of paper]

This suggestion follows the pattern of zooming-out. Mexico is surprising as it has not been suggested until Martin caught it out of the blue. After several unsuccessful attempts to state his suggestion as the conclusion he directly addresses Robert to get his support: "Don't you vote for that too, Robert?" Robert follows him: "Yes, yes that'll be all right," and Brian confirms: "We're going to Mexico." Linda seems to realise the situation: "OK, we're going to Mexico." She immediately puts the 'decision' on paper.

Is the decision a result of a democratic vote: 1 for Koala Garden and 3 for Mexico? Maybe this voting did pass with Linda, however, the decision was not accompanied by any form of argumentation. It was not advocated but stated. In fact, lack of serious advocating is an essential aspect of zooming-out, and it is part of the strategy of the resistance group. By refusing to make any argumentation, they prevent themselves from being trapped by any 'logic of schooling'. Furthermore, the choice of decision is an insult to Linda, who in fact puts forward an argument for her preference of destination.

The bizarre voting procedure can also reflect another element, the sexism that always seems ready to surface. Thus, the daughter of the family is introduced as a sex object, and, in case anybody should forget, her name would remind us. This sexism can also be reflected in the fact that Linda's opinion is not even worth addressing by an argument. A 'shouting over' is enough. And with loud voices the boys now prepare themselves for Mexico. Wonderful things are waiting for them.

Martin:	And shining sun out of clay and I don't know what not. And Indians. [points in the brochure]
Brian:	Above all Indians.
Martin:	They're cool. My mum and dad actually went into the jungle like to go horse-riding.
Brian:	On an Indian. [laughs and leans back]
Martin:	On an Indian, that's what the cowboys do. [leans back]
Brian:	They are out shooting Indians or what?
Martin:	They just said it was mad. And then my mum, it [the horse] just ran. So she couldn't keep up, so it just took off, then there was one of the cowboys that caught it, then she ran up front with the cowboy.
Brian:	I-haaaa.
Martin:	And then there was this monkey down there. It was more than two metres long. It was just like this.

With big gestures Martin demonstrates what a two metres tall monkey looks like. He makes monkey sounds and puts the tape recorder to his mouth:

Martin	Arrggghh!
Linda:	Martin!
Martin:	[makes a face and gives the thumbs up to the camera] 10-4.
Brian:	Linda, why are you screaming into it?
Linda:	Like hell I am.
Martin:	Linda, why are you...
Brian:	You're sitting all the way up there with your tits. [Linda puts the tape recorder to her mouth to demonstrate how Martin does]
Martin:	Linda. Hey er... [addressed to the observer]
Brian:	[laughs]
Martin:	She [the observer] is right over there looking at you.
Linda:	I know. She's not looking at all.

Sure, the observer is worried about the robustness of the technical equipment. However, this part of the conversation can be read as the splendid bizarre and amoral 'finale'. Everything seems to be in play here. The stream of free associations touches upon Indians, cowboys, Martin's father and mother, who once went to the jungle. The amoral nature of the perspective is emphasised by Brian's question: "Out shooting Indians or what?" A two meter ape enters the scene. The actual score is announced to be 10-4. We hear the natural sound of the animal. The 'neutral' observer is brought back into the picture. And only 25 minutes of the lesson have passed.

They go to Mexico

From an outside perspective the resistance group confirm their own label as "just the most provocative group". They call for a lot of attention because of their noisy behaviour and language use, which is not exactly drawingroom standards. This might be a big challenge to the teacher, who is responsible for making room for himself and for the other groups of students as well. In the 'Travel agency' project the teacher seems very patient and almost unaffected. Very calmly he asks the boys to "be more serious," but he treats this group respectfully and no different from the other groups and there is no sign of anger on his face. This might be one reason why the boys like him so well and why they actually do some work in the mathematics lessons.[110]

In what follows the teacher helps the group to go along with their idea of planning a trip to Mexico. As the boys want to know about the exchange rate of the Mexican currency, he suggests that they find it on the internet. The boys leave the classroom in order to go to the computer room. When they return they have gained some information which they did not find on the internet, though. Instead they have called a bank that informed them about the exchange rate of Mexican Pesos.

During the next three lessons the resistance group keeps the interest in Mexico. They find out how far away it is and how long the travel time is. They find the price of a hotel with breakfast included, they decide the date and time of departure and home journey. Last, they make a poster with their findings decorated with cuttings from some travel magazines. All along they keep zooming-out just like they did in the presented ex-

---

[110] This is not the case in some lessons other than mathematics, where these boys cause a lot of trouble for the teachers, and actually, some time after our observations, Robert is dismissed from school.

cerpt. The periods of the zooming-outs get longer and longer, and the boys are getting still more rude to Linda. For instance Brian farts holding the tape recorder close to his seat, shouting at Linda: "It smells better than you do under your arms." She leaves the group, but returns after awhile. On other occasions she reacts by throwing things at the boys or by shouting "shut up!" She actually endures their attacks for more than two lessons before she finally gives it up and asks the teacher if she could please join another group.

Gradually the out-zooming voices get too noisy, and the teacher suggests that the boys take a break and leave the classroom. Brian, who actually understands this as a punishment, complains that the teacher support to the group has been insufficient. Sulkily, he leaves the room together with Martin, while Robert obviously is getting interested in finding out about the exchange rate, and he succeeds in doing some exchange calculations supported by the teacher. Maybe Robert learnt something, but have we learnt something about the learning of mathematics?

We did the things we were supposed to do, didn't we?

After having studied the transcripts from the resistance group for a longer period of time, we decide to ask them how they have experienced the course. So more than half a year later we arrange an interview with the group including watching the video of the presented excerpt. Surprisingly, the students have a very clear memory of what happened that day. In fact, before having seen the situation on video, they are able to recall and retell several headlines as well as details when asked about the episode. No doubt, they have reflected upon this and upon their own performances. Robert's spontaneous comment, which appears to be crucial to the rest of the interview, is:

Robert: We did the things we were supposed to do, didn't we?

Linda stresses her negative experiences with the group, and Robert does not miss the chance to indicate that Linda, and not the boys, has been the obstructing part:

Linda: It was a hard day, because it was hard to be with them. They were fooling about. So I changed groups.
Robert: It was only when Linda left that we got started properly. That has to be said.

While watching the videotape the boys comment on the situation. First they look at the situation from a critical distance:

Robert: Are you like that in all classes? [addressing Brian]
Brian: This will have to be burned.

But after a little while they begin to repeat their own remarks, laughing at what they hear and see. Their ruthless treatment of Linda is repeated in the interview session, where they make fun of her spelling:

Brian: She [Linda] cannot spell properly, damn it, man. [laughs]

As we have seen in the presented excerpt, the boys are rude to Linda during the whole course. In the interview Linda has not blamed them for that. As the reasons for her leaving the group she has only characterised the boys as smart-asses. We want the boys to reflect on their own fellowship:

Teacher: How do you three boys think you handled Linda that day?
Brian: We might have been nicer to her.
Teacher: [mentions the story with the pimples] What do you think of a reception like that?
Linda: That was Robert.
Robert: I was only making fun.
Teacher: What role do you feel will be Linda's?
Brian: She can do things while the rest of us are just talking.
Linda: I make notes of what the others are saying.
Teacher: Is that fair?
Robert: Well, it's not unusual, is it? – for a girl? [laughs]

Robert excuses himself with the remark that he "was only making fun". Brian almost admits that Linda is the one who works, while the others "are just talking," but Robert keeps a sexist attitude with the remark, that having a secretary's role is not unusual – "for a girl". His laugh indicates that he is well aware of his rudeness.

Linda is rather quiet during the whole interview session. Once in a while she smiles, but she only speaks when asked. This can certainly be caused by her own serious reflections on the possible consequences of complaining. Martin is rather non-committal. His answers are "I don't know" or "I agree". Robert and Brian are the most eager to comment on the situation. But they cannot keep concentration very long, so the conversation is often interrupted by their zooming-outs. They begin to talk about something else or they whisper together. Once in a while Robert moves some tuck plates with sweets from himself to Linda, further on to

Brian and so on. In this and many other ways the interview session mirrors the observed classroom situation. However, they have not brought the keys, although another sound track is made up by the drumming sounds of some coke bottles made by Martin and Brian during the interview. This is not commented on.

The group members seem conscious about their behaviour during the observed mathematics lessons, so we want to know what makes them behave like this.

Teacher:	Why do you think you begin the assignment the way you do?
Robert:	That's because we're nervous. With the camera on.
Brian:	No, that's not it.
Martin:	That's the way we always begin.
Brian:	No, we only begin like that 90 per cent of the time.

The teacher gets three different answers to his question. Robert accentuates the videotaping which corresponds well with the fact that he was also very busy with the camera during the classroom observation. This is repeated in the interview session, as Robert (rhetorically) asks: "Do you realise that the camera is on?" Brian denies the influence of the camera, and Martin claims that this case is not exceptional. Brian cannot resist cracking a joke: "No, we only begin like that 90 per cent of the time." He later reflects on the difference in being part of the situation and observing it from outside:

Brian:	Well, when you're sitting there, it's fine, it's going. But when you're sitting here you can see that we're not really doing anything. Now we've almost found out what they are called.

By this final remark, Brian takes an ironic distance to their long argumentative procedure of finding the names of the members of the family. But the boys unanimously agree that they certainly do work:

Teacher:	Have you started?
All:	[promptly] Yes!
Brian:	We're doing what we're supposed to, but we're also doing other things.
Martin:	Mmm.
Robert:	Mmm. That's the way we always do it: Talking a bit, doing a bit. Talking a bit, doing a bit.
Brian:	That's what the teachers don't understand. They think you're not doing anything. They only see you fooling about.
Robert:	That's when you make the most noise. If the camera was on all the time they would have seen it all.

The boys are obviously quite aware of their own behaviour. They know that they do what they are supposed to do and that they do a lot of other things as well. They do not consider this as a problem, but they are well aware that teachers do. Brian and Robert have identical explanations: The teachers only observe the noisy behaviour, and Robert's suggestion that a tape recording would show both the noisy and the learning behaviour is very reasonable. As a matter of fact we as observers in the situation only noticed the noisy behaviour. Robert sticks to this argument, justifying himself:

> Robert: It's not as wild as it appears. The problem is the noise. The teachers can't complain when we manage to do what we're supposed to.

To the teacher question how mathematics lessons should be organised to please the students the resistance group agrees that: "It has to be fun while you learn." And they also agree that the 'Travel agency' project was not bad at all. Still, the project seems far away from catching the boys' intentions in learning. As Robert formulates it:

> Robert: We go to school in order to be with our mates. The high point is the breaks.

So perhaps the teacher attempts to please students with resistant behaviour are wasted efforts. They do not primarily go to school to learn, but to have fun and to socialise with their fellow students.[111] And from time to time this being together will incidentally result in some learning processes. Who knows?

INTENTION

Resistance groups can be found in many classrooms. As we have seen, there are some characteristic communicative patterns in their zooming-outs that we have described as: surprising, humorous, sexual, bizarre and amoral. And we could add self-ironic, teasing, challenging and certainly unpredictable. Obviously, a resistance group has a lot to do. It does not make much sense to think of the members of a resistance group as low performers. Not much literature in mathematics education pictures this

---

[111] See Valero (1998b).

kind of group. The literature on students with difficulties in mathematics normally portrays them as well-behaved students, who struggle with 'concrete material' and elementary exercises in order to overcome their handicap. This portrait does not apply to a resistance group.[112]

The theory of speech acts is gaining an extra justification by the observations of the resistance group: much more is done by means of language than just making descriptions. By their comments the group members do a whole lot of things. 'Getting in contact' appears almost exaggerated among the boys, but Linda is excluded from this contact, and so is the teacher. 'Locating' is taking place, for instance concerning the name and the age of parents and children, but the locating appears as statements and shouting over, and there are no advocating, inquiring questions or arguments. 'Evaluation' is explicit but heavily ironic as, for instance: "It is good that we can be so serious." As mentioned, there is no lack of 'thinking aloud' or of creative ways to escape the classroom agenda. The behaviour of the resistance group is a combination of zooming-in and zooming-out of the landscape of investigation that can be interpreted in terms of double-bind.[113] They will and they will not at the same time. Many of the IC-elements seem to be present, however, in a perverted form. Something fundamental is missing if the conversation is to be interpreted as a dialogue-based learning process.

What is missing in the previous conversation is somehow revealed by the zooming-outs. The students depart from an intended perspective, and introduce something different and unexpected. They present themselves with an ironic distance to what is going on. Certainly, departing from the expected route of associations is essential to any humour.[114] A zooming-in, however, represents the act of getting into the work-process again. Of getting involved. Participating in a dialogue presupposes involvement, and this involvement may establish a link between qualities of a dialogue and qualities of critical learning. We will characterise this involvement by referring to the notion of *intention*.

---

[112] Maybe we come closer to an interpretation if we look at the students as a minority group who cannot associate with the dominant culture of the classroom. See, for instance, Mellin-Olsen (1987).

[113] See Bateson (1972) and Mellin-Olsen (1987).

[114] Zooming-out could also take place in a quite different way. In Chapter 1 we described students' minimal-response strategies that prevent the students from taking responsibility for their learning process. At the same time these strategies allow them to stay on good terms with the teacher. Zooming-out via minimal-response strategy, though, does not disturb the classroom environment.

We could skip the observations of the resistance group as irrelevant for a clarification of learning mathematics. Apparently the transcripts do not document any process of learning. However, we find it relevant to consider the resistance group for several reasons. Although the resistance appears exaggerated, we find that resistance towards learning is a general phenomenon. This resistance need not take the direct and open form, as presented by the resistance group. Resistance can also take a moderate form, when students just show a disinterest in what is going on in the classroom, and maybe occupy themselves with other things. This form of resistance can explain many students' low performances. In fact, as we shall see later, resistance towards learning can be a healthy self-protection. In order to understand the processes of learning it is important to understand what involvement as well as disinvolvement could mean.

There is a basic assumption in broad sets of observations that students really want to learn, and that they are motivated to occupy themselves with the designated tasks. But this is in fact far from being the case. This brings us to consider the notion of intention as part of our conceptual framework. We find that the behaviour of the resistance group empha-sises the importance of including some particular studies of intentions-in-learning in any theorising of learning.[115] Such studies are not so easily made in cases where data-material is collected in well-functioning groups of students.

Intentions-in-learning. Actions are constituted by intentions. As we see learning as action and some learning as dialogic action, it becomes important to study intentions-in-action, and in particular intentions-in-learning. Considering the actions of the resistance group, intentions-in-learning are basically missing. Further, their conversation is no dialogue. Some of their speech acts may look like dialogic acts. However, dialogic acts presuppose the involvement of the persons in terms of intentions-in-learning, and they presuppose commitment to the content matter if dialogue is to be part of a learning process.

In Chapter 4 we have argued that a dialogue is unpredictable. One cannot know where it will bring you beforehand. Thus, intentions-in-learning involves participating in an open inquiry with the purpose of learning from the process. A clear example of this is found in 'Batman & Co.', where Mary and Adam struggle with the inverse spreadsheet. As we remember, Mary concludes the lesson with: "Today we really learnt something!" This may be understood as a report of some mathematical

---

[115] See also Skovsmose (1994).

facts being grasped. This would be a direct interpretation of 'learnt', but it can also be a report of the experience of *really* putting intentions into it: Today they have made their very best effort to learn. And they have done so together. Acts such as getting in contact, locating, identifying, advocating, thinking aloud, reformulating, challenging and evaluating all presuppose that the participants are involved. The acts that bring together an inquiry co-operation lose their significance if the persons are not putting their intentions into it. We see *intentions-in-learning as basic to carrying out dialogic acts* as part of an inquiry co-operation. In this respect, involvement becomes a precondition if qualities of dialogue are to turn into qualities of learning.

Intentions-in-learning are essential for the students' ownership of the learning process. The ownership is, among other things, established in terms of who has the possibility to direct and redirect the investigation. Students can be well-behaved and follow the teacher suggestions without any resistance, but this does not indicate students' ownership. When the teacher interrupted Mary and Adam, and presented a new possibility, there was no guarantee that they wanted to follow the new direction. The interruption could have become an interruption of the dialogue. However, it became a turning point as the students recaptured the ownership. Their intentions-in-learning were reestablished.

In order for the dialogue to continue, it is important that the intentions of the participants are continually modulated and adjusted to each other. Thus, getting in contact also means showing respect for the intentions of the other. Identifying has to do with why-questions, but not only with why-questions related to the content matter. They can also have the form: Why are you doing this? What is the point of this task? Dialogic acts include sensitivity to the intentions of the persons involved. Linda had some motives for the choice of Koala Garden at Gran Canaria as destination for the holiday trip, but her motives were certainly not acknowledged by the group. No modulation or adjustment of intentions were taking place. Being part of a learning process, dialogic acts help to integrate intentions as intentions-in-learning. Naturally, this is not a given thing. Students' intentions can go many ways. Students can act as a resistance group and not as learners and they can do so intentionally.

The students of the resistance group certainly had many intentions with their way of acting in the classroom. They had intentions of having a good time, intentions of enjoying themselves. They put their efforts into socialising, although on the boys' condition, but they had no clear intention to learn. Robert said so in the interview: "We go to school in order to be with our mates. The high point is the break." Inviting these students into a landscape of investigation of mathematical subjects may be a wasted effort. At any rate, it is important to be aware of the fact that many students are going to accept the invitation only on their own premises and not necessarily with the intention of learning mathematics.

Underground intentions. The resistance group contrasts Mary and Adam by not putting their intentions-in-learning into the project. However, they did not ignore the project and just occupied themselves with other issues. In Chapter 1, we described the process of zooming-in as a student activity through which the students try to accommodate their learning intentions to the situation. Zooming-out is different but, as already emphasised, related to zooming-in. The students relate themselves to the prescribed activity, but they avoid doing what is expected. Their zooming-outs serve as ironic remarks to the project, and to schooling in general.[116]

There are many other forms of resistance to learning that are less noisy. When the resistance to learning is kept hidden and not declared in public, then many non-learners can be considered by their teachers as 'nice but slow'. The point, however, might simply be that they do not put their intentions into learning. And there can be many good reasons for students not to do so. For instance, if a student experiences or expects that he or she cannot successfully compete with his or her classmates, then it might be a healthy self-protection not to put particular efforts into the learning process. Instead such students can make their own agenda. Or students may react to a quizzing communication of the teacher by minimising their contributions to the classroom activities and their responsibility for what is going on there.

Intentions connected with learning are far from the only set of intentions that the student has. A student can have intentions about avoiding to be noticed by the teacher, about sitting next to somebody, about joining the game in the next break, etc. Here we will talk about *underground intentions,* which refer to the students' zooming-out of the official classroom activity. Such intentions also flourish in the classroom, and they are connected with acting as much as other intentions, partly setting an alternative scene for what is going on in the classroom. It is not always easy to spot the underground intentions in the classroom. Apparently the students are calculating studiously, but this is only when the teacher is in their close vicinity. When the students find out that they can once

---

[116] Our discussion of intentions and underground intentions can be related to Mellin-Olsen's (1977, 1981) discussion of instrumentalism, and of I-rationales and S-rationales.

again make themselves invisible in the abyss of the classroom, their activities change.

We find it important to identify underground intentions in order to understand what many students in fact are doing in the classroom context. We must search for an understanding of their behaviour by trying to locate how they see their reasons for being involved, or not, in the classroom activities. Underground intentions are intentions, and consequently they can also be parts of acts. What we have described as zooming-outs are examples of such acts. But they are no simple acts of learning.

The position of the resistance group might be caused by the particular organisation of the project, the 'Travel agency'. Landscapes of investigation are supposed to provide a multifaceted invitation for the students. But such landscapes can also cause problems. Maybe the students find the suggested activities of the 'Travel agency' to be too childish. The students might be too old for planning a trip for a more or less imagined family. Maybe the fact that the teacher sets the scene can be interpreted in terms of authority and thereby invite resistance. Maybe it is important that a contextualisation makes some obvious challenges, also of a mathematical nature, that are clearly visible to the students. Thus, Mary and Adam were definitely challenged by the problem of constructing the inverse spreadsheet. It can also be that a clearer relationship to real life work-processes might have been relevant, in particular making the role of computers more significant. In fact, the continuation of the 'Travel agency' indicates this (see the first part of the sub-section 'They go to Mexico'). Basically this is guess-work, however, as the fact remains that it can be extremely difficult for some students to engage in classroom activities. If they do not accept an invitation into the landscape of investigation they cannot direct their intentions to learning. But certainly their underground intentions can be activated.

We can locate many types of underground intentions among students. The activities of the resistance group might as well be guided by priorities related to groupings outside school. In literature, a notion such as 'post-modern youth' has been presented (see Tarp, 2001). Some groups of young people may have difficulty in adjusting their intentions to the activities in school, when the tasks do not fit their 'world view'.

We must acknowledge the possibility that the organisation of schooling is not adequate for making all students active learners. Resistance may not address, first of all, the particular project but the fact that the activities take place in school. Should we accept the fact that school does not accomodate all students? Can some school contexts be diagnosed as not-suitable-for-certain-students, just as some students can be diagnosed as not-schoolable?

Resources of intentions. Intentions are formed on the basis of experience, impressions, prejudice, preferences, etc. Such resources of intentions we refer to as *dispositions.* A person's dispositions make up the raw material for his or her intentions. We see dispositions as individual, but at the same time as culturally determined characteristics of a person. When we look at learning as action we also use the concept of disposition to describe the source of motives for the student to enter a learning process. The student's dispositions for learning are thus indicative of the factual possibilities that the student holds for the school system and of the student's interpretation of these possibilities. Correspondingly, the students' dispositions make up a heavily structured framing condition for intentions-in-learning. The students expose such intentions in patterns and according to their notions about learning and going to school.[117]

The notion of disposition brings us to the notions of *background* and *foreground* of a group of persons (see Skovsmose, 1994). Let us consider the boys of the resistance group once more. How can we gain an understanding of their behaviour? There is much to be considered in relation to their background, for instance when trying to locate the roots of their sexism. And we can try to understand Linda's patience by finding out if she has older brothers and is used to coping with tough guys. However, we can also try to look for an explanation for their behaviour in their foreground. This means that we must consider how the activities in the classroom relate to their priorities that are constructed by their hopes, expectations and frustrations when they face the future.

In general, by the foreground of a group of persons we understand the way they interpret their possibilities, given the political, cultural, economic context and their own social position. Thus, foreground refers to the prospects of the person. Foreground is not simply a subjective term, because it is modulated by social conditions and other background issues. Equally, foreground is not a sociological fact, as it refers to an interpreted situation. A foreground is an experienced phenomenon. We find that the intentions of a person to a large extent reflect his or her foreground, or the foreground of the group of persons to which he or she belongs. From this resource, intentions are activated, or not. As a consequence, we also

---

[117] The parts of the students' dispositions that are important for the shaping of intentions in learning correspond to what could be called 'the students' learning plan' (Lindenskov, 1992).

consider the foreground when interpreting the actions of a person. Still, the background should not be forgotten. The foreground as well as the background may influence what a person might want, and what actions he or she might engage in. Both foreground and background represent resources of intentions (including underground intentions). This applies to any group, also to a resistance group.

An action has consequences, including consequences beyond the notions of the individual. The intention (being part of the action) reflects at least an inexact notion about some of the possible consequences of the action. At the same time the action and its consequences can end a circle (or open a spiral), because a significant restructuring of a person's dispositions are conditioned by that person's actions and the person's reflections on the consequences that these actions contain. In acting, dispositions are continuously changed. Freire, for instance, has emphasised the close connection between reflection and action (Freire, 1972, 76). We would suggest that action is connected not only with reflection but also with intention. That goes for learning as well.

When we are concerned with learners, we find it particularly relevant to consider their foreground. The general educational task is to present activities that the students can relate to their own possibilities and be involved in as acting persons. Much educational discussion has concerned the 'meaning' that students can associate to mathematical concepts and activities. Some research has associated resources for meaning as primarily having to do with the background of the students. Thus, many ethnomathematical studies have concentrated on the cultural and historical background of the students in order to identify activities which students might want to engage in. We find it problematic if background is considered as the only and primary resource for meaningfulness.[118] It is important to acknowledge students' foreground as a resource for bringing intentions into learning in order to establish meaningful learning for the students.

However, the foreground of many students does not allow them to be involved in a wide range of classroom activities. In this respect the resistance group can represent many other groups. It can be the group of silent girls, who need to protect themselves from the demands of the school by downplaying the importance of what is taking place in the classroom. More generally, we suggest that interpretations of, say, girls' performances in mathematics, do consider not only their background but also their foreground, including those possibilities which society and culture

---

[118] For a critical discussion of ethnomathematics, see Vithal and Skovsmose (1997).

allow girls to conceptualise as their possibilities. The resistance group can also represent a minority group of students, who not only bring a different cultural tradition to school, but who also face a different future than the majority, and who as a consequence ascribe meaning to their classroom activities from a different perspective.

In some cases a majority group of students have difficulties in associating meaning to school activities, and consequently they do not provide intentions in learning. Here we can think of black children in the previous apartheid South Africa. Many observations seem to document that black children performed much more poorly than white children. And white research in black education could interpret this as having to do with the cultural background of the children. Thus Herbert Khuzwayo (1998, 2000) has shown how white research has provided interpretations along the following line: the father of the black family plays a dominant role in the household, which implies that the creativity of the black children is hampered with the consequence that they are not well prepared for subjects like mathematics. In other words, the black children themselves bring with them to school the causes for their own failure in school. Not much to do about this! This is, however, a completely misleading interpretation. The black children live in a society where the white apartheid regime had simply stolen their future. Reconsidering this political crime, we reach a different understanding of the students' performance in school. And naturally we can definitely not ignore the most appalling material conditions of the black schools.

If the students have no possibility of connecting meaning in what they are doing in school with aspects of their former or their future life, then it may be difficult for them to direct their intentions towards learning. Trying to understand what the resistance group is doing must, consequently, also include an understanding of how they see their possibilities, and how the school activities relate to their aspirations and hopes. Reconsidering the interview with the resistance group, months after the project took place, however, does not reveal many clues as to how students can be brought into learning processes. This does, however, not change our general idea: If you want to interpret certain learning processes of today, then it is necessary to consider what the students might hope to do tomorrow.

The 'Travel agency' is exemplary for what many teachers experience and have to deal with. Entering a landscape of investigation also brings the teacher into a risk zone, where it becomes unpredictable what will happen. As mentioned previously, one possibility is to return to the comfort zone of the exercise paradigm with its well elaborated code of what to do and what to expect. Here students' underground intentions might be in operation but often less visible and less obstructive, and in case of difficulties the teacher can try to exercise a certain amount of bureaucratic absolutism. This might be a pragmatic, but in some cases reasonable way of pacifying a resistance group. Nevertheless, it remains an educational task to provide possibilities for students to direct their intentions to their learning activities, as such learning may have particular qualities. The possible resources of students' intentions must always be considered.

In many classrooms no teachers invite any students into a landscape of investigation. Nevertheless, the result, in terms of test results and marks, seems impressive. So why bother about the students' background and foreground and about directing their intentions to learning? The reason is that we are concerned about the students' involvement in the process of learning. It is important that students experience an ownership of the learning process. Such an ownership is essential if some of the qualities of dialogue are to turn into qualities of learning. In particular, it is difficult to imagine processes of reflection being integrated parts of processes of learning if students are not involved.

CHAPTER 6

REFLECTION AND LEARNING

The notion of 'reflection', and related terms, plays an essential role in several learning theories. Thus, in Piaget's genetic epistemology reflective abstractions are crucial.[119] Reflective abstractions are based on particular types of reflections, and to Piaget the constituting process of making abstractions is to carry out reflections. As mentioned previously, to Freire the notion of reflection is also essential, and he integrates reflection and action into the political powerful concept of *conscientização*, which represents a crucial aspect of literacy. Certainly the notion of reflection, included in *conscientização*, is much different from the Piagetian one. Following the Freirean methodology of teaching adults to read and write, learners not only have to recognise the syllables of particular words and to learn how to combine these syllables into other words, they also get invited to discuss the social context that the word might refer to. Reflections become an essential part of a developed literacy and it takes on a political dimension by addressing the broader context of the particular elements of learning. In this chapter we shall try to make our way into the notion of reflection by relating our discussion to the 'Caramel boxes' project.

We find that reflections are part of a dialogue. In particular we find elements of reflection in dialogic acts like locating, thinking aloud, identifying, advocating, etc. This means that we do not follow the Piagetian line, seeing reflections as carried out by an individual. We consider reflections referring to 'shared considerations', and we see dialogue as including processes of reflection. We will try to characterise further the nature of reflections, by addressing the 'scope of reflections', referring to what reflections can be about, the 'subject of reflections', referring to who it is carrying out the reflections, and the 'context of reflections' re-

---

[119] See, for instance Beth and Piaget (1966); Dubinsky (1991) and Piaget (1970).

ferring to the situation in which the reflections are fulfilled. By means of this clarification we try to show that dialogue, representing qualities of communication, and critique, representing qualities in learning, can be connected. We will return to this issue in Chapter 7. However, before we get that far, we will look at an example.

'CARAMEL BOXES'

The 'Caramel boxes' project takes place in the same class that did the 'Travel Agency' project, but we promise the reader that, in the following, we are not going to pay attention to any resistance group. The students are divided into groups, and this time each group is going to plan a factory production of caramel boxes. The teacher introduces a landscape of investigation. As a beginning the groups will have to construct two boxes, one twice as big as the other. In an 'industrial newspaper' handed out to the students it says: "As always you will have to consider the functionality and the price of the box. Please, do not forget that our factory has always taken a pride in satisfying the requests of our customers, and at the same time providing a good income for the factory."

This introductory task illustrates some mathematical possibilities established by the project: What does it mean that one box is twice as big as the other? Could it mean that the length of the sides is the double? That it is made by a paper double the size of the paper necessary for the small box? Or that the price of the content of the bigger box should be double the price of the content of the small box? The relationship between the length-factor, the area-factor and the volume-factor is yet to be identified.

The group we are going to follow is made up by Simon, Dennis, Lisa and Sara. Because of little space in the classroom this group is placed in a small room next to the classroom. The door between the two rooms is open, but the noise of the other groups does not disturb them. After a short while they agree to get started, and Sara makes a first suggestion:

Sara:	Isn't that supposed to be a quadrangular container?
Lisa:	Yes.
Sara:	Isn't that the one that takes the least? Then make one 1×1 cm and then one that is 2×2. Then that's twice as big.
Simon:	No.
Sara:	But it is.
Lisa:	Yes.

Sara advocates her suggestion in a questioning form. The suggestion of "quadrangular" may refer to the handiness of the box but also to something else. It could be the one that "takes the least" (paper for its production). She also has an idea of the size of the boxes, one being 1×1 cm, the other 2×2: "Then that's twice as big." Simon objects to that, but Lisa agrees with Sara.

However, instead of further inquiry at this interesting start, Simon, in what follows, suggests that they make a drawing to help them find out. Lisa suggests that they make one box of cardboard. At this stage there is a little confusion until they find out that they are supposed to produce boxes not only for one single caramel but for several caramels. They get some centicubes, which makes it easier to experiment.

From the very beginning they use different methods to examine the relation of the size of the two boxes: drawing, making a paper model and a model with centicubes. This concretising seems to be the reason why they get started immediately with the clues of the task. Some of the other groups start with long discussions of form and aesthetics of the boxes. The teacher shows up with some real caramels and asks the students if they could make some boxes that suit this special type of caramels. This action can be seen as a challenge, but also as a supportive reformulation of the task. The students begin experimenting by placing the caramels on the paper. They have accepted the invitation into the landscape of investigation, they are in the project, and they take control.

After a short while Sara once again takes the initiative. She advocates the idea of making boxes of 4 and of 8 caramels:

Sara:	I think we should make 4-packs… and 8-packs.
Lisa:	Yes.
Sara:	That's one with 4 and one with 8.
Simon:	Yes, I think so too.
Lisa:	OK, 4 and 8.
Sara:	How about we measure them? [the caramels]
Simon:	Well, how long are they now? About 3 cm, aren't they?
Sara:	No.
Dennis:	It is 2.
Lisa:	We don't use round figures here.
Simon:	[ic]
Lisa:	It is 3 cm long.

Sara now considers the size of the boxes in terms of volume: How many caramels should the boxes contain? The numbers 4 and 8 are accepted by the others. Obviously, her first suggestion: doubling the length of the sides means doubling the size of the box, is ignored. The presence of the real caramels may have changed this perspective. Sara also suggests measuring the caramels lying on the table: "How about we measure them?" Simon is supportive and estimates the length to be about 3 cm. But although Simon advocates his contribution with a tag questioning invitation and in accordance with Sara's proposal, he, as well as Dennis, are immediately turned down by Lisa: "We don't use round figures here." You can hear the voice of a controlling teacher in her objection, which becomes characteristic later in this episode. Perhaps this is the reason why Simon sometimes lets himself follow Dennis' attempts to zoom-out of the classroom agenda. As we shall see the boys' intentions in learning are not persistent.

One caramel is partly measured and partly decided to be $1 \times 2 \times 3$ cm. They produce some box models in centicubes and some in cardboard. The girls make their own model and the boys theirs. Simon presents one box made by centicubes to the group: "This is how big a 4-pack has to be... it should be... 2 high, 3 wide and 4 long." But Sara has an objection: "Don't make them in centicubes. Make them in cardboard." Simon answers: "Right, but we'll just make them in centicubes first." He seems to have a more formal approach to what they are doing. Anyway, the group comes to face the problem of area.

Simon:	We need... what's that called... we need the area of that... so we can find the area of the piece of paper, right?
Dennis:	Look, centicube of the year.
Sara:	Height × length × width.
Simon:	No, that's the cubic content.
Sara:	It's also the area... as far as I know. [in a low voice]
Simon:	It's not the cubic content we need.
Sara:	Well, no.
Dennis:	The area that's...
Simon:	You need the area.
Sara:	Right.
Simon:	How big is it on top, how big is it on the sides, how big is it... in front?

Simon has located the notion of 'area' as important to calculate the use of paper: "we need the area of that... so we can find the area of the piece of paper, right?" From this invitation the group tries to identify the principles for calculating the area. Sara seems not so sure about her own statement that height × length × width also gives the area, thus with low voice she adds "as far as I know". Simon explains his procedure by showing on the centicube model how to calculate the surface: "How big is it on top, how big is it on the sides, how big is it... in front?" The boys seem to be in a good mood. Dennis is about to make the centicube of the year, and they sing a well-known Cuban melody, 'Quanta la mera', that in a Danish version has been used in a commercial for 'Tom's caramels'. So what could be more appropriate?

These first steps in the project illustrate the difference between locating and identifying. The three pieces of the dialogue we have presented represent three different ways of looking at the problem of 'doubling' a box. It could mean doubling the sides, doubling the content, or doubling the surface. The perspectives are located, but more specific aspects of the perspectives are not identified. They may not even be realised by the students as being different. Mathematical ideas related to the doubling procedures are not crystallised and no why-questions are formulated.

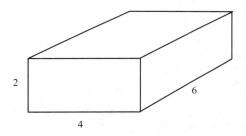

Figure 6.1: Sara's 8-pack box.

Sara accepts Simon's explanation about how to calculate the area but she wants to figure out what this can mean to her own drawing, which shows an 8-pack, the dimensions of which are $2 \times 4 \times 6$ (see Figure 6.1). Everybody looks at Sara's paper:

Sara:	OK, do I have to find all these? Do…?
Lisa:	Yes… you have to… How many are there on top?
Simon:	6×4
Sara:	6… 12… 24. [the calculation of 6×4]
Simon:	Right, good.
Sara:	24 on both sides.
Simon:	24 cm^2 on…
Lisa:	And then, how long is… How many is it down?
Sara:	8. [the area of the end of the box]
Lisa:	And that's also how many there are down there. [the other end of the box]

Simon:	How is it you make a cube?
Lisa:	16.
Sara:	16.
Lisa:	16, and how many are there here?
Sara:	There are 12. [the area of a side]
Lisa:	And how many… There are 12, that's 24.
Sara:	24? No 24 and 24 makes 48.
Lisa:	40… and 24.
Sara:	8… 24 and 48…
Lisa:	What's that? [Simon takes a calculator] That's… 72 cm^2.
Simon:	What did you say?
Sara:	72 plus… plus 16.
Simon:	72 plus 16.
Sara:	You can figure that out easily.
Dennis:	That's 88, I think.
Simon:	Yes.
Dennis:	Mmm.
Sara:	88, then the area is 88 cm^2.
Simon:	Yes…
Sara:	OK, and what do we do then?
Simon:	…on the outside.
Lisa:	Yes.
Sara:	But…
Simon:	88… cm^2, that's the area. So that's what all the piece of paper has to be altogether.
Sara:	Well, then we only have to…
Simon:	Then there has to be a folding of some sort.
Sara:	But, then I know, well then I know, I know, I know.

All four students are concerned about the calculation of the area of the surface of the 8-pack box, and they make it step by step, one box side at a time adding the numbers continuously. The sequence is characterised by thinking aloud, and here 'aloud' also refers to visualising and showing. The model helps them to identify the principle of calculating the area, and this calculation is carried out in a shared process, which includes inquiring questions, advocating, reformulating, completing of utterances and mutual confirmation. Thus, Dennis, who mostly participates on the fringe of the group discourse, comes up with the final result, a little cautiously, however: "That's 88, I think." Sara repeats and specifies the result: "88, then the area is 88 cm^2," and Simon repeats once again and points out: "88… cm^2, that's the area. So that's what the piece of paper has to be altogether." Every member of the group has taken part in the process of investigation, how the calculations have been made, what is the result, and what this means as regards the use of paper for the boxes. But referring to real box production they also have to consider some paper for the joining (see Figure 6.2). However, this does not provoke them to reconsider their previous calculation of the area. "Then there has to be a folding of some sort," Simon says. However, Sara has an idea about how to handle this. In the following minutes the students have some difficulties placing the model on the A4 sheet of paper with as little

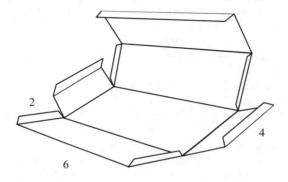

Figure 6.2: An 8-pack box to be folded.

waste of paper as possible. Once in a while Simon and Dennis drop out of the co-operation and talk about various other things, which makes the girls call them to order.

...but nobody wants to buy it

The group makes a division of labour. The boys are going to produce the 4 pack-box, while the girls make the 8 pack-box. The girls also prepare a poster with some describing text so that they can hang up their boxes nicely on the wall. At this moment the teacher arrives to see the group.

Lisa:	Look, there's our lovely poster. [addressed to the teacher]
Teacher:	You'll stick it on it as you go along?
Lisa:	Yes.
Teacher:	Clever.
Simon:	That's our new one that one, there's room for 4 caramels.
Lisa:	But look at all the others, they have made big ones. We have just made one for 8 caramels right here, right? and then one for 4...
Teacher:	But that's fine.
Lisa:	...right? The one for 8 and then the one for 4.

Lisa proudly shows their poster and their boxes to the teacher who praises their work: "Clever" and "But that's fine". There is contact right from the beginning. Then he raises a question:

Teacher:	Right. Did it meet the demands we made on the container then?
Sara:	That there is no wasted space? And... what does it say? [looks at the industrial newspaper] It should be... It should be a practical shape...
Simon:	Well it is, it is square.
Sara:	And should not be too expensive to make.
Teacher:	No.
Lisa:	And it isn't either...
Teacher:	No. Very well.
Lisa:	...because in that box Sara is making, a tiny one like that, there is room for 8, right?
Teacher:	Yes.
Lisa:	But of course, the more you have, the more or less you have to make, because there doesn't have to be all the ends, you see? If you have a box where there is room for 100, [illustrates non-verbally, also during the following] then you have a lot of 8's, because there are all those on, here you only need one up, you see? You see?
Teacher:	Right.
Lisa:	If we say there is room for 100 in this box here, right?
Teacher:	Yes.
Lisa:	And then if you have got one with 8, then there is all this inside. Which there actually isn't there, right?
Teacher:	Right. So maybe it is somewhat expensive to make after all, the small one?
Sara:	No.
Lisa:	Well, it's how you look at it, but who wants to... who wants to buy...
Sara:	...one with 100?
Lisa:	...really.
Sara:	Because then it may be expensive to make it, but nobody wants to buy it.
Lisa:	Yes, exactly.
Teacher:	Yes... but I think you'll have plenty of time for that. I think you should work on that idea, you should try to to... to pursue... it I think, you should try... what you're saying there... Lisa, right? Try.

The teacher does not directly intervene in the students' work, but he asks if they have considered the demands on the container. This makes the students reflect and reformulate: "That there is no wasted space?" and that it is not "too expensive to make". The teacher just confirms their reflections with no judgements or counter-arguments. Lisa widens her reflections by reconsidering the price, which would be relatively cheaper if the box contained a bigger amount of caramels, say a box with room for 100. The teacher challenges their approach: "So maybe it is somewhat expensive to make after all, the small one?" but his question is relativised with a marketing argument put forward by Lisa and Sara almost in stereo: "Well, it's how you look at it, but who wants to... who want to buy... one with 100, really?" Dennis has a tendency to zoom-out. He seems occupied with other things and he does not participate much in the dialogue.

In this sequence the teacher makes the students reflect upon their own thoughts and ideas. After getting in contact they identify, think aloud and reformulate their perspectives. The teacher lets them think aloud without intervening until he makes the challenge: "So maybe it is somewhat expensive to make after all, the small one?" The dialogue is ended by an evaluation and a teacher encouragement to pursue the marketing perspective.

We can observe several dialogic acts. They make up a process of inquiry, which we could also label a process of reflection. And this is a main point to us: *Dialogic acts also include processes of reflection*. We shall return to this point in the next chapter, as reflection provides a main link between dialogue and critique. Thus the dialogic acts of getting in contact, locating, identifying etc. all include reflections.

The price...

The box production continues. The boys have made a model in cardboard which is a little too small for the caramels the teacher gave them. The girls protest and claim that they will have to make a new box. Simon, on his side, claims that his model is mathematically correct. Lisa: "OK, you have cut and drawn it a bit tight." Dennis then comments: "She always has to complain, that woman." Dennis humorously reacts to Lisa's behaviour, not to the content of her objection, and he is ready to change their model: "Then we just make it a little bigger." Simon is not ready to give up his perspective. To Simon it is not important to make a model, but to make the exact calculations: "I can't be bothered to make a new one... now that I have already done it."

The girls counter-argue that he will have to consider the size of the real caramels, not just of the centicubes. This shows the girls' production perspective as opposed to Simon's more formal perspective. The dialogue has turned into a discussion which is closed by Lisa, who takes the role of a controlling teacher and gives the orders in a rather condescending tone of voice: "You have to try to start all over again and then don't care about the one you have made. Try figuring out how much it hangs outside. That will probably be the hardest... to you at least." She wins the fight. The boys have to give up their resistance and make a new box. After this episode the boys zoom-out on other interesting things as, for instance, who Jimmy (a friend of theirs) is dating at the moment.

Lisa leaves the group to find the teacher. The girls are finishing their poster when the teacher comes in, and they show him one of the boxes:

Teacher:	Is there room for 4 in that one over there?
Lisa:	No, not in the caramel. It's because they are making the box.
Teacher:	I see!
Lisa:	It hasn't been put up yet.
Teacher:	That's all right... then you have at least made... two containers, and you have met the first demand...
Lisa:	Yes.
Teacher:	...because... what have you made?
Sara:	Two extra ones.
Lisa:	One is twice as big as the other.
Teacher:	And what does twice as big mean?
Lisa:	That there is room for twice as many.
Teacher:	That there is room for twice as many in it.
Lisa:	Yes.

Again, the teacher interference is characterised by an inquiring attitude towards the student perspective. First, he tries to locate it: "Is there room for 4 in that one over there?" and make them reflect upon what they did: "what have you made?" Further he wants Lisa to explain: "And what does twice as big mean?" and he paraphrases her answer: "That there is room for twice as many in it?" He does not evaluate right or wrong but he challenges the group by introducing a new possibility:

Teacher:	Yes... could you try to consider something about... [interrupted by entering pupil] Could you try to consider something about er...
Simon:	Yes.
Lisa:	The financi... The price... No, we can't.
Teacher:	Yes that might be possible to do too.
Lisa:	Of the box... no...
Teacher:	Yes.
Simon:	Er, how much is a cardboard box like this?
Lisa:	How much is a sheet of cardboard like this?
Teacher:	You'll set a fixed price on it.
Lisa:	What?

Teacher:	You can decide for yourselves.
Simon:	Then it should say: If a... a sheet of card...
Lisa:	...cardboard.
Simon:	...a sheet of cardboard...
Lisa:	...costs 1.25.

Before having finished the question the teacher is interrupted by Lisa who makes a proposal of investigating the price. However, she refuses this proposal herself immediately: "The price... No, we can't." The teacher confirms this possibility, although this was not exactly what he thought of. This is indicated by the word "too". We never come to know what the teacher actually had in mind because the students choose to consider the price of the cardboard, and the teacher follows their new route of investigation. The students ask for the price of a piece of cardboard, and when they are allowed to decide their own price, Lisa suggests 1.25 Kroner.

Then the students begin to measure how many boxes can be made out of one piece of paper. Lisa notices that there will be some waste. Here the teacher interferes with a challenging question: "Should we try to calculate it more precisely?" When they are going to find out how many boxes they can make out of one piece of cardboard, they discover the problem that they have already assembled their models. They need to spread them out in order to measure precisely how many can be placed on the paper. But the girls have a quick solution to the problem. They can cut the tape from the boys' model!

Probably as a reaction to this infringement the boys seem to zoom-out for a while, making some slightly ironical remarks about the girls: "We must be happy to be in such an good group with such excellent members," Dennis remarks. "Yes, the girls are very clever, indeed," Simon adds. While the boys talk a little about Dennis' birds, the girls go along with the calculations. By means of some experimenting they come to the result that 7 small 4-pack boxes can be made from one piece of cardboard. They write the result on the poster. And they calculate the cost of producing a box. Lisa: "...1.25 divided by 7 equals 0.1785714... OK, one costs this much." The boys are called to order: "Behave yourselves and assemble that box!" Sara leaves the group to call for the teacher, and the girls explain how they just calculated the price of the paper for a 4-pack box to be 0.18 Kroner. "Have you made good use of the paper?" the teacher asks, and both Lisa and Sara confirm. And they have considered the aesthetics and the functionality of the boxes as well.

Can you calculate how much wasted space there is?

The introduction of the price of the paper might have complicated the discussion, but the students want to concentrate on the amount of wasted paper. The teacher is still around.

Teacher:	Can you calculate how much waste there is?
Sara:	No.
Simon:	Yes, I suppose we can.
Lisa:	Yes, we can do that.
Teacher:	How should you do it?
Simon:	If you draw all of them.
Lisa:	You draw them completely like this. The boys can do that.
Dennis:	Sure thing.
Lisa:	You have to draw it completely as many times as it can lie here. It has to roughly... you can roughly see these lines, right? Then it goes all... then it has to go all the way to the edge...
Sara:	...and it should be able to lie there 7 times.
Teacher:	Yes.
Lisa:	...and then you draw it afterwards.

There are supposed to be 7 boxes produced out of one piece of paper. But how much waste of paper, then? Is it possible to calculate this? The teacher challenges the students. Sara refuses the question, but both Simon and Lisa have zoomed-in on the task and confirm: "Yes, we can do that." The teacher asks for their method: "How should you do it?" and again he gets identical answers from Simon and Lisa: "If you draw all of them." Further, Lisa promptly tries to convert this idea into action: "The boys can do that." "Sure thing," is Dennis' friendly-ironical remark. With no further discussion Lisa begins to instruct them how to do.

A mathematical procedure has been identified, but the teacher wants to challenge this procedure:

Teacher:	Could you in fact calculate it... without putting it down ...if you wanted to?
Dennis:	We could actually do that.
Sara:	Well we know there is room for 7, and that... we can, we can calculate how many... we... no, hang on... stop, stop, stop, stop! [reaches forward and takes the cardboard from Simon who is drawing the basic shape] We can find the area... or... the area of this, right?
Simon:	It is actually a bit smaller.

Lisa:	...and then find the area of it, and then you multiply that one by s... I mean, that the area of that one multiplied by 7, and then you see...
Sara:	...and then find the area of this, right? The area of this you multiply by 7, and then you see how much there is, then you can see how much wasted space there is...
Teacher:	What do you think of that? [looks at Dennis]
Lisa:	It was correct.
Simon:	It is correct.
Dennis:	It is correct.
Teacher:	Shouldn't we give it a try?
Lisa:	Yes.
Simon:	Then the number you get out of it has to minus.
Teacher:	That's good... that's good.
Lisa:	That... just try. You just do that.
Sara:	Can you just figure out some area from this?
Teacher:	Yes, very good.
Simon:	And you're allowed to use the calculator.
Teacher:	Very good. That's good. [the teacher leaves the group]
Simon:	The area of this.

The teacher obviously wants the group to identify a different procedure as well. But this suggestion is put forward indirectly and hypothetically: "Could you in fact calculate it... without putting it down?" and with no demands "if you wanted to?" This time Dennis and Sara are the ones to grasp the perspective, and Sara shows an eagerness of voice, words and gesture: "No, hang on... stop, stop, stop, stop!" She takes the paper from Simon who is already completing Lisa's orders of drawing the models. The girls formulate their algorithm almost simultaneously: They suggest taking the area of the box multiplied by 7 and subtract this from the area of the piece of cardboard: "then you can see how much wasted space there is." The teacher does not directly confirm this idea but asks Dennis what he thinks. He waits a little with his answer, which makes it possible for him to adopt and paraphrase the answer of the others: "It is correct." A new method has been identified.

Sara's exclamation: "No, hang on... stop, stop, stop, stop!" indicates that she has become aware of something remarkable. She has located a possibility. She might be on her way to identifying a mathematical idea. This identification is not colonised by the teacher. He does not present particular clues to the group, the identification stays as a dialogic act, and the students remain owners of the inquiry process. Again we see that re-flections appear as essential elements of dialogic acts. In particular, *dialogic acts include collective reflections.*

By relating reflections to dialogic acts we make a particular interpretation of reflections. As mentioned, the notion we are proposing is different from the one related to Piaget's genetic epistemology. In his case reflections are characterised as a process related to the individual, while we consider reflections that are carried out in a process of co-operation. In this way reflections become an integrated aspect of an inter-action.

The teacher asks the students to give it a try, and he praises their work before he leaves. Simon takes the lead in calculating the area of the 4-pack box (see Figure 6.3).

Simon:	10 cm long... and... 4 cm wide. 40 times...
Lisa:	18 Ore.
Sara:	Actually you can also just calculate this... 4, there are 4...
Simon:	Yes.
Sara:	...plus 6, no, there are 8, isn't that right...? No... are there not 4 here? no, there are 6.
Simon:	There are 8 there, and there are 6 there, and there are 6 there, there are 12 there. 12 on top of 40 that is 52.
Sara:	[during Simon's sentence]: 12... 12... 12... – 12 plus 8... 12 plus 8, what's that?
Simon:	52×7... 52.
Sara:	12 plus 8.
Dennis:	That's 20...
Lisa:	Then I measure what the area is with this one. [the ruler]
Sara:	12 plus 8.
Dennis:	That's still 20.
Sara:	That's 20 plus er...
Simon:	52×7 that's 364, then we only have to find the area of this one.
Sara:	That's what I'm doing. Hang on. Well are you sure it's 64?
Simon:	Yes 364.

All four members of the group are engaged in collective reflection when calculating the area of the surface of the small box. Sara is apparently somewhat insecure in her attempts. She has some suggestions that she turns down herself at once without waiting for the reaction of the others: "...plus 6, no, there are 8, isn't that right...? No... are there not 4 here? no, there are 6." Simon is the one who takes the lead. He seems to be sure of the procedure and he is a bit ahead of the others with his calculations. For instance, he has already found the area and is about to multiply with the number of boxes, while the others are still concentrating on adding up the area. But at the same time he seems willing to explain his method explicitly: "There are 8 there, and there are 6 there, and there are 6 there,

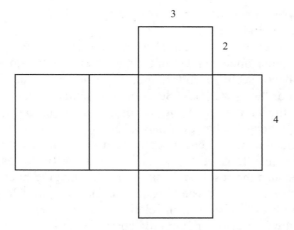

Figure 6.3: An unfolded 4-pack box.

there are 12 there. 12 on top of 40 that is 52." and "52 × 7 that's 364, then we only have to find the area of this one."

Lisa follows his direction, and the following calculation about the area of the A4 cardboard is made by the two of them in co-operation. They start by measuring the length and the sides of an A4 piece of cardboard:

Lisa:	This one is 29 and a half times 21... 29 and a half times 21.
Simon:	29 and a half times 21...
Lisa:	Yes, then the area of this one.
Simon:	...times 21?
Lisa:	Yes.
Simon:	Yes... equals 600 and something.
Lisa:	No.
Simon:	That one minus... minus...
Lisa:	364.
Simon:	I know.
Lisa:	...equals...
Simon:	That is the wasted space...
Lisa:	There are...
Simon:	...in cm^2.
Lisa:	There are 255 and a half... point 5... wasted space... on a sheet.

Lisa has the calculator, and Simon closely follows her calculations by thinking aloud, reformulating and confirming. The length and breadth of an A4 piece of paper is measured to be 29.5 and 21 cm, and $29.5 \times 21 = 619.5$ and $619.5 - 364 = 255.5$.

Lisa is about to write the result on their poster when Sara interrupts. She does not quite understand. Simon makes an attempt to clarify, but Sara does still not seem to understand, and she keeps questioning him about the area of the 4-pack box. So, Simon patiently explains once again how they got the 52 cm^2, showing her on the drawing, but it looks like Sara wants to manage at her own pace. The boys, then, zoom-out of the discussion and begin an eager conversation about football. In the meantime, the girls finish the calculations and the poster as well. The teacher appreciates the result and asks some challenging questions about the amount of waste: "A wasted space like that, is that a lot of wasted space, do you think? What is it in relation to how much one box fills?" The group, however, does not really come to reflect on his question because the bell goes.

Were you surprised by anything?

As a conclusion to the project the teacher and the group get together after the lunch break to evaluate the group activities. First, Lisa reformulates the story about the production of boxes – one twice as big as the other. How they calculated the price and the wasted paper. Then the teacher wants the students to reflect on the adequacy of the paper size:

Teacher: …could you arrange that paper in another way, fitting it bet-
            ter with what you are making for these boxes? Have you
            thought in those terms? Is it possible to imagine that you told
            the people producing this cardboard: We don't want to buy
            from you, because your dimensions are awkward? Is it possi-
            ble…?
Sara: Yes, but that is how a sheet of A4 is.
Teacher: Yes, but wouldn't it be possible…?
Lisa: You can actually, you can make… you can probably make a
            special sheet, but that's more expensive. Then they also have
            to charge more for the boxes.
Teacher: Yes it might mean it gets more expensive, but could you think
            of dimensions better than the A4?
Lisa: Yes, yes that… yes, that… one shaped after them, no, but
            there would be wasted space too.
Sara: Yes, but there you could kind of…
Teacher: Do you think, do you think… would there be less if you could
            use these big ones? [pulls out a big sheet of cardboard]
Sara: It is a bigger area, so you could better… I don't know.

Simon:	There is actually, then there is actually… you can actually of course make more here, but there is actually er… more wasted space too.
Lisa:	There will be wasted space too.
Dennis:	Mm.
Teacher:	Yes.
Sara:	But it's not certain there is just as much.
Lisa:	But it might be actually, like there are just sometimes… there is just as little hanging out, so it all becomes wasted space, because you cannot actually make like a bit of a half box, can you?
Teacher:	No.
Lisa:	So it might be better.
Teacher:	You instinctively think that it will be better with the big one.

First, Sara rejects the argument of "awkward dimensions" of the paper: "Yes, but that is how a sheet of A4 is." But Lisa catches the point as the teacher sticks to his question. She argues that they would have to make special sheets, which would be more expensive and as a consequence the boxes would be more expensive. The teacher accepts the argument but at the same time he tries to maintain the process of locating: "Yes it might mean it gets more expensive, but could you think of dimensions better than the A4?" Lisa confirms in the first place, but counter-argues that there would be waste of paper anyway. At this point the teacher challenges the students more directly by placing a big piece of cardboard on the table: "Do you think, do you think… would there be less if you could use these big ones?"

The students are not quite sure. Sara's remark: "It is a bigger area, so you could better…" could indicate that she is aware that a clue is hiding somewhere, but she gives up: "I don't know." Simon claims that they could make more boxes, but there would also be more waste of paper. Sara is not quite sure: "But it's not certain there is just as much." Maybe the idea is located, anyway. She is supported by Lisa whose argument relates to the flexibility of placing the boxes, so that there would not be: "just as little hanging out." Again the teacher repeats the result of their reflections: "You instinctively think that it will be better with the big one." Somehow a new possibility has been located, but no attempt is made to crystallise a mathematical idea, like: whereas 7 unfolded boxes can be placed on an A4 size of cardboard, maybe more than 14 unfolded boxes can be placed on an A3 size. Instead the teacher changes the direction of the subject.

The teacher now wants the students to consider the size of the boxes as related to each other. In particular, if the volume of one box is double the volume of the other, is the paper needed for the construction of the first one then also double the paper needed for the construction of the other one? So, the teacher is inviting reflections that might lead to the identification of particular mathematical ideas.

Teacher:	Yes, what can you say about the two boxes? How are they in relation to each other?
Simon:	This one, it is twice as big as the small one.
Teacher:	Yes, what about use of paper?
Simon:	Then that one of course is higher. [points at the big one]
Teacher:	How in relation to? How much bigger?
Simon:	No it's actually the same.
Lisa:	No.
Teacher:	Did you discuss this?
Lisa:	It has less.
Sara:	But it has, if you were to take like…
Simon:	It means using more paper, because it's bigger… the wrapping.
Sara:	Yes, but I mean if you were to…
Lisa:	…you were to make two of these ones [puts her hand on the small container] and one of this [puts her hand on the big container] one then…
Sara:	…yes, then it would, then it would be more of this one. [puts her hand on the small container]
Lisa:	…then it would use more paper [small container] because this one [big container] would also have a piece of paper over the middle here.
Simon:	Mm.

Simon explains the size of the boxes with the argument that one box contains twice as much as the other. The teacher accepts his answer and continues: "Yes, what about use of paper?" Simon promptly points at the big box: "Then that one of course is higher," but he seems to regret it when challenged by the teacher: "How much bigger?", so he says: "No it's actually the same." (referring to the height of the boxes). Here the teacher addresses the whole group: "Did you discuss this?" which gives Simon some time to reconsider and come up with a final answer and argumentation: "It means using more paper, because it's bigger… the wrapping." The girls, who once again seem to complete the arguments of one another, claim that making two small boxes takes more paper than making one big box. Simon seems to be a little insecure with the conclusion, and the discussion continues for awhile, when they consider the price of the paper to be used.

During the investigation the students' reflections could naturally have been provoked more directly by questions like: Isn't it surprising that while the volume of the small 8-pack is double the volume of a 4-pack, then the carton used for producing an 8-pack ($88cm^2$) is not double the carton used for producing a 4-pack ($52\ cm^2$)? Why could this be? Faced with such direct challenges, however, the collectivity of the reflections might be lost or materialised as possible answers to teacher-set tasks.

The teacher rounds off the evaluation by the following question:

Teacher:	Were you surprised by anything?
Dennis:	That we are so great.
Teacher:	Is there anything… is there anything of this you wouldn't have been able to have said this morning, but that you can say now, because you have been through all this?
Lisa:	Yes, but then I guess we didn't know about the wasted space.
Sara:	It is like, when you see, when… [ic]
Simon:	I didn't think, I didn't think there was less wasted space on that one. [the big one]
Sara:	That's right, because when you look at it like there were 600 something cm^2 in this one.
Simon:	619 and a half.
Sara:	And then, and then when you see 255, well it's actually not so much, so when you draw it, then it's actually quite a bit, it's almost half, isn't it?…
Teacher:	Yes.
Sara:	…because there is still room… I mean there is room for 7, right? But there is room for almost twice as much if they were square for example.
Teacher:	There you have it! Dice, that is…
Sara:	Yes.
Teacher:	…instead. Yes. That means that would have been better. Yes it matters about the shape.
Lisa:	Yes it matters, but you know…

The teacher question: "Were you surprised by anything?" appeals to the students' overall reflections, and the specification: "Is there anything of this you wouldn't have been able to have said this morning, but that you can say now, because you have been through all this?" leaves a direct possibility for the students to evaluate and express what they have actually learnt. Simon and Lisa both mention their discovery about paper waste, and Sara agrees. She continues by specifying the amount of waste compared to the paper used for the boxes: "…it's almost half, isn't it?" which makes her reconsider the functionality of the box: "But there is room for almost twice as much if they were square for example." (Sara's formulation appears ambiguous, but we read it as if 'square' refers to the form and volume of the box.) The teacher confirms and reformulates her reflections: "There you have it!" And he emphasises: "Yes it matters about the shape." Lisa agrees, but takes the evaluation in a new direction.

In the following conversation, the girls reconsider if more boxes might be made when putting them upright. They discuss this for a while, supported by Simon, but come up with the same conclusion, that they would have to assemble smaller pieces of paper in order to get more boxes and less wasted paper. They confirm the teacher conclusion that this recognition results from the process: "This means there are actually some of these things that you cannot survey from the beginning?" And, finally: What have the group members learnt about the relation of volume and area? They have not mentioned this point by themselves, so in the concluding interview the teacher asks directly: "Were you surprised that when it [the size of the box] was doubled the use of paper wasn't just doubled?" Lisa rejects the teacher question in the first place: "Not really," but she changes her mind immediately by saying: "We had not thought like that."

REFLECTION

The 'Caramel boxes' project illustrates how the students express and reflect on what they think in a collaborative process of inquiry, the four of them together and when the teacher is present. And we have seen how this process has helped them address their problem.

Reflection means considering at a conscious level one's thoughts, feelings and actions. In general, any dialogic act may be accompanied by reflection. The act can be addressed by a reflection, and it can support a reflection. In the project 'Caramel boxes' we have observed an inquiry co-operation. The process has contained a variety of dialogic acts. However, in our presentation of the episode we have not so much concentrated on labelling the particular dialogic acts, instead we have tried to emphasise that such acts are accompanied by reflections. We see reflections as an integral part of any action, and collective reflections accompany inter-action also in terms of dialogue. In order to clarify further the notion of reflection, we will consider different aspects of the concept. We will consider what can be addressed by reflections, who is carrying out the reflections, and in what context the reflections are carried out.

Scope of reflections. Reflections can concern almost everything, even when we concentrate on mathematics. The students can reflect on the result of some calculations. They may be worried if the result seems wrong. Have they misunderstood something? Would they get into difficulties in the next examination? etc. Reflections have a *scope*, and we shall try to clarify dimensions of this scope, first of all with reference to the project 'Caramel boxes', although we also refer to the previously presented projects. We shall comment on six dimensions of scope of reflections.[120]

First, reflections may concern a particular mathematical calculation. The students can consider if they in fact have done the calculations in a reasonable way. Have they got the right answer? Have they used the right algorithm? Has somebody else got the same result? Should they ask the teacher to check their result? Such questions all address particular mathematical aspects of a problem-solving process. In mathematics lessons, structured by the exercise paradigm, many student reflections seem to be focused on questions of this type. We have also observed examples of this type of reflection in the 'Caramel boxes' project where the girls seem concerned to check the calculations of the area of wasted paper (while the boys engage themselves with different issues).

We have also observed situations in which reflections of this type are not present. As a result of constructing the inverse spreadsheet, Mary and Adam came to the result of 63.93 Swedish Kroner. However, this result was never checked against the result 63.75 Swedish Kroner, which was available during the whole process.

Secondly, the students can consider not just if they have calculated things correctly, given the algorithm, but also if they have found the appropriate procedure. As we have seen, one way of approaching the problem concerning the waste of paper is to place the shapes of the unfolded boxes on the A4 piece of paper, and then calculate the area in between. Naturally, the in-between area becomes a most complex figure, and to calculate this area appears difficult. But the teacher suggests a certain way of looking at the task. It is possible to calculate the area of one unfolded box. Then it can be estimated how many of these boxes can be placed on one piece of paper. This is a question of doing a good puzzle. The students find that 7 such unfolded boxes can fit into a sheet of A4 paper. When the number 7 is estimated, the procedure is simple, and the waste paper is calculated to be 255.5 cm^2. However, the result of the calculations provokes some extra thought. Could the amount of waste paper in fact be 255.5 cm^2? This surprises the students. In this sense, reflections

---

[120] In Skovsmose (1994) six entrance points to reflections have been presented. They correspond with the dimensions mentioned here. See also Christiansen, Nielsen and Skovsmose (1997).

may concern the adequacy of an algorithm in a specific context. Are there some better ways of making the puzzle with the 7 unfolded boxes? The students are asked to consider if using an A3 piece of paper instead of an A4 would more than double the result. Even though only 7 pieces could be placed on an A4, more than 14 could be placed on an A3. And this could provoke a new consideration about a more realistic process of producing boxes, where an 'infinite' size of paper is at hand. As we have seen, this possibility was not really investigated by the students.

Reflections and the adequacy of mathematical procedures definitely also occurred in 'Batman & Co.'. The whole process that brought Mary and Adam's long walk to an end was a process of reflection, which addressed the adequacy of a mathematical procedure. Different dialogic acts expressed their reflections. New possibilities can be located and alternative mathematical principles can be identified as part of a process of reflection.

Thirdly, reflections may have to do with the reliability of the solution in a specific context. Does the calculation make sense? Is there anything that surprises the students? Even if the calculations are done correctly and the accountability of the techniques is established, it need not be the case that the result can be trusted. This kind of reflection is addressed when the students consider the waste of paper. How could it be that in fact 255.5 cm^2 were wasted, when it seemed obvious that more could have been used? We know that a 4-pack box only needs 52 cm^2 of cardboard for its construction. Almost half of the A4 paper is wasted, as Sara remarked. This kind of reflection addresses in broader terms the performed calculation. Does it make sense? Are the results reliable for the purpose they have in mind? Is it necessary to design production of a box in such a way that a bit more than 40% of the paper is wasted – even though this is what the students' calculations show, and even though the girls have checked the calculations an extra time? In order to make it possible for students to raise questions of this type in school, it is important that mathematics is contextualised in such a way that they see a purpose for such investigations.

In Chapter 7 we shall discuss further the notion of reliability, which we consider an important issue to be addressed by reflections when we have mathematics in mind. Reliability addresses the trustworthiness of a mathematical calculation, which somehow is going to be used in an extra-mathematical context. When the activities in the classroom are settled in an exercise paradigm, the question of reliability cannot easily be addressed. Instead the ideology of certainty arises to obstruct such reflections. Thus, it is also important to introduce landscapes of investigation with real references.

Fourthly, reflections could address the question if it is appropriate to use a formal technique at all. Do the students in fact need mathematics in order to handle the proposed problem? Could they find an answer without mathematics? Is the result of a mathematical calculation more or less reliable than an intuitive interpretation of the situation in question? These questions draw attention to the fact that formal techniques and mathematics are not necessary tools for clarifying all kinds of questions. In some cases an intuitive way of handling a specific problem may be preferred. It is an important experience for students that they are sometimes able to find out things without mathematics. In fact this was what happened when the students t the end of the interview started considering that the boxes could be assembled from smaller pieces of paper, and that such a procedure would have made their calculations of waste appear irrelevant.

A nice example of reflections addressing the relevance of using a more formal mathematical method in order to solve a problem occurs in the project 'What does a Danish flag look like?'. When the students had to place the white cross on the red piece of paper, and do it exactly, certain mathematical calculations seemed appropriate, and the teacher headed for this in the quizzing intermezzo. But for all practical purposes, the procedure of making a dot a bit outside the red paper on the desk that is still visible after the white cross has been placed, seems adequate enough for answering the question: What does the Danish flag look like? It is only when more principal aspects of doing 'proper' geometric constructions are considered that the students' empirical method appears irrelevant.

Fifthly, we can imagine more basic questions for the use of mathematics. The first three types of reflections seem to accept as a given the relevance of using mathematics. (And taking this as a given is natural, as the tasks are organised in a school context of learning mathematics.) The fourth type of reflections questions the relevance of a particular use of mathematics. However, we can think of mathematics in a much wider sense as being an integral part of our every-day life. If reflections are to support critical learning of mathematics, then it is essential that the scope of reflections becomes considerably extended. Students should also have an opportunity to address the way mathematics operates as part of our everyday environment. To Freire reflections must address the sociopolitical context of the learners. In general, critical learning means extending the scope of reflections. In the project 'Caramel boxes' we did not observe the scope of reflections extended in a 'critical' direction.

Maybe the reflections addressing the amount of wasted paper could have included more general considerations concerning ecological issues. The project could illustrate that by means of mathematics it might be possible to identify new designs of a production (in this case the production of boxes). But in the actual project this possibility was not realised. In fact, a difficult problem has yet to be considered: What could extending the scope of reflections mean when we have critical learning of mathematics in mind? How can we provide meaning to mathemacy so that it can act as a 'parallel' to literacy? We will elaborate on this issue in Chapter 7.

Sixthly, we should never forget that reflections can go in many directions, which, apparently, have nothing to do with mathematics, but which definitely are relevant to the learning process. Underground intentions are always operating in the classroom and turn the students' attentions in new directions. Thus, the interview with the resistance group some months after the 'Travel Agency' project has finished reveals the group as reflecting students: "We did the things we were supposed to do, didn't we?" And we would not be surprised if Linda's reflections did address the uncomfortable learning situation more than the learning content. So, by reconsidering the whole conversation of the resistance group, we might, nevertheless, come to learn quite a bit about reflections. Not reflections which address mathematical issues, but reflections which address the whole learning situation.

Subject of reflections. Reflections concern something, the scope of reflections, but they are also performed by somebody, the *subject* of reflections. The subject of reflections can be an individual, but certainly also a group. We are interested in *the collectivity of reflections,*[121] in particular in dialogically based collective reflections.

However, let us first add some comments about individual reflection. Following the Piaget inspiration into radical constructivism, we come to meet the 'lonely learner'. The basic epistemic processes take place in the individual. Naturally, the individual can be stimulated, and the learning environment can be considered stimulating, but the very 'construction of knowledge' becomes an individual undertaking. Reflections, then, come to refer to processes by means of which the individual reconsiders his or her operations. Glasersfeld has emphasised the notion of 'viability' as an

---

[121] Other terms have been suggested for this type of reflections. Thus, Valero (1998a) talks about co-flections. Cobb, Boufi, McClain and Whitenack (1997) also use the term *collective reflections* to describe the communal activity of reflecting on mutual actions. Collective reflections are verbalised in a 'mathematising discourse' that produces mathematical insight and knowledge.

important characteristic of knowledge, and reflections come to address
the viability of certain patterns of action and thinking. Still, 'viability' is
to be judged by the individual. Reflections can prepare processes of accommodation, where assimilated schemes of actions and thinking
become readjusted. But processes of accommodation and assimilation are
also individually undertaken. In this way the subject of reflection becomes strongly individualised. We shall return to these considerations in
Chapter 8.

We suggest that the subject of reflections need not be an individual,
but that reflections can be based on interaction of two or more people.
Reflections can be an expression of an interaction. When we want to emphasise the collective basis of reflection, we will talk about collective
reflections. Naturally, we would never deny the existence and the relevance of individual reflections, also for certain processes of learning.
What we have in mind is that reflections based on interaction, supported
by a dialogue, might provide the process of learning with certain qualities. We find that collective reflections open an important link between
dialogue and critical learning.

In the project 'Caramel boxes', we find several examples of collective
reflections. One example is found where the students are going to figure
out the area of the box. Simon advocates and invites: "We need... what's
that called... we need the area of that... so we can find the area of the
piece of paper, right?" Sara makes a suggestion: "Height × length ×
width" and Simon paraphrases "Height × length × width..." This reformulation highlights Sara's suggestion and invites further examination.
Sara keeps her perspective: "It's also the area..." for awhile, but seems to
hesitate as she adds in a low voice: "... as far as I know." Simon relates
to Sara's idea: "It's not the cubic content we need," and in this way he
affirms that there is something relevant in her suggestion, that her formula relates to the volume, but also that they are looking for something
different. Simon maintains the collectivity of reflections, as a sharp correction to Sara's suggestion could have broken the flow of the dialogue.
Then Simon makes a clarification of area by formulating the question:
"How big is it on top, how big is it on the sides, how big is it... in front?"
In this case the reflections address the questions of which formula can
be the appropriate one to choose. The reflections provide an identification. And the dialogic aspect of this identification is clearly maintained
by the nice use of reformulating, challenging questions and thinking
aloud.

During this clarification, Sara and Simon not only get in contact, they
also stay in contact. In fact, it does not make sense to separate what is
happening into two compartments: Simon's reflections and Sara's reflec-

tions. The reflections are an expression of the interaction, and they accompany their inquiry co-operation. This is the reason why we emphasise collective reflections as an analytical unit. Thus, we describe reflections linked to an inquiry co-operation as collective reflections. Naturally we could analyse reflections from an individual perspective, but then we would address something quite different. It is not the case that collective reflections are 'made up' only by the participating individual reflections. We do not find that collective reflections can be reduced to the sum of individual reflections. Collective reflections also emerge from the interaction.

The calculation of the area of Sara's 8-pack box represents a beautiful example of shared reflections expressed in a process of thinking aloud and a careful identification of each step to be taken. In this way, the students ask and answer why-questions concerning the procedure in use. In general, the way the teacher addresses the students also helps to ensure the collectivity of the reflections. He does not judge their reflections but uses a reformulation of their own conclusion to challenge their perspective: "So maybe it is somewhat expensive to make after all, the small one?"

More generally, we find that dialogic acts from the IC-Model represent particular aspects of a collectivity, which include and support reflections. Thus, identification can mean an identification of some mathematical ideas, and in this way help to constitute an object of reflections. Thinking aloud may ensure that reflections become public. Reformulating may support the collectivity of reflections. Challenging means broadening the scope of reflections. Evaluating means almost literally a reflection. Collective reflection creates new ideas and understandings that could probably not have emerged without collectivity. Neither of the persons involved can be said to produce them. They rather emerged in between.[122] In Chapter 4 we stated that new perspectives may be constructed as part of a dialogue. Constructing new perspectives and making collective reflections are closely connected activities. The co-operation and collective reflections between Mary and Adam in 'Batman & Co.' is one of the most excellent examples of the in-between construction of new perspectives and ideas. And we have experienced the writing of the present book as another example.

---

[122] Alrø and Kristiansen (1998) and Kristiansen and Bloch-Poulsen (2000) have stressed this aspect of collectivity in dialogic learning.

Context of reflections. Reflections have a scope, they are performed by somebody, but certainly by somebody in a certain context. In mathematics education a dominant element of this context is the 'logic of schooling'. This logic provides an agenda for the activities in the classroom and frames the interaction between students and teacher. The exercise paradigm first of all invites reflections with a mathematical reference and with a 'strategic' nature.

Just imagine the situation in a traditional mathematics classroom: the teacher asks a question that the students are supposed to answer. A certain student could feel uncertain whether his answer is correct. Should he raise his hand? Well, it is not really necessary because he already has raised his hand twice within the last five minutes. It is not that long time ago the teacher asked him (and he answered correctly), so most likely the teacher will not ask him again. He does not really run a big risk by raising his hand in ignorance. And he could give a good impression. On the other hand, some of his friends might find him a bit too eager to raise his hand and to please the teacher. Such considerations do not address any issues of content matter. They can instead be seen as provoked by the logic of schooling that fits the exercise paradigm. In other words: the scope of reflections can be extended in many different ways, depending on the context of reflections.

One idea related to the introduction of landscapes of investigation is to provide a situation that invites different types of reflection. However, landscapes of investigation do not guarantee that particular reflections will occur. Both aspects are clearly illustrated in 'Caramel boxes'. On the one hand, issues related to the reliability of a mathematical procedure become addressed in a profound way. Such reflections could hardly emerge within an exercise paradigm, where the primary task of the student is to find the right answer, the algorithm being an unquestioned given. It is interesting to observe how the students address the calculations of the amount of wasted paper. This scene-setting invites new types of reflection, in particular the one-and-only-one-answer-is-correct assumption is not in operation as the learning context. On the other hand, issues that seem directly related to the students' investigation are ignored or not considered as relevant.[123] There seem to be some obstacles to reflection.

---

[123] Landscapes of investigation may provide resources for reflection, but other resources can naturally be found. Mathematical concepts can be represented in different ways. Much discussion of the use of computers in the classroom has concerned the following: To what extent do semi-physical representations of mathematical objects help the students to discover properties of mathematical objects? In this way we can see the computer as part of the resources for providing opportunities for reflection.

The context of reflections can facilitate reflections, as well as producing obstacles. Thus, at the very beginning of the project, Sara suggested that the length of the small box could be 1, and the length of the sides of the double box, could be 2. Simon's prompt answer to Sara's guess is "no". Travelling in a landscape of investigation, the students become interested in a particular approach. Some alternatives are carefully considered, others simply ignored as the students just pass along a certain route of investigation without noticing alternatives that seem so close by. One possibility in such cases is that the teacher enters the scene and tries to draw the students' attention to some paths in the landscape, which they would, otherwise, have passed by, as was the case in 'Batman & Co.'.

Let us see what could have been pointed out in the 'Caramel boxes' project. The students have calculated the area of the 8-caramel box to be 88 cm^2 and the area of the 4-caramel box to be 52 cm^2. Interesting! The volume of the big box is certainly the double of the volume of the small box, but the surface of the big box is not double of the surface of the small box. It is somewhat smaller than the double. Has this to do with an inaccuracy of the calculations and the measurements? Strange, isn't it? Had the two boxes had the same proportions, then interesting properties were waiting to be located. The notion of 'double' could have been explored by some challenging questions. Then the students might have discovered that there is a big difference between interpretations of 'double as big as' in terms of (1) length of sides, (2) area of the paper necessary for its production, and (3) volume of the box. This could have led to a conceptual clarification of a similar nature as we indicated with relation to 'fill' in the project 'How much does a newspaper fill?'. Conceptual clarification is closely linked to processes of locating, identifying and crystallising mathematical ideas. And they are a direct expression of reflection.

Possibilities for making reflections can be obstructed by seemingly insignificant decisions. Thus, particular details of the contextualisation have implications for which route of investigation is made available. The bigger box should contain double the number of *caramels*, and then it would be natural to consider the 8-caramel box as a 'double' 4-caramel box, and it had the dimensions $2 \times 4 \times 6$. Naturally, it would not have made much sense to multiply the length of the sides of the small box by $\sqrt{2}$ to get the

---

The discussion in literature has, however, concentrated on the possibilities of making reflections with a mathematical reference. But computers in the classroom may also facilitate other kinds of reflections.

dimensions of the big box, as the boxes were going to contain caramels. But if the boxes were going to contain ice cream, or soda water or pop corn then the situation would have been quite different. A seemingly neutral element in the contextualisation, caramels, may have a great impact on the route of investigation. If the project had not considered boxes for caramels, but boxes for popcorn the route of reflections could have taken a quite different turn.

REFLECTION AND INTENTION – EXPLOSIVE CONCEPTS

We have tried to clarify the term reflection by considering the scope of reflections, the subject of reflections and the context of reflections. In the previous chapter we have discussed the notion of intention in terms of intentions-in-learning, underground intentions and resources of intentions. By doing so we do not pretend to give a sharp and clear characteristic of reflection, nor of intention. These are open concepts. The meaning of open concepts cannot be pointed out by straightforward definitions. However, dealing with open concepts is not unusual, as much theory building deals with open concepts.

There is, however, one more aspect to be considered with regard to notions like reflection and intention. Any clarification of such concepts will relate to apparently more complex concepts and less clarified than the original concepts themselves. Thus, intention is related to the background and foreground of a person or a group, and this again is related to the interpretation of the possibilities provided by the political, cultural and economic context. And a clarification of reflection could bring us to consider the notion of political action in a technologically structured socio-political environment. When a clarification of a concept almost immediately brings us to refer to concepts apparently much broader and much more complicated than the concept in question, we will talk about an *explosive concept*. Both reflection and intention are such explosive concepts.

We have tried to cope with this explosiveness by carefully referring to classroom situations in our clarification of the concepts. Clearly, we could have referred to many other and very different situations as well, not to forget the possibility that we could have elaborated a more systematic philosophically based clarification of the concepts.

Add to this, we can imagine a great variety of reflections, which we do not refer to in our rather mathematics-related considerations of reflections up to now. The students can certainly reflect upon the situations in which they are involved. The resistance group did this with many references to the tape recorder, etc. The students can pay special attention to what is happening outside school. Dennis is rather quiet, sometimes. What is on his mind? Is he reflecting upon his performance in mathematics? Or is he considering who may become his girl friend? Being in the resistance group Linda has certainly reflected a lot: 'How to cope with being in this group? Should I ignore what they are saying?' She gives up her personal interest, going to Gran Canaria, without any strong arguments, which may also be grounded in reflections: 'Well, let me try to get the best out of it. Things are lost anyway because I'm in this group. Try not to make a fuss about it.'

We can as well imagine that very different motives and intentions are acted out in the classroom. Why did Mary and Adam in 'Batman & Co.' in fact occupy themselves so intensively with the task? Could there be other explanations than the one that they really have put their efforts into the learning process? Could they for instance have been interested in impressing the teacher? As for Adam this might have been the case, because the teacher gave him a special invitation to participate that day. Could they have been particularly interested instead in working and sitting close together in front of the computer? We do not find any evidence that this could be the case. Our point is naturally not to find out, but simply to emphasise that the notion of both reflection and intention are not only broad and general. They are explosive, and consequently they must be handled with care.

Previously, we have tried to characterise dialogue in terms of inquiry, risk and equality. Reconsidering these terms we must conclude that dialogue is an explosive concept as well. So also is the notion of critique, which we have used now and then, and which we shall try to clarify more carefully in Chapter 7.

Although reflections can concern almost everything, we cannot conceal that something essential is missing so far. Where is the political dimension of reflections? If the content of reflections is to find some similarities with the concept of reflection connected to Freire's concept of *conscientização*, then we cannot be satisfied with the scope of reflections developed with reference to the projects presented so far. If we want to establish connections between the concept of dialogue and critique via the notions of intentions and reflection, then the scope of reflections we have considered seems too narrow. This brings us to the next explosive concept, the concept of critique.

CHAPTER 7

CRITIQUE AND LEARNING

Could a critical learning of mathematics be grounded in dialogic acts which presuppose that students' intentions are brought into learning processes, and which build on detailed reflections on mathematical content matter issues? Certainly, it is difficult to imagine that critique can be supported by a school mathematics tradition where a teacher is lecturing, where bureaucratic absolutism flourishes, where parts of the students' learning processes are 'forced', and where their reflections first of all are determined by issues related to the exercise paradigm.

As discussed in the previous two chapters, intention and reflection represent two important aspects of dialogic acts. Dialogic acts are acts, and as such they presuppose the involvement of the participants. As a person's intentions make up part of his or her actions, a person's intentions-in-learning become part of a dialogic process of learning. Actions without reflections are blind, according to Freire, and we agree that reflections make up part of dialogue as well. Dialogue takes place in interaction, and this brings us to consider not only reflections, but also collective reflections. Basically, we find that intentions and reflections represent two underlying connections between dialogue and critique.

Critique has to do with making judgements, but we are not going to draw heavily on the idea that critique, first of all, means making negative evaluation. Critique can be positive as well as negative. We see critique as having to do with making a distinction. In a critique we can address e.g. actions, proposals, ideas, theories, methods, concepts. There seems to be no limit to what can be addressed by a critique. In particular, we can try to clarify what it could mean to address mathematical ideas and actions based on mathematical clarifications in a critique. When doing so, as part of an educational enterprise, we talk about critical learning of mathematics. And the question is to what extent such learning can be grounded in dialogue.

Critique presupposes involvement. We cannot imagine anybody being forced to be critical or being critical by mere chance. As a consequence, we see intentions-in-learning as essential to any learning, which can be labelled critical. If we consider the interpretation of reflection suggested in Chapter 6, we might doubt whether the scope of reflections, exemplified by the project 'Caramel boxes', is broad enough to constitute a critical activity. Naturally, a proposed algorithm can be addressed by a critique, say for being efficient or non-efficient, but we see critical learning as including also broader and more fundamental issues of a critique. This brings us to consider, from a sociological perspective, what the challenge of critique could mean.

THE CHALLENGE OF CRITIQUE

The discussion of what might follow modernity has initiated a discussion of post-modernity, late modernity and reflexive modernisation as well as risk society.[124] According to Ulrich Beck: "In the age of risk, society becomes a laboratory with nobody responsible for the outcomes of the experiments." (Beck, 1998, 10) The difference between the 'classical' logic of scientific discovery and technological development is breaking down: "The logic of scientific discovery presupposes testing before putting into practice. This is breaking down in the age of risky technologies. Nuclear technologies have to be built in order to study their functioning and risks. Test-tube babies have to be born in order to find out about the theories and assumptions of biotechnologies. Genetically engineered plants have to be grown in order to test the theory. The controllability of the laboratory situation is lost. This causes serious problems." (Beck, 1998, 14)

Not only does the difference between scientific discourse and technological development break down, but certainly also the difference between traditional scientific priorities and economic interests. In this way we are facing risks, not simply caused by nature, but produced as part of technological development: "Risks are man-made hybrids. They include and combine politics, ethics, mathematics, mass media,

---

[124] See, for instance, Bauman (1989); Beck (1992, 1995a, 1995b); Beck, Giddens and Lash (1994); Castells (1996, 1997, 1998); Franklin (ed.) (1998); Giddens (1990) and Lyotard (1984). The presentation in this section draws on Skovsmose (1999). The notion of risk related to 'risk society' is different from the notion of risk related to 'risk zone'. However, we do not think that this ambiguity causes much confusion.

technologies, cultural definitions and precepts." (Beck, 1998, 11) Risks include mathematics. Giddens makes a similar point, although without mentioning mathematics: "Manufactured risk is risk created by the very progression of human development, especially by the progression of science and technology." (Giddens, 1998, 28) And he adds: "Manufactured risk is expanding in most dimensions of human life. It is associated with a side of science and technology which the early theorists of industrial society by and large did not foresee. Science and technology create as many uncertainties as they dispel – and these uncertainties cannot be 'solved' in any simple way by yet further scientific advance. Manufactured uncertainty intrudes directly into personal and social life – it isn't confined to more collective settings of risk." (Giddens, 1998, 28)

As presented by Beck (in Beck, Giddens and Lash, 1994), reflexivity refers to social, economic, scientific and technological feedback processes. The results of our production make an impact on society far beyond the intended impact. Reflexive modernisation emerges because of the tremendous success of the industrial society, a main characteristic being that we face intended as well as unintended results of our own production. Reflexivity induces manufactured risks. However, the processes of reflexivity can be objects for considerations, and this brings us again to the notion of reflection. We might in fact be able to reflect upon the processes of reflexivity, but we face a general problem of great significance for our entire social epoch. While the processes of reflexivity are strong and powerful and, according to Beck, create a risk society, then the processes of reflection appear weak and fragile. Reflections might be unable adequately to interpret reflexivity including the production of risks and the new scope of possible implications of our technological actions. Reflections might be unable to cope with the dynamics of reflexivity.

Natural sciences, and mathematics in particular, have had an enormous influence on the way technology, in all its aspects, becomes part of our environment. This idea has been discussed in terms of the *formatting power of mathematics*, which claims that mathematics is not only a neutral descriptor of social, natural or technological facts. Mathematics constitutes resources for technological constructions (bridges, coffee machines, traffic regulations, airline security systems, queuing systems for hospital operations, decision systems, insurance policy, marketing strategy, security systems in e-mail communication, etc.).[125] Mathematical rationality helps to establish new connections between scientific thinking and, for instance, industry and economic interests. The formatting power of mathematics signifies the break down of the difference between the classical logic of scientific discovery and technological development. The formatting power of mathematics is a part of the processes of reflexivity, also referred to by Beck. Mathematics provides intellectual and scientific resources by means of which technological inventions are conceptualised, analysed and realised. In this way, mathematics becomes part of our environment.

In 'Cultural Framing of Mathematics Teaching and Learning', Ubiratan D'Ambrosio makes the following statement about the new role of science, including mathematics: "In the last 100 years, we have seen enormous advances in our knowledge of nature and in the development of new technologies. [...] And yet, this same century has shown us a despicable human behaviour. Unprecedented means of mass destruction, of insecurity, new terrible diseases, unjustified famine, drug abuse, and moral decay are matched only by an irreversible destruction of the environment. Much of this paradox has to do with the absence of reflections and considerations of values in academics, particularly in the scientific disciplines, both in research and in education. Most of the means to achieve these wonders and also these horrors of science and technology have to do with advances in mathematics." (D'Ambrosio, 1994, 443)

This remark states the paradox that science appears to exercise a double function: It is a source for both wonders and horrors. But how can the development of human knowledge in its sublime form – as science and mathematics in particular are supposed to express – be associated with despicable human behaviour? This certainly seems to be a paradox.

D'Ambrosio claims that most of this paradox has to do with the absence of reflections, both in research and in education. We shall pay particular attention to this remark. We shall try to face this paradox by considering the claim that the (blind) production of wonders as well as of horrors has to do with the lack of reflections, including in mathematics education. Naturally, we do not know in particular what this lack of reflections might mean, but in what follows, by commenting on the project 'Terrible small numbers', we shall try to explore what broadening the scope of reflections in mathematics education could include.

---

[125] See, Skovsmose (1994, 1999) and Skovsmose and Yasukawa (2000) for a discussion of the formatting power of mathematics. See also Applebaum (1995); Keitel (1989, 1993); Keitel, Kotzmann and Skovsmose (1993) and Yasukawa (1998).

We will also refer to facing the 'D'Ambrosio paradox', as the *challenge of critique*. Is it possible, within the mathematics classroom, to support such powerful reflections to meet this challenge? By talking about the challenge of critique, we make our first step in trying to clarify the notion of critique. It means an activity, which addresses 'wonders' as well as 'horrors'. It seems obvious that the examples of reflection, as presented in Chapter 6, need much further development, in case reflections should develop into critical activities that could address social aspects of reflexivity as, for instance, manufactured risks. A basic characteristic of critical mathematics education is to face the challenge of critique.

Later in this chapter we will return to the notion of critique and try to show its relationship with 'dialogue', 'intention' and 'reflection'. We see a critical activity including critical learning, as founded in a particular form of interaction, namely dialogue. Involvement of the learner, as expressed by intentions-in-learning, and the considerations of the learning, as referred to by the scope of reflections, are essential resources for critical learning and for the development of mathemacy. Learning mathematics critically means in particular that certain issues of reflection have to be considered, and 'Terrible small numbers' may serve to illustrate what this could mean.[126]

'TERRIBLE SMALL NUMBERS'

During the 1970s, a heated discussion for or against the introduction of nuclear power took place in Denmark. It was argued that a nuclear power plant was 'almost not dangerous'. At least, statistics showed that the probability for the worst possible scenario to occur (on a certain power plant within a period of one year) was a terrible small number; let us call it p. The counter-argument emphasised that this very small number p was not estimated correctly, that essential scenarios for accidents had been ignored, and that the 'real' p was considerably bigger. Nuclear energy was not introduced in Denmark. It was, however, introduced by our neighbour, Sweden, and for some bizarre reason, one Swedish power plant, Barsebäck, was placed on the Swedish side of the Sound just

---

[126] The original Danish title of the project is 'Farlige små tal'. In a Danish dialect the connotations of 'farlige små tal' are ambiguous. The numbers are 'terribly small' and what they represent is terrible, they are 'terrible numbers' as well. We want to keep this nice ambiguity when choosing 'terrible small numbers' as our translation.

opposite Copenhagen. In nice sunny weather Barsebäck is visible from the sea front of Copenhagen. Obviously, one reason for the positioning of Barsebäck has been that it was assumed that the p in question in fact was terribly small. But as stressed by Beck: "Nuclear technologies have to be built in order to study their functioning and risks."

After Chernobyl, it became clear that it is not only an accident on Barsebäck that may affect Denmark. A closer look at the map will reveal that accidents on nuclear plants in our neighbouring countries may have disastrous effects on the Danish environment. We certainly live in a risk society. However, this is not particular to Denmark. The generous distribution of risks is part of the process of globalisation. Thus, industrial production, which is heavily polluting, is exported to Third World countries.

Pollution, however, is a risk phenomenon everywhere. Over Christmas 1999 in Denmark, a father and his son died of salmonella poisoning after having consumed a cake with raw eggs in it. Other incidents including salmonella have caused serious food poisoning. In the previous years this problem has grown, and almost everybody in Denmark has heard about or know of people who have been infected by salmonella. But how can problems connected to the incidence of salmonella be connected to learning mathematics critically? And how can these problems be presented in a form that can be experienced as relevant by teen-age students?

Here we will refer to a project work, 'Terrible small numbers', that took place in a 9th grade with 15-16 year olds.[127] We present the general idea of the project and some episodes from the classroom. One particular question is how to provide a simple representation of eggs, some with salmonella and some without. Naturally, eggs can easily be represented on paper, but a more tangible interpretation seemed appropriate. A great number of photo film cases were collected. Each case represented an egg (see Photo). A centicube was put into each case, a yellow one would indicate that the egg was healthy, while a blue cube showed that the egg was infected.

The intention was to develop a particular landscape for critical reflections by concentrating on two issues related to mathematics in action: reliability and responsibility. Critical reflections indicate a problem with the scope of reflections developed so far. If we in educational

---

[127] This project includes co-operation between Henning Bødtkjer, Mikael Skånstrøm, Morten Blomhøj, Helle Alrø and Ole Skovsmose. Results from the project have been presented in Alrø, Blomhøj, Bødtkjer, Skovsmose and Skånstrøm (2000a, 2000b, 2001). The project 'Terrible small numbers' has been repeated in several classrooms.

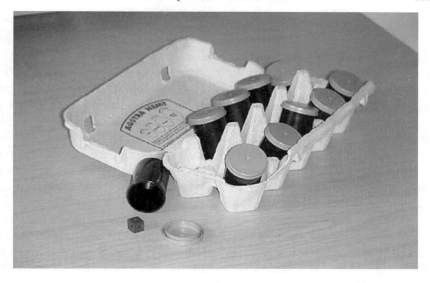

Sample of 'eggs' (Photo: Mikael Skånstrøm)

practice, also want to face the challenge of critique and to be aware of the D'Ambrosio paradox, we have to address broader issues by reflections. It is important always to consider the extensions of the scope of reflections. In Chapter 6 we presented 6 dimensions of scope of reflections. By the fifth and sixth dimension in particular we indicated what it could mean to make critical reflections.

As mentioned, we shall try to clarify further the notion of critical reflections by paying special attention to two issues: reliability and responsibility related to mathematics 'in action'. The notion of *reliability* can be related to the question: to what degree can we expect a sample 'to speak the truth' about the whole population? This question can be clarified by statistics, but we find that it may provide an entrance to further clarification, as reliability (of a sample) is part of a more general question: How reliable is a conclusion, based on calculations and mathematical modelling? As citizens we face the results of many mathematically based decisions, but how can we interpret the nature of their justification and their technological impact? To what degree are such decisions trustworthy? The risk society seems to be established by decision making with particular reference to numbers – some of which may be terribly small.

The issue of *responsibility* relates to the fact that many actions, related to technological constructions in a broad sense, include mathematically based decision making. As already indicated, the thesis of the formatting power of mathematics claims that mathematics is an essential ingredient of a technological imagination, which helps to identify a scope of technological alternatives; that mathematics is necessary for any detailed investigation of certain properties of a technological construction; and, finally, that mathematics is present in the resulting technological construction. If it is to make sense to distinguish between horrors and wonders, it becomes important to consider critically the basis and the implication of the decisions that are made with reference to numbers and figures. For instance, how are we supposed to act in a situation where we only have a limited knowledge of the possible implications of the action? What does responsibility mean in such a situation?

It is important to consider the exemplarity of these discussions. The point is not just to open a discussion of reliability and responsibility which refers to a particular example, although we are going to refer to such a particular example in what follows. It is important to point out general aspects of mathematics in action and of the formatting power of mathematics, and make these aspects accessible for critical considerations taking place in the mathematics classroom. We suggest that addressing issues like reliability and responsibility may show a way for mathematics education to face the challenge of critique. This could provide 'critical learning of mathematics' with a more specific meaning. So, back to the first part of the project 'Terrible small numbers'.

RELIABILITY

"Some happenings are almost not dangerous," the teacher says and points to the bicycle that is flung in the middle of the classroom. The rider (a teddy bear) has obviously been thrown off. Everybody knows that biking to school involves the risk of being thrown off the bike, but the risk is so small that it does not seem worth considering. As a matter of fact most students and their parents seem willing to run the risk. But how big is the risk, and what happens when you ride a bike throughout one week? Or a month? Or a full year? The teacher and the students make some calculations on the blackboard.

These calculations serve as an introduction to the idea that if the probability of being thrown off a bike on a trip to school is estimated to be, say, 0.0001, then the probability for being thrown off one or more times after taking 500 trips can be calculated as:

$$1 - (1 - 0.0001)^{500} = 0.0488$$

(and not, as first suggested by some of the students, as 500 times 0.0001).

Another example is used to introduce the term 'sample'. The teacher pulls a bulb out of his bag: "What about this? Can I be 100% sure that it works? Has the producer checked it? What do you think they have done?"

Peter:	They probably try it out once in a while, maybe once for every one hundred.
Ida:	They take a random check?
Teacher:	What does that mean?
Ida:	They test some once in a while.
Teacher:	What if they work?
Ida:	Then they assume that the others also work.
Teacher:	How often do they have to do that?

After a few more examples the teacher introduces the salmonella story. The students are going to work on the project for three days, two lessons per day. The students are presented with a box containing 500 'eggs', the photo film cases, of which 50 are infected by salmonella. The mixing of 50 blue eggs and the 450 yellow eggs is done openly in the classroom. The students know the mix, and they are asked to take a sample of 10 eggs in a tray, observe the result, and return the eggs to the box. Each group has to repeat this procedure five times. The reason why the mix was done with simple numbers – 50 out of 500 were infected, and not with, say, 47 – was that it had to be simple to get an expectation of the sample result. Could it be the case that the eggs were properly mixed, and that a sample nevertheless showed 3 blue eggs? The intention was that the students came to realise that a particular sample of 10 eggs need not tell the whole truth about the population from which it is picked. The

Group	Salmonella infected eggs				
1	0	3	1	1	1
2	0	2	2	1	1
3	1	1	1	1	3
4	0	0	1	0	4
5	3	2	2	3	2

Figure 7.1: The number of salmonella infected eggs in the different samples collected by each of the five groups.

teacher writes the results of the samples in a diagram on the board (see Figure 7.1), and asks the students to consider the results. There are obviously different results. What do the samples actually show? The groups are left in an open landscape of investigation.

We had figured out a percentage of 10%

We concentrate on the work of a group with four students, Oscar, Peter, Anna and Ida.[128] They start to copy the diagram (Figure 7.1) in their field notes. What to think of these figures? What to do? Anna and Ida are in charge, while Peter and Oscar make small-talk. The teacher comes to their table, and Peter addresses him:

Peter:	OK, do we figure out the percentage?
Anna:	Do we?
Teacher:	I don't know, try. Now you've had this information [ic]…
Anna:	Do we just do something?
Teacher:	…then there have been these random tests. What do you think you see? Any comments about that? [ic] [the students talk at the same time]
Ida:	We can see that…
Peter:	…that it is a bit more than the 10% we had figured out.
Ida:	Well it's between 0 and 3 we get every time… well 4, there is one with 4
Peter:	That's accidental.
Anna:	Yes, we can't use that really. [towards Ida]
Ida:	We *can* use that.
Oscar:	Then we have… lowest and highest value… then we need the average.

As the teacher arrives, the group obviously wants him to tell them what to do: "OK, do we figure out the percentage?" but the teacher wants to challenge the students at another level. He does not reject their proposal, but asks them to try it. And he invites them into an open landscape of inquiry by his opening questions to the results: "What do you think you see? Any comments about that?" These questions do not disclose a certain direction of an exercise. In the first place, the challenge for the students is to define their own way into the landscape and to reflect on the result of their calculations. They seem to look for some calculations to make. Should they put the results in percentage? Although they do not quite agree as to whether they can use the information "…that it is a bit

---

[128] A fifth student, Julie, joins the group on the 3rd day.

more than the 10% we had figured out," they actually manage to define two tasks during these very first minutes of the group work: They intend to calculate the frequency of salmonella, and they intend to calculate the average: "Then we have... lowest and highest value... then we need the average."

Group	Salmonella infected eggs					%
1	0	3	1	1	1	12%
2	0	2	2	1	1	12%
3	1	1	1	1	3	14%
4	0	0	1	0	4	10%
5	3	2	2	3	2	24%

Figure 7.2: The percentage of salmonella infected eggs.

After a short while the students have calculated the percentage of infected eggs in the five samples for each of the five groups (see Figure 7.2).

It doesn't hold!

What do they intend to do with the numbers in this table? Ida, Anna and Oscar follow a plan, while Peter comes to wonder about the outcome of the experiment:

Ida: And what then?
Oscar: Then we have to find the average.
Anna: Then we'll add it all up and divide by 5.
Ida: Yes.
Peter: I just don't, I just don't understand why it has to make *more*...
Ida :   12+12+14+10+...
Peter: ...all the time, instead of some of them making 0.
Ida: 2,3,4... [counting aloud]
Peter: That ought to make 10%, right? There is 10, but there is never anything below that... No, it's [pointing to the result from the notes] strange, because it doesn't... it doesn't hold...
Oscar: That's probably just a coincidence.

[...]
Peter: ...because it can only make 10%, and the only one that
                holds is that one [the result from Group 4] and all the rest
                of them are more than that. It is strange that none of them
                are below.
                [...] I for one don't want to eat eggs again.

While the other students continue the calculations, Peter keeps reflecting
why there are no samples under 10 %. His wondering attitude can be seen
in his expressions "I just don't understand" and "it is strange". The others
do not seem to care much about his wondering, as Oscar declares:
"That's probably just a coincidence." No need to reflect on this
phenomenon. Finally, Peter draws his own conclusion: "I for one don't
want to eat eggs again."

The students get involved in calculations that appear reasonable, given
the 'exercise perspective', for instance maintained by Oscar in the
comment: "Then we have... lowest and highest value... then we need
average." Remembering what they already know about statistics, they
make themselves busy, and they calculate the average to be 14.4%. But
something feels wrong. They experience a need for locating a point of the
task. In particular, Peter does not seem happy with the calculation of
average, so he addresses the co-teacher, who comes to the table:

Peter: Do we just try to find out as much as possible?
Co-teacher: As much math as possible, you have to try to... come up
                with as many comments, as many estimates, about how it
                gets to be sensible, and when it cannot be used. What
                speaks for one solution, what speaks for another solution.
Peter: OK.
Anna: Well, of course.
Co-teacher: That's the purpose... to get some considerations going.

Directly addressed about what is expected from the students the co-
teacher explains at a general level: "As much math as possible." What is
expected are the students' "comments" and "estimates" that they can
make about the samples. There are no instructions of exercises and no
direction of a path into the landscape of investigation. There are no hints
whatsoever that the students might benefit from paying attention to
certain aspects of the numbers presented in Figure 7.2. The students are
supposed to find their own way through. The co-teacher's reluctance to
provide clear guidelines is part of the frame for the project, as the
planners (including the authors of this book) of 'Terrible small numbers'
were interested in figuring out how the students would react to general
invitations to making reflections.

In the following, Peter repeats his objections to the results, and he begins to wonder if the teacher could have made a mistake. Perhaps he did not mix the eggs properly. Perhaps the incidence of infected eggs is more likely to be found at the top. In other words, he is trying to locate a good reason for the unexpected result. Anna suggests that they make a new test in order to see if the average at the top is bigger than the average at the bottom:

Anna: Couldn't we try to go to the *bottom* again. What? Oh well, from the average of the *top* it's 14.4, [laughing] and the average of the bottom is some smaller figure.

Peter: Then it's a smaller percentage and not 10%... [4 sec.]

Anna: ...which would be logical.

Peter: Yes, which it *is*...

Ida: ...which is the most likely, is that OK then?

Oscar: That's not the most likely [ic] That *is* not the most likely.

The students do not actually do a new test, but they communally reflect on the apparent result of such a sample. Peter and Anna agree upon the logical argument that there might be less than 10% salmonella in a bottom sample. That would be "the most likely". But Oscar objects to that argument: "That *is* not the most likely." It is not easy to guess the point of Oscar's objection. Anyway, they have formulated the thesis that the density of blue eggs is higher at the top of the trolley than at the bottom. This will explain that the average percentage of the samples is calculated to be 14.4%, and it would solve Peter's problem. Or would it?

The teacher has arrived and overheard the students' last comments.

Teacher: You don't think I mixed them well enough?

Ida: No you didn't, did you?

Peter: [to teacher] No, we think there are too many on the surface, because otherwise that figure there can't be right...

Teacher: It doesn't correspond with that?

Peter: ...well, yes, it does correspond, but it's only... a bit unlikely that it would be just that. Because the average for all the groups is 14.4 and none of them is below 10% average and 10% ought to be the most likely figure [ic], but if we did *a lot*, if we made a lot of tests, then it would be 10%, I think.

Anna: If we started with the bottom and they were all mixed well.

The teacher reformulates the students' arguments about him not having mixed the eggs properly and about the reliability of the results, but he does not reject or comment further on their claims. Peter repeats his considerations about probability and adds a generalised conclusion: "but

if we did *a lot*, if we made a lot of tests, then it would be 10%, I think."
He advocates the point that the more samples the more reliable results.

In this way, Peter makes a reference to the 'Law of Large Numbers', a
much discussed issue in the philosophy of probability. This law states
that when the same experiment is repeated over and over again, then the
calculated relative frequency for the outcomes of a specific possible event
will 'stabilise' around the probability of the event. The Law of Large
Numbers can be interpreted as an empirical statement, supported by
observations and not maintaining any logical or mathematical necessity.
However, the Law of Large Numbers also refers to a mathematical
theorem, which can be proved within the mathematical theory of
probability.

As an empirical statement the Law of Large Numbers addresses a
series of repetitive events, where the outcome varies in an unpredictable
manner. The Law states as an empirical fact that out of such short-term
chaos a long-term regularity emerges. If A refers to some particular
outcome, n to the total number of experiments, and n_A to the number of
occurrences of A, then the relative frequency of occurrence of A, n_A/n,
seems to tend to some limiting value as $n \to \infty$. The limit of this relative
frequency we call $P(A)$, the probability of the event A. However, the
notion of probability can also be developed from a purely mathematical
point of view, and Bernoulli's Theorem represents the mathematical
counterpart of the empirical formulation of the Law of Large Numbers.
Bernoulli's Theorem is also referred to as the Law of Large Numbers. In
fact, it is possible, in cases like the salmonella experiment, to do a purely
mathematical calculation of the value which the experimental frequencies
approximate.

The students' comments about the samples are certainly relevant.
However, they do not consider the fact that we cannot expect a sample to
tell the exact truth, but only to provide indications. Even if the teacher
had mixed everything perfectly well, the different samples would
probably have given different indications. The students interpret the
experienced 'unreliability' of the samples as caused by the teacher's bad
mixing, and not as an aspect of the method itself. And what could be
concluded in a case where the mix of blue and yellow eggs is not known
in advance? The general situation, when using samples, is of course that
no 'correct result' is known. Knowledge about the population, be it eggs
or bulbs, is based only on the indications of the samples. In most cases, a
complete control is impossible. We can only control 'something', but we
still need to form an opinion about 'everything'. Drawing the conclusion
about 'everything' based on investigations of 'something' constitutes a
basic problem of reliability. Given the observation that a particular

sample is not a simple truth-speaker, how then to operate in situations where samples provide the only access to knowledge about the total population? The theory of statistical inference deals with this issue.

This part of the project did not bring the students to consider the fundamental issues of reliability. However, sometimes they seemed to get close to considering such issues. It was like they were passing interesting sites, but without noticing them. In an evaluation of the project work Ida makes the following comment: "We were Group 3, and we got a reasonable result, it was only at the end that the figure was different from what the groups reached. The average result from the 5 groups was that 14.4% of the eggs were infected by salmonella. The expected mathematical result would be that there was salmonella in 10% of the eggs, because the trolleys had 450 eggs without salmonella and 50 eggs with salmonella. In our group we assumed that the reason why the salmonella figure was so high was that the teacher had put in the salmonella eggs last and not mixed them well enough. And when all groups took eggs from the top they would take too many salmonella eggs in relation to how many there really were."

You've left us in the dark

The co-teacher has made a spreadsheet to make virtual samples. So, instead of carrying out the tedious task of collecting the 10 film-box eggs and opening each one to check if it contains salmonella or not, the students only need to push the F9-key, and a sample of 10 eggs is provided. The teacher has prepared the groups with the question: How many samples will do? One more push on the F9, and they have added a new sample to their data material. The students concentrate on those samples that are free from salmonella, and they observe that this percentage does change, as they collect more and more and more F9-data. (There appears to be no particular stated reason for the students to concentrate on the percentage of salmonella free samples. They might as well have studied the percentage of samples containing exactly one blue egg. This would have told them how many of the samples in fact were revealing the truth about the whole mix of eggs.) The process of collecting F9-data could be continued almost forever.

Ida:	Well what are we going to *use* it for? [sounds resigned]
Peter:	It's *math*, isn't it, it's no good for anything.
Anna:	[yawning] That's not math. We're given everything at no cost.
Oscar:	Why do we have to take another one?

A remark from each of the four students, which indicates that none of them sees the point of what they are doing. They are ready to zoom-in on a task, but it seems difficult to locate one. Anna grasps the microphone of the tape-recorder, which in this situation also represents the teacher:

Anna:	Mikael, you've left us in the dark. Mikael, [speaks directly into the microphone] a small comment from group 3, you've left us in the dark, we don't get this at all. Thank you. Now he knows.
Peter:	Well we could talk about some math for them, I guess.
Anna:	Right, right, right, I'm just going to find out what the hell this is all about.

The tape-recorder does not provide much help, and the suggestion "Well we could talk about some math for them" (the "them" being among others the authors of this book), only perpetuates their problem. They have to find their way locating a path into the landscape of investigation and trying to identify an interesting perspective for further inquiry.

A little later, Peter takes the initiative to explain to the others: "Look, we try to count how many samples have got 1 salmonella egg in it." In this way Peter tries to formulate a more general task than just investigating the frequency of the salmonella-free samples. However, they concentrate on their original task.

That's what makes it difficult for a lot of people to understand calculus of probability

The students concentrate on examining the frequency of salmonella-free samples. They have investigated quite a number of samples. The chance of getting a salmonella-free sample is estimated to be 35 %. They wonder if 35% is a stable frequency, or if it will be stabilised at a different level when they examine more samples. They decide to investigate that question further.

Peter:	Let's try with 1000 [samples] to see whether that's gonna be more precise. [...]
Anna:	Well then we might as well... might as well have taken 200
Oscar:	No you can't, it's just more...
Peter:	It's more accidental with 200.
Ida:	It may be more accidental, but it's the same thing, bloody hell. It doesn't change. It doesn't matter then if you take 30 million or...

Peter:	If you do it once again you can't be sure it'll be 35 again, right? If you do the test again, right, it may well be that you, it may be that you...
Ida:	But can't you see that the most precise figures must be those that occur... many times? [4 sec.]
Anna:	Right, right of course.
Peter:	The more tests you make, the more precise figure you'll get. [...]
Ida:	Right, but can't you see that the difference from 100 to 1000, that's 1%?
Oscar:	But it could be bigger, couldn't it?
Ida:	But it *isn't*.
Oscar:	OK, but 100 is probably also enough, but if, if you want to be absolutely sure, then you just take 1000, right?
Ida:	And if you want to be *absolutely* sure you just take all of them.
Peter:	Well, yes of course [laughing], but 1000 that's... [it is not always clear if the students refer to number of eggs or number of samples]
Ida:	Yes but...
Peter:	...at any rate it's safer than 100
Ida:	...that's not always so, if you have 1 million eggs, then it doesn't matter whether you test 100 or 1000 eggs...
Anna:	Yes but you don't know if it's the same until you've tried.
Ida:	...because it may still be the last ones that are all infected by salmonella. [sighs loudly] Yes but that... that doesn't make all...
Peter:	Yes that's what makes it difficult for a lot of people to understand calculus of probability.

It looks like the group is split up in two parties here. The girls argue that the frequency is stabilised, so they defend the Law of Large Numbers from an empirical perspective. As Ida claims: "It doesn't change. It doesn't matter then if you take 30 million or..." In other words: a short-term chaos can produce a long-term regularity. The boys present the opposite argument. The boys' key argument is that when we have to do with an empirical regularity then another try might give different results. The result of the experiment is "accidental". Peter argues: "If you do it once again you can't be sure it'll be 35 again, right?" Ida defends her idea: "Right, but can't you see that the difference from 100 to 1000, that's 1%?" and Oscar defends his view: "But it could be bigger, couldn't it?" that is immediately shut down by Ida: "But it *isn't*." Here we observe principal statements about the Law of Large Numbers. Either the calculated frequency converges towards a specific value, because of a 'deep necessity' (which could be interpreted to be of mathematical nature), or we have to do with a coincidence, meaning that a continuation of the experiment could create a different result. It is not simple to accept that a series of experiments, consisting of selecting samples at random, can produce a regularity in the long run.

Number of samples	Frequency of salmonella-free samples
10	60%
30	50%
50	46%
100	36%
200	35%
500	36%
1000	35%

Figure 7.3: The group result.

However, with reference to the numbers shown in Figure 7.3, they find that the frequency of salmonella-free samples stabilises at about 35%, and that further experiments could reveal more precisely at which value it stabilises.[129] The uncertainty is how many experiments are needed in order to provide a good guess of the value of stabilising, in other words a guess of the probability of selecting a salmonella-free sample.

It seems like the students also tend to switch between different perspectives (maybe not really being aware of this, as the perspectives have not been properly located). Ida sees no big difference between 100

---

[129] In an accompanying text to the diagramme, Ida writes: "As you can see from the observations the figures are very much alike after 100 samples, and if that is calculated mathematically, it's about the same figure. The risk of getting a salmonella egg is 10% and thus there is a 90% chance of getting a salmonella free egg. The calculation is accordingly $0.9^{10} \times 100 = 35\%$." Ida's calculations are based on drawing samples with replacement, different from the procedure they actually used. However, given the large number of eggs to select from, the calculated value will be approximately the same.

and 1000 samples, which makes Oscar state an interesting point of view: "OK, but 100 is probably also enough, but if, if you want to be absolutely sure, then you just take 1000, right?" This question could have shown an entrance to a new landscape of investigation. The issue is not examined further but only rejected by Ida who claims that in order to be quite sure you will have to examine "them all". Peter tries to make a compromise: "but 1000 that's... at any rate it's safer than 100." But still the girls are not convinced. No matter how many samples are selected you will never know the exact number of infected eggs: "because it may still be the last ones that are all infected by salmonella." By this argument the Law of Large Numbers is acknowledged as an empirical statement. It is possible that an event, even with a small probability, will take place.

In the presented discussion the students try out different arguments, although only loosely related to a perspective. We do not observe a genuine inquiry co-operation. The students show no openness or inquiring attitude. This becomes obvious in their 'yes, but' pattern of communication that is a common feature throughout this sequence. They seemingly accept the argument and tag-invitation of the other by replying 'yes', but the argument following the 'but' has nothing to do with or is in opposition to what has just been said.[130]

In the end, the discussion is overruled by Peter's teacher voice: "Yes that's what makes it difficult for a lot of people to understand calculus of probability." This remark indicates that Peter continues to see their task in mathematical terms. It seems too difficult for the group to make a 'reflective turn': to start asking inquiring questions *about* mathematics. In many situations the teacher has invited this turn: "What can be said about the numbers?" and "How many samples will do?" etc. The problem, however, is not that the students do not raise questions of particular relevance for opening a deeper reflection about issues of reliability. The difficulty is rather due to the fact that such openings are easily ruled out (by the students' implicit exercise perspective) as a digression from the relevant and expected task. So, one important conclusion is that making a reflective turn needs a support in the locating, identifying and challenging of issues that are relevant to reflect upon. The students, who travel through a landscape of investigation, almost stumble over relevant issues, but they are not able to identify and examine their potentials.

If the students had realised that their disagreement is caused by differences of perspectives and these perspectives had been properly located and identified, it might have led to a reflective turn and to a critical re-

---

[130] 'Yes, but'-communication is described by Berne (1964).

flective questioning of these perspectives. It never comes to that. The group members do not show an openness to inquiry and they miss the possibilities of locating new connections that a dialogue might have provided. And there is no teacher present who could have challenged the students in that way.

The students continue by trying to formulate the conclusion based on their observations of the convergence of the percentage, as shown in Figure 7.3.

Oscar:	I'll write down how the salmonella-free frequency changes, that's one of the questions.
Peter:	It's unstable at first but when you get down around 100 and 1000 it stays around 35. [...]
Oscar:	Write... it's unrelia... unreliable at first, no, how the hell does one put it?
Peter:	Unstable at first, but it isn't unstable, it just gets smaller and smaller.
Oscar:	Yes it's only one case... but that could be [ic] Well, so we write 'unstable at first', but...
Peter:	But in theory that can be 1000, right?

The boys take the initiative to write down the result in mathematical terms: "I'll write down how the salmonella-free frequency changes." In their efforts to use the right mathematical term they consider the difference between "unreliable" and "unstable" but they do not get to a final identification of the terms. The students have finished their task, but nevertheless they seem left on a side track. There is no indication that they have located what the point of the whole investigation could be. They are involved, but there is no other indication of their intentions-in-learning. In particular, what could be the point of identifying the 35%?

Different possibilities

In order to provide some meaning to the 35%, we can consider again the result presented in Figure 7.1. Instead of calculating the percentage (12%, 12%, 14%, 10% and 24%) related to each group, the students could have considered the total number of samples that have 0, 1, 2, 3, and 4 occurrences of salmonella infected eggs. The result is shown in the second column in Figure 7.4. Thus, we see that of 25 samples 10 contained exactly 1 salmonella infected egg, which would be 40%.

How can it be that samples selected in this way only tells the 'truth' of the whole population in 40% of the situations? This question is a principal entrance to a consideration of the reliability of samples. If the

Salmonella infected eggs	Number of samples	Frequency of samples	Calculated frequency
0	5	20%	34.5%
1	10	40%	39.1%
2	5	20%	19.5%
3	4	16%	5.6%
4	1	4%	1.0%
Total:	25		

Figure 7.4: The frequency of samples with 0, 1, 2, 3 and 4 salmonella infected eggs.

real distribution of salmonella infected eggs was not known, what then would be the best guess, given the results as presented in column 2? Naturally, the idea is not to introduce the students to the whole terminology of statistics, but simply to open considerations of the reliability of conclusions about the whole population based on observations of samples which the figures in the second column of Figure 7.4 may provide.

It is also worth considering if these results somehow can be checked by 'pure calculations'. The calculations can be based on the formula for the hyper-geometric distribution.

$$P(n) = \frac{\binom{50}{n}\binom{450}{10-n}}{\binom{500}{n}}$$

This formula is not available to the students, but it is worth considering if it would be possible to introduce them to the idea that pure calculations might be able to bring about the same results as their experimental work. It might be possible to present the existence of a formula that provides results, which appear 'identical' to their empirical findings.[131] The results of applying the formula are shown in the third column of Figure 7.4. In particular, it is found that the probability of getting a sample with exactly one infected egg is 39.1%, quite close to the experimental based estimation of 40%. We can also see that while the students' empirical data, based on the manual selection of the samples of film boxes, show that the probability of getting a salmonella free sample can be estimated to be 20%, the calculation shows 34.5%. The question can then be raised if the empirical result shown in the second column of Figure 7.4 could happen with any reasonable probability.[132] It could be discussed if it makes sense to suspect the teacher of not mixing the eggs properly, or if some groups of students could be suspected of not collecting their samples at random.

At one point Peter suggested that they make a broader investigation of the frequency of the samples.[133] This could have brought about a new and improved version of the first column of Figure 7.4. In this way the result of the experiments and of calculations could have been related. However, they investigate only one figure empirically: the frequency of salmonella-free samples. Instead of the 20%, they found it to be 35%, almost the same as the calculated 34.5%. A reasonable question would be whether further F9-experiments would show a clear approximation to the rest of the figures in the second column in Figure 7.4. This would have made a strong input to the examination of both the experimental and the mathematical aspect of the Law of Large Numbers, and the students would have got adequate material for further considerations of reliability.

By pointing out these possibilities, we try to show that this part of 'Terrible small numbers' brought the students quite close to considering essential points concerning reliability of conclusions made with reference to samples. But the students showed no clear idea about this. As mentioned, the set up of the project presupposed that the students should not receive any straightforward guidance concerning their reflections. We were interested in observing what would happen when the students were brought into a landscape of investigation where reflections on mathematical reliability were possible. Now we must conclude that the teachers' inquiring and challenging questions are important. As in 'Batman & Co.', where the teacher provides a turning point in the students' investigation, it seems important that an identification of issues

---

[131] In fact Ida made such calculations.

[132] This question could open for a discussion of the χ^2-test.

[133] See the final lines of the section: "You have left us in the dark."

takes place. Making a reflective turn seems to presuppose that issues for reflection have to be located and, in particular, perspectives identified.

Maybe a relevant perspective cannot be located among the student perspectives. However, as emphasised in Chapter 4 in our clarification of the notion of dialogue, perspectives need not only be explored, they can also be constructed. This is one of the essential features of a dialogue based inquiry co-operation. In the previous section of 'Terrible small numbers' we can observe resources for such a construction in the students' many different remarks and arguments. We can also find resources in the very landscape of investigation. Still it is clear that a process of constructing new ways of considering the issues and the tasks were not embarked upon, and consequently it was not possible to make a proper mathematical crystallisation.

We see now the particular relevance of the dialogic acts of locating, identifying and challenging. The students get involved in reflections which concern a basic and essential topic, but the learning potential of their co-operation seems almost eliminated, as principal issues for inquiry are not adequately located and identified. Their discussion takes place in a conceptually muddy area with absence of critical reflections. It seems that such reflections need much more teacher support in order to be realised. Let us now look at the second part of 'Terrible small numbers'.

RESPONSIBILITY

What does it mean to act in a *responsible* way, when we have the possibility to apply a mathematically expressed insight as a basis for decision making? It is clear that responsibility does not simply mean checking the mathematical calculation one extra time. Responsibility in this situation includes something different. It presupposes an understanding of the context in which the mathematically based decisions are made. How do the calculations support making a certain decision? Could the decision be justified or questioned for other reasons?

In the following sequence of 'Terrible small numbers', the groups are presented with two lots of eggs: Spanish and Greek eggs. Each group acts as merchants. The groups have to decide which lot they want to buy, but they do not know the 'quality' of the eggs. Each lot contains yellow eggs and blue eggs, but only the teacher knows the mix. What samples do they want to make? Which and how many eggs do they want to buy?

To investigate all eggs is not possible. It does not even make sense, as eggs opened by Quality Control cannot be used again. Furthermore, each group has to buy the number of eggs they want to check. The price of the Spanish as well as of the Greek eggs is set to be 0.50 Kroner each. The Salmonella Control charges 10 Kroner per sample. The eggs can be sold at 1 Krone each. The teacher also provides each group with 1000 Kroner. The students have to estimate how many eggs they want to check, and on this basis make their budget.

Samples mean, you know, that we are not making any money…

First the students consider making 25 samples of size 10 of each lot. They easily calculate that the quality control will then cost 500 Kroner (25 ×10 × 2), but this will be very expensive compared to the profit they would have.[134] 1000 Kroner is not much for a merchant to do business and this causes some problems as it puts heavy limitations on their financial activities. As a matter of fact they would not earn anything at all by that operation. When they pay 500 Kroner for the samples they have 500 Kroner left to buy 1000 eggs that can be sold for 1000 Kroner. So there will be no profit at all, as Peter concludes: "We do not lose money, and we do not earn money either." But he also spots some problems.

Peter:	Then we have to take fewer samples. Samples mean, you know, that we are not making any money.
Anna:	We are making some, aren't we?
Peter:	No.
Anna:	Well OK. But then we have to take 20 samples. How much is that then?
Peter:	That's 400, isn't it?
Oscar:	Then we have 100 as profit.
	[smalltalk, in low voices]
Peter:	20 samples, right, that's 40 tests in all.
Anna:	Well right.
Peter:	Times 10, that's 400.
Ida:	Then we get 1200 eggs… that's 1200 Kroner. Then we earn 200 Kroner… I thought we were to make 10,000 Kroner on this…
Anna:	You're not supposed to make money buying Christmas presents either, are you?
Peter:	[laughing] Too bad!

---

[134] The students even ignore that they also have to pay 0.50 Kroner for the eggs they want to check. This would have added 250 Kroner to their costs.

Through a joint calculation the students realise that reducing the number of samples to 20 of each lot will give them a small profit of 200 Kroner. "Then we earn 200 Kroner... I thought we were to make 10,000 Kroner on this..." No big deal! The limitation of the disposal of money seems to be a limitation for the motivation of the students and the very reason why they do not seem to bother and engage themselves in the task. In other words it becomes a limitation for their *intentions-in-learning*.

A basic idea is clearly located: In order to do business, you have to reduce the costs, and the salmonella control is an obvious candidate. This idea is clearly related to the set up of 'Terrible small numbers', but it represents a general condition. The 'salmonella control' can be interpreted as any kind of 'quality control' and in any form of business the interest in maintaining quality and the concern for maximising profit tend to contradict each other. In this situation mathematics is in action in order to clarify the conditions for decision making.

How about just quitting those samples?

Peter's suggestion, to take fewer samples, is not forgotten, but a more radical solution is also possible:

> Oscar: How about just quitting those samples, just forgetting that there is something called salmonella?
>
> Anna: We can see as it progresses if the results are mixed, [eager] right, right, listen: If we take...
>
> Ida: Does it matter how many we take, because we only need to know which eggs we should pick?
>
> Anna: Right.
>
> Peter: Well, but we also need some samples.
>
> Ida: Right, but we don't need to take 20 samples each, because we can already see after 10 samples which of them contain most salmonella.
>
> Oscar: No, because it may be accidental with 10 samples, right?
>
> Anna: No, because you can see... [ic]
>
> Ida: But we can't afford that either, so it doesn't matter.

Oscar suggests a radical solution: "How about just quitting those samples, just forgetting that there is something called salmonella?" We do not get to know whether this proposal is a consequence of too little profit or too little engagement, but the others obviously pay no attention to it. Instead they begin to discuss how many samples will do. Anna has an idea: "...right, right, listen: If we take..." She wants to pay attention to the process: "We can see as it progresses if..." Ida clarifies that they need not make a decision in advance about how many samples they need to take in order to know which lot they want: "Right, but we don't need to take 20 samples each, because we can already see after 10 samples which of them contain most salmonella." his *minimal-number-of-sample strategy* that is somehow located by Anna and Ida is a powerful idea, but it is not explicitly identified as a mathematical idea in the group interaction. The minimal-number-of-samples strategy is sound to the extent that the Law of Large Numbers is in fact in operation. When the convergence becomes visible, then it is possible to draw conclusions. Oscars' counter-argument that 10 samples will give an arbitrary result represents a doubt about the existence of this convergence, and this revives their previous discussion.

Anna and Ida's argument is remarkable. In many cases it is essential to collect a minimum of samples. One reason for this can be ethical. Imagine two different procedures for medical operations being considered. Which one is better? Samples are produced by simply carrying out the two operations – sometimes the one, sometimes the other. But it seems highly dubious to continue producing samples, when it seems possible to conclude that one is better than the other. Naturally, the experiment can continue and provide well-justified material to tell that one operation is better than the other. An alternative strategy, as soon as it seems possible to draw a conclusion, is to carry out all operations in the way that is indicated to be the best. This alternative might not be the best for research, but certainly the best for the next person in the operation queue. Another reason for collecting a minimum of samples before trying to reach a conclusion can also be economic, as is suggested by Ida. This argument is also put forward in many cases. The minimal-number-of-samples strategy has an exemplary value. Quality control is a simple area for reducing costs.

The discussion of 'How many samples?' is directly related to the previous discussion about the Law of Large Numbers. When we increase the number of samples, we increase our certainty of making the proper estimation, but how long does it make sense to increase the number? Doubling the number of samples taken means doubling the costs of the quality control. And, doubling the number of samples means halving the...? Or how is it? Peter opens the topic:

Peter:	But doing 20 we halve the risk of mere accidence. [compared to a situation with only 10 samples]
Anna:	*No* that's just not true.
Oscar:	Yes it is.
Anna:	We don't halve the risk... No because there are more eggs... more than 40.
Oscar:	But we have twice as many, we have, we are twice as sure.
Ida:	That's right, but we can't halve the risk...

Peter:	Yes we halve the risk in relation to only taking 10. [the pupils speak all at once]
Anna:	Well you are twice as sure as last time.
Ida:	No, I don't think so.
Anna:	But you *are.*
Peter:	That's clear.

Peter states the thesis, that doubling the number of samples (going from 10 to 20) means halving the "risk of mere accidence". Oscar does a reformulation. Doubling the samples means that we can be "twice as sure". Peter and Oscar combine two ideas: First, that more samples mean more certainty (in the conclusions to be drawn), and secondly, that 'more certainty' can be expressed by a simple proportionality: doubling the number of samples means doubling the certainty. The first part of this thesis appears reasonable, but the second part is problematic, as it tries to connect something well-defined, 'the number of samples', with something much more subtle, 'the degree of certainty'. The thesis is also refuted immediately by Anna and Ida: "*No* that's just not true" and "No, I don't think so." It might well be the second part of the thesis, Anna and Ida react to, although Anna seems to give in to Peter's reformulation: "Well you are twice as sure as last time." Ida, however, is still not convinced. The issue is essential but also difficult to tackle.

Ida:	You can't be twice as certain, because it's [ic] It will *still* be accidental, and it won't be twice as certain because...
Peter:	It's twice as certain as when it is 10.
Ida:	No it's 10 more than 10. It's not twice as many.
Oscar:	Is 10 more than 10 not also twice as many as 10? [smiling]
Ida:	*Listen* to me, will you, you bloody *never* do. [exclaiming]

Ida introduces a new argument that has to do with the meaning of 'certain'. It is not possible to be "twice as certain". The very notion of 'certain' seems problematic in this context, as certainty will never be reached. A coincidence will always be possible. This point is only met by Peter's repeating the thesis of proportionality. Ida then expresses herself a bit cryptically: "No it's 10 more than 10. It's not twice as many." It might be the case that Ida has sensed that there is something problematic in their use of proportionality. However, this idea is not explicated in Ida's formulation, and Oscar ironically returns the remark by referring to the logic of her 'surface-statement': "10 more than 10" are certainly "twice as many as 10." Not surprisingly Ida exclaims: "*Listen* to me..."

In this part of the conversation it would have been nice to observe dialogic acts such as, reformulating, locating and identifying. Instead of responding to the surface-logic of Ida's statement, another possibility would have been to try out some inquiry. It would have been important for them to locate that there can be some fundamental difficulties associated with their formulation of the thesis that there is a connection between the number of samples and the degree of certainty. This consideration is crucial for clarifying in what sense the reliability of conclusions drawn from samples may increase as the number of samples increase. The important thing here is not the question who is right, but the way they are stuck with the same problem for a long while without any development in perspectives and understandings. They do not engage in a dialogue but in a discussion in terms of 'smashing to pieces'.

Nevertheless, in this discussion the students come to touch the statistical notion of 'power', which refers to the quality of a statistical procedure. If, say, a choice has to be made between the Greek and the Spanish eggs, and if (as the students later concluded) 13% of the Greek eggs are infected by salmonella, while 3% of the Spanish eggs are infected, then the power of the procedure in use is measured by the probability that the Spanish eggs in fact would be selected. Thus the power of the selected process is 1, if the procedure is sure to come to the right conclusion (the procedure could simply consist of checking all the eggs). Making the decision by throwing a coin, would be a procedure with power 0.5. Referring to the Peter-Oscar thesis, the first part of it can be reformulated as the more samples the more power (and this is a sound part of their thesis). The second part of their thesis appears to be: Doubling the number of samples means doubling the power. This is the problematic part of their thesis. A much more complex relationship exists between number of samples and power, and this is indicated by Ida but not followed up in an inquiry co-operation.

The group authority is clearly represented by the boys, who continue to follow their own way, and they let Ida pull herself out of the group work for a long period of time. Anna returns to the great idea: the minimal-number-of-samples strategy.

Anna: What if we take 10 samples first, and then check if there's any big difference, and if there isn't really, then maybe we *can* stick to 10 samples, or if it doesn't drop very much, or if it doesn't change very much.
Peter: Then let's do 20.
Anna: But we don't have to decide on that now.
Oscar: Then we'll earn... if we take 15. [samples]
Peter: Then we'll earn a little more.
Anna: But isn't that...
Peter: "Which samples do you wish to take?"... which samples? [Reading from a worksheet]

Oscar: I think it says "How many samples?" we wish to take. [5 sec.]
            Shall we take 15? Well let's just take 10.
Anna: Let's just get started. So we take 1 sample...

Anna makes a clear formulation of the minimal-number-of-samples strategy. As a kind of compromise she suggests starting with 10 samples. Peter seems to ignore her suggestion when stating: "Then let's do 20." Anna makes the principal claim of the strategy: "But we don't have to decide on that now." The idea is simply to include new samples until it is possible to draw a conclusion, and then terminate the experiment. Oscar suggests a compromise, which would mean a compromise in terms of numbers, but which would not acknowledge the strategy, as suggested by Anna. Peter follows up by pointing to economic aspects, which support Oscar's suggestion (but which in fact would serve as a better justification of Anna's idea). Anna still makes the principal argument: "But isn't that..." and she would probably have continued "unnecessary to make the decision about the numbers of samples in advance". Oscar reformulates his compromise: "Shall we take 15? Well let's just take 10." And as he is obviously addressing Peter, it comes to serve as a compromise, not as an acknowledgement of Anna's idea. But Anna does not give it up: "Let's just get started. So we take 1 sample..."

Reshaping the landscape of investigation

The teacher has realised the consequences of the limited financial conditions he gave the groups, so the next day he presents some new guidelines for the investigation. The groups are allowed to decide for themselves how much money they want to use, and they are supposed to make a budget and to consider their sample results. The price of the eggs is still 0.50 Kroner each for both Spanish and Greek eggs. The price of the salmonella control is not 10 Kroner per sample but 10 Kroner per egg! And the controlled eggs cannot be used for sale. So the questions are: How many eggs do you want to buy? How much profit do you go for? And what would be the text on the egg trays? The merchants are supposed to make money, but they are also supposed to consider some moral questions of responsibility. What would they tell the consumer about salmonella?

Our group is immediately confronted with a new problem. They have not quite finished taking samples of the Spanish eggs, and the egg mix from yesterday is no longer available. As the students cannot take the missing samples they have to do some virtual ones. Ida is opposed to the boys' pragmatic suggestion of guessing at a sample result. Such an approach would obviously spoil the whole possibility of showing that the minimal-number-of-samples strategy could work. She wants to calculate the average of the samples they have already made in order to give a reliable result. The students do not try to understand each other or to reach a mutual agreement. Immediately they end up in a quarrel that makes Ida pull herself away from the group activities. And the boys continue as the group authorities. (The authors of this book suffer with Ida. It would really have been a great idea to see how few samples they would have considered enough to make an indication of the quality of the Spanish and the Greek eggs.)

It is, one way or another, clarified that the Spanish eggs seem to be of the best quality. According to their more or less reliable numbers, the Spanish eggs contain 3% salmonella eggs, whereas the Greek eggs contain 13%. Combining the results from yesterday with the 'invented' samples from today, it has become somewhat unclear how many samples they in fact have used. Anna and Julie (who has come to join the group after not having been present the days before) ask for the boys' method. In the end they have investigated 100 Spanish eggs and 100 Greek eggs in order to reach the conclusion to buy the Spanish eggs. And, as mentioned, the price of the Salmonella Control is 10 Kroner per egg!

Oscar:	That's real expensive, isn't it?
	[...]
Peter:	That's also because he's [the teacher] raised the prices of samples... it was 10 Kroner *per* egg, wasn't it?
Anna:	But if it's 10 Kroner per egg, do we also have to pay 50 Ore... for each egg?
Julie:	Yes apparently.
Anna:	He hasn't said anything about that.
Peter:	Yes, I think we have to, because it's the ones we've already tested, that costs 10 Kroner pr. egg... that is besides...
Anna:	That means first you have to buy an egg, and then hand in an egg.
Oscar:	...that you also have to pay for.

The group has decided that they have 10,000 Kroner to begin with. Now they (except for Ida who has zoomed-out and put her head on the table) are ready to make a budget. How much money have they used until now? They have to pay 10 Kroner per egg for the samples. 200 eggs make 2000 Kroner, but they also have to buy the eggs for the test at 0.50 Kroner each. This is not quite clear to Anna: "But if it's 10 Kroner per egg, do we also have to pay 50 Ore... for each egg?" Peter confirms, and Anna has to reformulate for herself: "That means first you have to buy an egg, and then hand in an egg." The tricky thing is that they have to buy the eggs for the samples, but they are not for sale as they are destroyed in the

The start:		10,000 Kroner
Eggs for the control:		100 Kroner
Costs of control:	2,000 + 100	2,100 Kroner
The rest:	10,000 - 2,100	7,900 Kroner
Spanish eggs bought:	7,900 × 2 = 15,800 eggs	
Spanish eggs sold:	15,800 × 1	15,800 Kroner
Profit:	15,800 - 10,000	5,800 Kroner

Figure 7.5: The budget.

process of control. Such eggs are only negative on the budget. Another reason why the samples are that expensive today as compared to yesterday is that "he's raised the price of samples".

The boys take the initiative to make a budget. After paying the salmonella control, they have 7,900 Kroner at their disposal. All group members including Ida, who has mentally returned to the group, participate in making the budget. They supply each other with contributions that lead to the following conclusion: 7,900 Kroner makes 15,800 eggs that can be sold for 15,800 Kroner. The samples and the eggs they have bought cost 10,000 Kroner and Anna concludes: "Then we have earned 5,800." Their budget is shown in Figure 7.5.

This part of the process is obviously no big challenge to the group, as they agree upon the procedure immediately. So far so good.

'The Woman with the Eggs'

The students begin to act like 'the woman with the eggs'– a fairy tale by Hans Christian Andersen about a farmer's wife who, on her way to the market, imagines what she would be able to buy if she sold the eggs she has got in her basket that she carries on her head. As soon as the budget is available, it becomes possible for the students to imagine further business done.

Oscar:	Well then, but if we are to do it again, then we have, you see, the Spanish eggs we have to buy, and then we'll just spend all our money.
Ida:	And then we have to spend all that 5,800 too, or what?
Oscar:	And then we multiply by 2, and then we have it. That's…
Ida:	And then it's just going on with 2, and then you subtract 5,800 and then you buy the double, and then you've spent 5,800, and if you don't take any more samples, then you get 5,800 again, and then you don't make any money.

Anna:	[ic] why do you have to halve?
Ida:	because… well no, we don't.
Peter:	No you only have to multiply by 2.
Ida:	But that's because we have to subtract it, because we've used it there.
Oscar:	You only have to multiply all of it by 2.
Ida:	No no no no no.
Peter:	If it was as easy as that, if it was as easy to do business, right?

The group starts a thought experiment. What if they use the income of their first business to buy some more eggs? This is initiated by a question from Ida: "And then we have to spend all that 5,800 too, or what?" She is, however, not convinced that they will make any profit: "And then it's just going on with 2, and then you subtract 5,800 and then you buy the double, and then you've spent 5,800, and if you don't take any more samples, then you get 5,800 again, and then you don't make any money." Her argumentation seems to lead to the conclusion that they will never earn anything: As soon as they have got 5,800 Kroner they invest them in eggs, and earn a new 5,800 Kroner which also ends up in eggs. Where is the profit? However, she regrets her calculation as she is challenged by Anna. The students seem eager to participate in the thought experiment. 5,800 Kroner multiplied by 2, then you can get 11,600 eggs that can be sold for 11,600 Kroner and your profit will be another 5,800. And so on and so forth. Ida is still not convinced that they will get any profit, and Peter claims: "If it was as easy as that, if it was as easy to do business, right?" It seems too good to be true.

After some further discussion, Ida becomes convinced, and she explicitly draws a parallel to the fairy tale in her evaluating remarks: "If we kept on this way it wouldn't take long to make a pile of money, but we never do. It's like that story that was read aloud to me when I was very young about the woman with the eggs who is so proud and has so many good dreams, but happens to hold her head too high and loses all her eggs on the ground so that they are broken along with all her dreams."

Almost salmonella free eggs

The group now has a plan of how to make money as merchants. One question is still left: What would be the text on the egg trays? They have to have a reliable text in order to guide the customers. This opens a new scope of reflections.

Oscar: We have to make a slogan.
Peter: OK... salmonella free Spanish eggs.
Oscar: They are not salmonella free.
Anna: Well, then we'll go on calculating.
Peter: We've finished calculating.
           [...]
Peter: We need a slogan for our egg trays.
Oscar: For our egg trays...
Teacher: But it mustn't say anything wrong.
Peter: Mustn't it say anything wrong?
Oscar: It mustn't say salmonella free Spanish eggs.
Peter: Ah well, 3%.
           [...]
Peter: But it doesn't sound very groovy that you say...
Oscar: Almost salmonella free eggs.
Peter: ...almost salmonella free eggs, and there's... 3% [laughing]
           salmonella free eggs.
Teacher: No that's a problem.
Anna: No you can't say that, 3% with salmonella, that's 97%.
Teacher: Eat only 9 of them!
Anna: You can also just say 'Spanish free farm eggs'.
Peter: Free range chicken from Madrid.
Anna: It's not chicken.
           [laughing together]

The boys are ready to prepare a slogan for the egg trays while the girls have not finished the budget yet. Peter has a first suggestion: "...salmonella free Spanish eggs," but Oscar immediately objects to that: "They are not salmonella free." The teacher shows up and claims that they are not allowed to write anything wrong on the trays. Oscar repeats his objection, but Peter does not seem to care about 3% salmonella: "Ah well, 3%." But it is a problem to write that the eggs are "almost" free of salmonella. Instead they choose to characterise the hens positively: "Free range chicken from Madrid."[135]

Afterthoughts

We have just witnessed a breakdown between scientific interest and economic priorities. On the one hand, the students' investigations have brought them to conclude something about the quality of the Spanish eggs. On the other hand, their business interests make it difficult for them

---

[135] The project 'Terrible small numbers' continues, but we stop our presentation of the project here.

to state this in a clear voice. At a previous stage of the project we have also observed the tension between scientific and economic interests, when Oscar suggested just to quit sampling. If we try to reach some well-justified conclusion, the cost will spoil the economy of the business. So, in order to make profit, it becomes essential to skip the dream of getting a 'final' certainty in the investigations. The minimal-number-of-samples strategy emerges as a kind of compromise between these two interests.

'Terrible small numbers' has brought the students into situations where they can carry out investigations and produce arguments which are exemplary for the way science and mathematically based decision making are operating in society at a larger scale. It becomes clearly illustrated how scientific principles and economic interests may often be in conflict with each other, with the result that new risk structures are established, as alluded to by Beck. The way the students handle the labelling of the egg trays illustrates an essential mechanism: the commercially based distribution of risks. The customers may get cheaper products, but they may also run into new risks, which only at certain moments reveal their nature.

Mathematically speaking, risk can be described in the following equation: $R(A) = P(A) \ C(A)$. Here A refers to an event. The risk associated with the event A, $R(A)$, is calculated as the product of the probability, $P(A)$, that A will take place, and the consequence, $C(A)$, of A taking place. This naturally presupposes that both $P(A)$ and $C(A)$ can be put in numbers. In the case of salmonella infection, A can mean the event of a certain person being infected. The $P(A)$ means the probability that he or she gets infected. The $C(A)$ refers to the cost of being infected (the loss of income for instance), and the $R(A) = P(A) \ C(A)$ represents the risk. Such considerations are general and can be applied to any form of risk consideration. When $P(A)$ can be estimated as particularly small, we have to do with what we have labelled a 'terrible small number'. This opens up the general issue: if $P(A)$ is terribly small whereas $C(A)$ is big, could then the mathematical risk calculated become misleading? Could it be that even though $R(A)$ appears small, the risk is not acceptable anyway?

From the analysis of the project, it is clear, however, that *the students did not experience the exemplarity of their activities*. To them the activities appeared first of all as confusing tasks: the teacher has produced something 'dark'. The overall structure of the project, however, seemed to be clear to the students. Thus, Oscar and Peter made the following summary in their evaluation of the project: "When we traded in eggs we could choose between two kinds of eggs: Spanish and Greek ones. In order to find out about the quality of the two different kinds we had to take samples. Each sample cost 10 Kroner and each egg that we had to break cost 50 Ore, so we were forced to consider how few samples we could get away with and still get a reasonable result. We took the samples and found out that the Greek eggs had a salmonella rate of 13%, and that the Spanish eggs had 3%. Consequently we decided of course to buy the Spanish eggs, as the price was identical. Selling price 1 Krone."

We have, however, carefully to examine why the experience of exemplarity was lost. What prevented this situation from developing the richness of critical reflections which, at least from an analytical point of view, can be identified as potential for this landscape of investigation. 'Terrible small numbers' *in principle* provided topics for reflection, which *in principle* may face the challenge of critique. But as experienced by the students, the reflections were not developed into any powerful ideas of critique.

One year after our classroom observations we taped an interview with Anna, Ida, Oscar and Peter. During that year we had been transcribing their conversation, we had analysed details and elaborated drafts for the present chapter, whereas the students had concentrated on a whole lot of other things. So their memory of the details of the project was not that distinct. For instance Anna and Ida could not recall the minimal-number-of-samples strategy. However, the interview clarified some issues related to the project.

In the interview Figure 7.2 was presented to the students, and they recognised the experiments which produced the numbers. The interviewer presented the possibility of comparing the results of the empirical investigations (in Figure 7.2) with mathematical calculations. Further, the formula for calculating $P(n)$ for each value of n was also presented to the students. Although a long time had passed, the students easily grasped these possibilities. In fact they stated that they would have preferred that these possibilities had been presented during the project.

This returns us to the idea of constructing perspectives. When in Chapter 4 we characterised dialogue in terms of inquiry, we emphasised that a perspective can be explored, suspended as well as constructed. During the project 'Terrible small numbers' we did not observe shared explorations. The students did not establish a 'spirit of investigation'. One reason for this can be that no proper perspectives from which to conceptualise the inquiry were located and identified. However, after reconsidering the whole process, we come to doubt if some adequate perspectives were 'represented' among the students, waiting for identification. It might be that perspectives were in need of being constructed. We read the students' afterthoughts as an indication of this need. The construction of perspectives can be of particular relevance when we are in search of critical reflections. This means that the scope of reflections is widened radically, and this may include the interference and challenge of a teacher. The possibility of the students' ownership of the inquiry does not exclude a construction of a new perspective, assisted by the teacher, as is illustrated by Mary and Adams co-operation in figuring out about the inverse spreadsheet.

During the interview with Anna, Ida, Oscar and Peter, the notion of quality control was also brought to their attention. In this way the exemplarity of the salmonella control was spelled out. This also appeared as a new idea to the students that they would have liked to have had presented to them during the project. The importance of considering a minimal-number-of-samples strategy was also presented during the interview. Thus, the example of choosing between two different forms of heart operations was referred to in order to illustrate that the interest of obtaining scientific certainty not only can come to contradict economic interests, but also human values. Again the overall conclusion is the same: In order to broaden the scope of reflections, it may be important to construct new perspectives, and a teacher challenge or input may facilitate this process. Dialogue is essential.

CRITIQUE

We will return to the general idea that certain qualities of communication, which have been expressed in terms of dialogue, support certain qualities of learning, which we refer to as critical learning of mathematics, and which is represented by mathemacy. In particular, we shall try to clarify relations between the four notions: dialogue, intention, reflection and critique.

In Chapter 4, dialogue was characterised in terms of making an inquiry, running a risk, and maintaining equality; and the dialogic acts included in the IC-Model specify further our notion of dialogue. By being acts, dialogic acts bring us to consider the notions of intention and reflection. However, intention and reflection also relate to the notion of *critique* (with respect to learning). Thus intentions concern the participants' involvement in the process of making a critique, and reflections concern the issues that can be addressed by a critique. Putting these issues together we find that dialogue represents interpersonal resources for critique and critical learning. The conceptual relations are illustrated in Figure 7.6, and we shall try to clarify these relations in greater details.

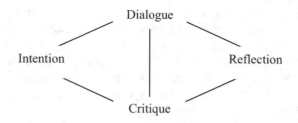

Figure 7.6: Some conceptual relations.

Intention and critique. We have been concerned about collective reflections, referring to reflections carried out in a process of co-operation. An inquiry co-operation also presupposes that intentions become explicated and adjusted to each other. In several of the presented projects we can observe examples of adjustment of intentions in order to ensure the collectivity of the task. Working together does not presuppose that the intentions of the participants must be identical. It is important, however, that intentions-in-learning become shared, maybe leaning towards each other. In this case it could make sense to talk about collective intentions.

A critique is not simply an analytical activity. It means more than detached contemplation. Critique also includes action. It presupposes involvement that represents a personal or a collective foundation for making a critique, and intentions-in-learning become a defining element in any critical learning. A process of learning critically cannot be a casual or a forced activity. It is not possible to prescribe that anybody should be critical.

This brought us to consider the importance of leaving the exercise paradigm and entering landscapes of investigation, which could supply invitations for the students to participate in inquiry processes. The proper test of a landscape coming to serve as a landscape of investigation is whether the students in fact accept the invitation. An eager zooming-in indicates that the students are concerned about the issues presented. A zooming-out indicates the presence of a reluctant learner. In the case of the resistance group this zooming-out became so hectic that it disturbed the whole classroom activity. Reluctance turned into active resistance.

Although the students in 'Terrible small numbers' accepted the invitation and tried to locate a task, they seemed to do so with less enthusiasm than, say, Mary and Adam did in 'Batman & Co.' or Simon, Dennis, Lisa and Sara in 'Caramel boxes'. However, in 'Terrible small

numbers' there are many indications that the students were trying to
locate a point of focus. As was the case in 'How much does a newspaper
fill?' the students were trying to zoom-in on the aim of their activity.
They made different attempts, once by searching into the exercise
paradigm by trying to treat the numbers of Figure 7.1 as if they belonged
to a normal exercise. We definitely also observed some zooming-outs of
the process. Thus, after having been seriously not understood, Ida rests
her head on her arms on the table.

We prefer to use the word intention and not motivation, although in
many cases these two notions overlap considerably. Motivation has been
developed within the paradigm of behaviourist psychology that tries to
follow the paradigm of natural science in identifying causes for actions
and behaviour, and motivation can be identified as a cause of a biological
nature. We do not try to follow this line of thought. Instead we consider
the motives and the dispositions of the acting person, and this brings us to
consider the background and in particular the foreground of the learners.
Establishing the learners' intentions-in-learning means paying particular
attention to the learners' background and foreground. Rogers (1994) suggests a person-centred learning. Dewey (1963) finds that the experimental
mode must substitute the teacher based lecturing. Freire (1972) emphasises that banking-education has no place in his approach to literacy. And
Mellin-Olsen (1987, 1989) emphasises that students must be owners of
their learning processes. Such critiques of traditional school based education can be summarised in the claim that critical learning cannot be a
forced activity. Critical learning presupposes intentions-in-learning. Critique presupposes ownership.

In our discussion of the different events in the dialogic process, we
observed the importance of the teacher 'handing back' to the students the
ownership of the process. When the teacher challenged Mary and Adam
and the new possibility of turning the spreadsheet upside down was located, the project could have come to be a 'teacher project', which Mary
and Adam then had to cope with. But during the process of locating and
identifying, a basic equality between teacher and students was maintained, and it became possible for the students to renew their ownership
and to proceed with the investigation as being their investigation. A direct
and forceful challenge can make the students pull back their intentions-
in-learning, and different underground intentions can be produced. In
'Terrible small numbers' the teacher did not challenge the students' ownership of the process. However, it was clear that the students did not
always want to stay as owners of the process. Thus, when they dealt with
issues of responsibility, their ironical distancing from the activities made

sure that they did not become personally involved. And this provided an obstacle to developing a critique in more detail.

Freire paid special attention to how to establish collective intentions-in-learning, and he carefully contextualised the key terms upon which the teaching of literacy was based. As mentioned, reading *tijolo* became associated with the understanding of the social, economic and political aspects of brick building. A particular reason for the efficiency of his method is that Freire made it possible for the learner to be the involved in the process of learning. The basic condition for the Freire-approach to critical learning is the careful involvement of the students. This is a general aspect of any critical learning, and in this way intention and critique become conceptually connected.

Reflection and critique. When it is assumed that the content of what is learned serves an ultimate good, then reflections can concentrate on intrinsic aspects of the learning process. Thus, some learning theories have been concerned about 'learning obstacles' and 'students' misconceptions', and the reflections discussed refer to how the students think about their conceptions and misconceptions. However, when we try to face the D'Ambrosio paradox, i.e. to face the challenge of critique, it becomes important to broaden the scope of reflection. In the discussion of the scope of reflections in Chapter 6 we presented six dimensions of reflections. If we should face the D'Ambrosio paradox, it is important that all these dimensions become developed as part of the educational processes.

Following the exercise paradigm, the students can make their calculations, and their results can be checked. Also in this case we can imagine several issues for reflection. The students can be concerned about their results. Are they correct? They can be concerned about the number of exercises set by the teacher. Will they finish before the bell rings, or will they need to do a lot of homework? Reflections can concentrate on particular elements of mathematical calculations, and certainly such reflections can be complex. However, we have been particularly concerned about expanding the scope of reflections. Reflections cannot simply address issues concerning, say, correctness of particular calculations (as was discussed in Chapter 6 with reference to the project 'Caramel boxes'). Reflections, then, come to relate to the notion of sociological imagination, as presented by Wright Mills (1959). They can address important aspects of our technologically formatted environment. In this way, the whole enterprise of mathematics becomes addressed in a reflection. Reflection may turn into a critique, and the scope of reflections has to be broadened in order to provide for critical learning of mathematics.

We have tried to illustrate what it could mean to broaden the scope of reflections and to address more fundamental aspects of mathematics, by highlighting the discussion of reliability and responsibility. Reliability is a general aspect of dealing with mathematics and the result of calculations. When actions can be carried out with reference to calculations and numbers, then we always have to consider the issue of reliability. As is also illustrated by 'Terrible small numbers', the idea is not to emphasise that 'numbers are unreliable'. The point is only that the issue of reliability cannot be ignored. The issue of reliability concerns all levels of mathematics. It can concern a simple calculation belonging to an everyday practice. It can concern more advanced mathematical modelling. And it can concern the use of advanced mathematics in an everyday context. The same is the case with respect to responsibility. Issues of responsibility can concern all situations where decisions based on calculations have to be taken. One point of 'Terrible small numbers' was to illustrate what a discussion of reliability and responsibility could consist of. In this way we want to show what a broadening of the scope of reflections could mean.

The scope of reflections can naturally be broadened far beyond mathematics and far beyond the issues we have considered. In general, we find that 'scope of reflections' is an important issue to consider in any critical activity. That we have concentrated on mathematics related issues, is only a limitation related to the nature of our study. We are trying to discuss what a critical learning of mathematics could mean.

We do not define reflections as an organism's self-reflections caused by recognition of non-viability. Thus, the Piaget-Glasersfeld approach (which we are going to discuss further in the next chapter) relates reflections to the individual's reorganisation of his or her conceptual framework, caused by a process of accommodation. However, we do not think of reflections as being 'caused' by specific phenomena. Reflections are *carried out* by somebody. Reflections refer for instance to ethical considerations. Reflections are not a semi-biological process addressing obstructions for viability, but a complex cultural process. That reflections must be 'carried out', indicates the close relationship between intentions and reflections. Reflections presuppose involvement.

We have talked about the collectivity of reflections, as illustrated in the project 'Caramel boxes'. If we reconsider Mary and Adam's co-operation, we can notice that collective reflections are represented almost throughout the whole process. An inquiry process includes a series of dia-logic acts, which are simultaneously a manifestation of reflections.

Collective reflections can naturally turn in many directions. However, we find that they are essential for establishing critical reflections. In this way reflection and critique become conceptually connected.

Dialogue and critique. Dialogue refers to certain qualities of communication. Critique refers to certain qualities of learning. Intentions and reflections refer to essential aspects of both dialogue and critique. Critique can only be carried out as an intended activity, and reflections can turn into a critique. We see dialogue as a communicative foundation for critical learning.

By characterising dialogue as a process of inquiry, we have already emphasised that dialogue has an epistemic content. By emphasising that dialogue is risky, we acknowledge also the non-predictability of getting to know. By claiming that dialogue presupposes equality, we emphasise that the role of a teacher cannot consist in simple 'delivery' of knowledge, if we want to talk about critical learning. We here try to clarify further the relations between dialogue and critique by considering the dialogic acts of the IC-Model. These acts can be seen as a preparation for critical activities. We find that dialogic acts, on the one hand, represent elements of a dialogic process and, on the other hand, represent elements of critical learning. In order to clarify these connections further we comment on each element of the IC-Model.

The process of *getting in contact* is essential if equality between students and teacher is to be maintained, and if the rituals of the school mathematics tradition are to be broken. An act of getting in contact can be seen as a way of acknowledging that the students' intentions-in-learning are important. The students should be treated as persons (and not as pupils). A critique is not 'delivered' to students, it must be carried out by the students. Getting in contact can mean an acknowledgement by everybody of their participation in the process to follow. It signifies the importance of being involved. This act helps to put intentions-in-learning.

Locating refers to the process of opening spaces for investigation and becoming aware of the fact that several perspectives can be possible. Locating can be facilitated by what-if questions. Locating may help to relate mathematical terms to familiar, but not specialised terms, as we observed in the project 'How much does a newspaper fill?' The mathematical concepts of area and volume were related to the concept 'fill'. A locating of mathematical concepts and ideas among non-mathematical ones is one condition for broadening the reflections on mathematics in use. More generally, the resources for critique must be found within the horizon of the persons involved. Or, if this is not possible, a perspective has to be constructed. Without the process of locating, the teaching-learning process easily turns into processes of information delivery. Thus, locating has much to do with the ownership of the learning process. Locating may help to maintain intentions-in-learning. This is essential in case a learning process should come to contain such energy, as is illustrated by Mary and Adam.

Identifying may also help to broaden the scope of reflections. Identifying is essential in order to specify particular mathematical ideas. It is essential also that the perspective of 'the other' is always considered as a possible resource for further inquiry. This is essential in mathematics if we consider the ideas – for instance much emphasised by the ethnomathematical approach – that anybody is in possession of mathematical knowledge. By relating to this knowledge, mathematics education can become empowering for the students involved. Identifying could mean the identification of an idea like the minimal-number-of-samples strategy or of the statistical notion of power. Identification can mean that the students enter the process of learning as owners, also of some of the mathematical ideas.

Advocating refers to the act of presenting lines of arguments. This is essential in order to develop a possible justification. But advocating includes suspending perspectives in the sense that the argumentation does not maintain a truth. Advocating means openness to other interpretations as well, and this is important to critique. Advocating represents an important and rational part of any critical activity. We do not see a critique as only an emotional statement of like and dislike. A critique is based on some sort of justification, and advocating means to try out a justification. Naturally, there can be advocating which does not bring us forward towards a critical activity, but we cannot imagine a critical activity, without it being rooted in some advocating.

Thinking aloud refers to the process of making mathematical reasoning and reflections public. Thinking aloud helps to verbalise ideas that otherwise would not have come to the surface of communication and inquiry. Thus, thinking aloud is important for critical ideas to be located. Thinking aloud is also a direct expression of making a critique a public and collective concern. It is difficult to imagine the development of collective and critical reflections if there is no thinking aloud.

The process of *reformulating* means dwelling for the purpose of further (critical) investigation. We have seen reformulating also as an emotional act, making it possible to 'stay in contact'. Reformulating has much to do with focusing, directing and redirecting the educational process which means that reformulating directly concerns the ownership of the process. Reformulating can thus be seen as a dialogic act which helps to explicate intentions and to co-ordinate the motives of the co-operation. This helps to establish collective intentions that are essential for critical learning.

We find that *challenging* is essential for locating new possibilities and for provoking new ideas. Thus, in 'Terrible small numbers' the students were directly involved in basic problems concerning mathematics in action, the problems of reliability and responsibility. However, the issues were not addressed directly. The exemplarity of the tasks was not observed by the students and we find that the teacher's challenging questions could have provided a critical turning point in the investigations. Such turning points are of particular relevance in mathematics, as challenging can mean a most direct way of expanding the scope of reflections, but a challenge can also provide direct obstruction for the involvement of the students. In the project 'Caramel boxes', we saw some very elegant forms of challenging. The teacher participation in the dialogue appears to consist mainly in his listening and his few confirming comments: "Yes," "Yes" and "Well, yes". Nevertheless, this provides a challenge, and it helps the students to identify new possibilities. In other words: challenging is a dialogic act which in a direct way can provoke a critical activity.

Evaluating is essential when we consider the sources of intention, the dispositions of the students. An evaluation can help to relate their activities to their aspirations and expectations. Evaluating is a dialogic act, but also a critical act. In fact, we can consider every dialogic act represented by the IC-Model as part of a critical activity.

By critical learning we understand learning based on a process where dialogic acts, as just described, play an essential role. We find that dialogic acts enrich the process of learning, in particular, by establishing intentions-in-learning and broadening the scope of reflections. We find that dialogue is an interaction which provides (a visible) basis for critical learning. Dialogue is the 'public' part of a critical learning process.[136] Here it is tempting to refer to the Vygotkian terminology (we will return to Vygotsky in the next chapter): the interpersonal aspects of the dialogue turn into intra-personal and constitute processes of knowing. In particular, dialogic qualities become epistemic qualities. We see critical learning as grounded in a collaboration in terms of dialogic acts. In particular, we see mathemacy as a competence which represents a critical learning of mathematics.

---

[136] There is no doubt that dialogue can lead to many things other than critical learning. However, in our analyses we have concentrated on elements of dialogue which can be supportive of critical learning.

We do not see some principal difference between processes of critical learning, depending on particular topics, mathematics, language, history, etc. Considerations related to literacy may be close to considerations related to mathemacy. The particularity of learning mathematics has to do with the particularity of the landscapes of investigation. It might have to do with the particular issues that are located, identified, advocated, etc. There might be some particular forms of advocating that we can designate as characteristic of mathematics. But this does not change our main point, that those dialogic acts which we have identified in particular landscapes of investigation support critical learning in general.

THE CHALLENGE OF CRITIQUE – TOO DIFFICULT?

One of our intentions with the project 'Terrible small numbers' was to establish a landscape of investigation that could invite students to make critical reflections about mathematically based decision making. This appears most important if the challenge of critique is to be considered. This challenge demands that the intensity and the scope of reflections have to be developed considerably. However, could it be that critical reflections addressing wonders and horrors of science, including mathematics, are not really possible to locate in a mathematics classroom? This is certainly one possibility that needs to be considered. There might be issues so complex that they cannot be approached by students wandering in a landscape of investigation, although this landscape in principle provides resources for critical reflections.

'Terrible small numbers' does certainly not confirm that it is possible to meet the challenge of critique in classroom practice. (Although the interview with the students indicates that the project contained potentials that were not realised.) But the project can serve the purpose of clarifying some of the particular difficulties related to realising the critical learning of mathematics. We will consider some of these.

There were no strong structural limitations in the project, as the school where the project took place does not emphasise the value of the school mathematics tradition. Instead, the school and the students are ready for experimental projects. However, also in this case we find that the school mathematics tradition produces obstacles for making a critical turn. Breaking away from this tradition, including its bureaucratic absolutism linked to the exercise paradigm, and inviting students into a landscape of investigation, may provide resources for critical reflections about mathematics in action, but as 'Terrible small numbers' demonstrates:

This is not so simple. Although neither the project nor the school were located in the school mathematics tradition, this tradition is not completely absent. For instance, when the students experienced uncertainty about their task, they tried to establish a zooming-in by looking for tasks that make sense as part of the exercise paradigm. This may be due to the fact that this school is only for 8th to 10th grade students, and many students come from schools where they are used to traditional school mathematics. Ida indicates this explanation in her evaluating comments: "When I entered the room I thought at first that I'd ended up in a perfect group. I was in the same group as Anna, Peter and Oscar, the best in the class at math, but I don't know if it was just me not being up to it or what, but all the time I got irritated with them and didn't understand what they were doing. All the time I wanted to find both the answer and the reason for the answer, but they were more interested in just finding the answer and move on."

Possibly, the difficulties of making the critical turn can have to do with the particular contextualisation? The students could consider the contextualisation as childish or longwinded. Peter and Oscar indicated this point in their evaluating remarks: "It was a good way to learn about calculus of probability, because it was easier to understand when we had something specific to relate it to (the eggs). At least we think that will help many to understand it. It was also rather good to have both 'the eggs' and the spreadsheet, but without the latter it would have been very longwinded." The project and the specificity in the form of photo film cases were tried out in a different classroom with 13-year-old students. Here the concretisation made good sense, but to older students the possibility of making experiments with samples on the computer seems more motivating. On several occasions the students distanced themselves from the contextualisation by ironic remarks, although their zooming-outs were small and elegant compared to the bombastic zooming-outs made by the resistance group. Also particular aspects of the concretisation could have served as obstructions. For instance, the first limitation of the budget of 1000 Kroner seemed to de-motivate the students. Working in semi-reality the limit of 1000 Kroner might appear a detail, but in real-life trading efforts are not really worth it if you can only make a small profit. Students of 15 or 16 years are well aware of that. Although landscapes of investigation may invite the making of a rich variety of reflections, particular difficulties related to even seemingly insignificant aspects may provide obstructions.

Maybe the invitation into the landscape of investigation was too open. As already mentioned, it was part of the design of the project that the students were not guided by the teacher pointing at particular issues worth considering. Guidelines for investigation and reflection were not specified. So maybe an open landscape of investigation can be too open and in this way over-challenging to the students. Furthermore, our observations lead us to conclude that when tasks are presented to the students in this open way, they do not establish the critical turn by themselves. Developing a critique must be considered an elaborated cultural process, at least when we consider a critique that is supposed to face the challenge as presented by D'Ambrosio. This brings us back to the importance of constructing perspectives which can guide the inquiry process.

Could the problem of making the critical turn become related to the fact that dialogue was not a clear aspect of the communication among the students? This is definitely a possibility that is also considered by Peter and Oscar in their evaluation of the project: "Mostly our group worked well, but there were times where we argued and didn't quite understand each other." When some new ideas were presented, the ideas were often left along the mainstream of the conversation (in most cases defined by the boys). As mentioned, we did not observe many dialogic acts by means of which we have characterised an inquiry co-operation. We have also characterised inquiring questions and reformulation as ways of staying in contact during the process. Perspectives were rejected before being examined, and this might be a reason why the emotional atmosphere turned negative and why they missed some interesting inquiries. However, several ideas were located during the process. Or almost-located? The students came to formulate the minimal-number-of-samples strategy, but this was never acknowledged or identified. They formulated a thesis related to statistical inference: The reliability of the statistical results increases with the number of samples. This thesis provides an excellent entrance to an inquiry of reliability and to the notion of power. The Law of Large Numbers was stressed, and somehow it was related to the possibility of carrying out the minimal-number-of-samples strategy, as well as to the quality of sample-based reasoning. The students had in front of them data (Figure 7.1) that contained the relevant information for an introductory consideration of reliability. They were involved in calculations that in direct ways expressed a confrontation between scientific reliability and economic interests, and in this case the minimal-number-of-samples strategy was presented as a mediating approach. In this way the students almost identified essential issues of mathematics in action. But certainly their exemplary value was not identified.

Maybe the problem has to do with the missing dialogue between the students and the teacher. In particular we must consider possibility for the teacher to make challenging questions and assist in constructing alternative perspectives. In the case of Mary and Adam, we saw this approach in operation. Here the teacher made a clear intervention in the students' communication, and the challenge made it possible for Mary and Adam to locate other possibilities that did exist, to identify a particular mathematical idea (the inverse spreadsheet and that the percentage will change when the step is taken in the reverse order), and to operate on the basis of this identification. We talked about establishing a turning point in the investigation. In 'Terrible small numbers' the teacher's and the co-teacher's challenges were much 'softer'. They did not establish any turning point in the students' investigations. When no identification takes place, then it becomes difficult to address why-questions. The identification of a certain perspective is relevant. This could also have changed the atmosphere of the students' interaction. When perspectives are not identified, the discussion may appear as a quarrel or as a 'smashing to pieces', accompanied by negative feelings, for instance of not being understood. In order to be included in the inquiry process ideas need to be highlighted. Issues for reflection have not only to be located they must also be identified.

After considering these difficulties in making a critical turn, it might well be asked: Why worry about this? Even if critical mathematics education might be an attractive approach to many, it might turn out to include too many difficulties. Why not give up facing the challenge of critique? We shall address this question in the next and final chapter, where we consider the nature of a critical epistemology. In particular, we shall try to clarify the point of trying to develop a critical epistemology for mathematics education and in this way support the development of critical mathematics education.

CHAPTER 8

CRITICAL EPISTEMOLOGY
AND THE LEARNING OF MATHEMATICS

We have been, and we are still, trying to clarify the notion of learning mathematics critically, and now we want to reconsider where this search has brought us. We will look more generally at issues which, with philosophical connotations, can be referred to as epistemology. Thus, Piaget refers to his approach as 'genetic epistemology' – 'genetic' emphasising that he, first of all, considers the personal growth of knowledge and not, as in classical epistemology, the sources and the justification of knowledge.[137] When we have in mind specific learning contexts we can talk about theories of learning, or theories of getting to know. When we consider more general aspects of how a person or a group of persons can engage in a process of getting to know, we choose to talk about epistemology.

In this chapter, we shall concentrate on conceptual aspects of our journey. In particular, we are going to clarify our position by considering how epistemologies can include mono-logical, dia-logical, non-critical, as well as critical elements. We shall discuss in what sense the theoretical position we have tried to develop can be referred to as a critical epistemology.

MONO-LOGICAL EPISTEMOLOGY

Piaget tries to reconcile empiricism and rationalism, the two classic approaches to epistemology, the first claiming that the resources for

---

[137] For a presentation of genetic epistemology, see the section written by Piaget in Beth and Piaget (1966) and Piaget (1970).

knowledge are found in sense experiences, the latter that human rationality is the resource. Initially, Piaget makes a distinction between logico-mathematical experience and physical experience the latter being the one that constitutes knowledge about physical objects and phenomena. According to Piaget, this knowledge is rooted in the physical properties of objects. Logico-mathematical knowledge (mathematical knowledge for short), however, is not rooted in such properties; it has a different empirical root. Mathematical knowledge, he says, is rooted in actions on physical objects. Human beings can rearrange physical objects, and they are able to reflect on their operations with objects. Mathematical knowledge is grounded in such reflections. Here we also find the rationalistic element in Piaget's epistemology. It is not the case that mathematical knowledge grows directly from operations on objects (and certainly not from the properties of the objects themselves, which could have turned his theory into empiricism). Operations also have to be reflected upon. Piaget talks about reflective abstractions that are grounded in operations on objects. By means of such resources we produce mathematical knowledge. According to Piaget's genetic epistemology, mathematical knowledge has an empirical root in our operations on objects and a rationalistic root in reflective abstractions addressing these operations.

The picture that Piaget draws of the growth of mathematical knowledge has many implications for mathematics education. Thus, structuralism gets theoretical support, because Piaget's argumentation indicates that a harmony can be established between mathematical structures, in particular as they were identified by the Bourbaki-group, and the natural growth of mathematical knowledge. Piaget's epistemology was taken as justification for the mathematical reform of the 1960s. Another implication of Piaget's epistemology relates to the notion of construction. A reflective abstraction is an activity performed by the individual, and this leads to the idea that mathematical knowledge is in fact constructed by the individual.

Genetic epistemology, however, faces the following question: How is it possible to imagine a construction of mathematical knowledge by the individual, as mathematics seems first of all to be characterised by its uniformity and not by its individuality? If mathematics is constructed by the individual we should expect an enormous variety of different forms of mathematical knowledge. Piaget discusses this question, and he makes a distinction between the 'psychological subject' and the 'epistemic subject'. He claims that the epistemic subject is uniform, and not characterised by individual features. The epistemic subject contains the common human aspects of knowledge construction, and Piaget claims that this epistemic subject is the subject that produces mathematical knowledge. In this way Piaget tries to solve the problem of how to interpret the uniform nature of mathematical knowledge. By his solution Piaget expresses his rationalism, because rationalism faces a similar problem: How is it possible that the soundness of rational thought seems independent of the individual? The assumption of rationalism is that if human beings apply reason in a proper way, then different human beings will come to the same conclusion when they apply reason to the same set of assumptions. *Ratio* provides a uniform tool for logical reasoning. This line of thought is repeated in Piaget's suggestion that reflective abstractions, as carried out by the epistemic subject, guarantee that we construct the same mathematics.[138]

Reflective abstraction, carried out by the epistemic subject, is crucial to Piaget's genetic epistemology. This notion provides Piaget's constructivism with a sort of individualism. The individual has access to the mechanisms for constructing mathematical knowledge, in the sense that the epistemic subject ensures that everybody constructs the same sort of mathematics. Mathematics is thus an expression of a uniform capability of human construction. The reason that we come to the same conclusions in, say, geometry is not that the geometric concepts and notions are created by a social process, but instead that the individual human beings have a share of *ratio,* which operates in a uniform way in the individuals. The human construction of geometry can be taken care of individually.

Radical constructivism emerges from a particular reading of Piaget. According to Glasersfeld (1995, 18), the model of constructivism he has proposed highlights that knowledge cannot be received but is an activity built up by the cognising subject. Furthermore, Glasersfeld emphasises that the function of cognition is to organise and reorganise the experiential world, i.e. the world as it appears to the individual. Thus, knowledge does not address aspects of a real world. In philosophical terms, the denial of an ontological reality which knowledge is about can be associated with idealism, as has been suggested by, for instance Berkeley, Hegel, McTaggert, Bradley and others elaborating on a metaphysics of idealism. Without any ontological commitment, it becomes natural to Glasersfeld (1995, 14) to adopt the biological terms of 'viability' instead of the notion of truth in order to characterise knowledge: "Actions, concepts, and conceptual operations are viable if

---

[138] Social constructivism also tries to formulate a solution to the millions-of-mathematics problem (see, Ernest, 1998a).

they fit the purpose or descriptive contexts in which we use them. Thus, in the constructivist way of thinking, the concept of viability in the domain of experience, takes the place of the traditional philosopher's concept of Truth, that was to indicate a 'correct' representation of reality."

This brings Glasersfeld to emphasise the instrumentality of knowledge. With reference to Piaget, cognitive changes take place when operative schemes are changed in a process of accommodation. And Glasersfeld (1995, 68) emphasises: "On the level of reflective abstraction [...], operative schemes are instrumental in helping organisms achieving a relatively coherent conceptual network of structures that reflect the path of acting as well as thinking, which, at the present point of reference, have turned out to be viable." This is a clear statement of the consequences of the radical constructivist idea that knowledge is instrumental and that the notion of truth can become substituted by viability. Knowledge becomes similar to other tools that the individual has developed in the process of growth. Knowledge can be judged as functional in a similar way as hands are functional with respect to the individual's operations in the world of experiences. In this sense, the instrumentalism of radical constructivism becomes associated with a strong individualism. The learning subject is an individual, as the experienced world is individual.

The notion of dialogue does not play any role in Piaget's epistemology for clarifying the growth of mathematical knowledge. Reflections on operations with objects are carried out by the epistemic subject which, operating in isolation as an integrated part of the individual, ensures the uniform nature of the developed mathematical knowledge. Dialogue does not play any role in describing the nature of reflective abstractions. We can rather characterise Piaget's epistemology as *mono-logical*. By this we mean that the basic mechanisms for constructing mathematical knowledge are to be found in the individual and not in the interaction between individuals.

We are neither following radical constructivism in its idealism,[139] nor in its instrumentalism or individualism. However, we are definitely

---

[139] We shall not embark on the discussion of idealism versus realism. However, in Skovsmose (1994), a realist position is indicated. Here we just want to emphasise that realism in epistemology does not presuppose that knowledge cannot be constructed. Certainly it can be so also when knowledge is about something. Furthermore, what knowledge is about need not be any 'eternal', if not Platonic, reality. The reality can be organised, reorganised, constructed and reconstructed by myriads of constructive processes.

inspired by Piaget and radical constructivism in suggesting that the learner is acting in a process of getting to know. And when we, in Chapter 1, emphasise the interpretation of learning as action, we refer to an important point in the Piaget-inspired radical constructivism. We are also inspired by the overcoming of the school mathematics tradition, which is supported by radical constructivism making the classroom open for inquiry processes.[140] However, we do not share the interpretation of the nature of action guiding an inquiry co-operation. Piaget's notion of operation is far from our interpretation of dialogue. We do not see such actions in individualist terms, but as a particular kind of inter-acts, namely dialogic acts.

DIA-LOGICAL EPISTEMOLOGY

We can contrast a mono-logical epistemology with a Vygotskian perspective, which assumes that cognition is constituted by cultural processes.[141] This brings us to consider communication and dialogue as being elements of an epistemology. Lev Vygotsky was concerned with higher mental activities, i.e. processes that are uniquely human. He did not want to follow any reductionist approach, which breaks such processes into smaller units claiming that complex mental processes can be seen as a combination of elementary processes. This reduction is in accordance with the empiricist tradition trying to describe the complexity from the simple, and to describe cognition as a result of a set of mental operations, like associations, which bring unity to sense impressions. Vygotsky also refutes another aspect of reductionism, which claims that in order to understand social processes we have to understand individual processes, as society is made up by individuals. Thus Vygotsky is opposed to the whole scheme of positivist reductionism, which tries to reduce sociological concepts and explanations to psychological, psychological concepts and explanations to biological, and via chemistry to end with physical concepts and explanations as a basis. Finally, Vygotsky refuses any mind-body dualism, inspired by Descartes' distinction between two substances: 'res extensa' and 'res cogitas', the first referring to the body, the latter to the soul. This dualism has brought

---

[140] For a summary of what constructivism could mean in practice see Steffe (1991).

[141] See, for instance, Moll, L. C. (ed.) (1990) and Vygotsky (1978).

psychology, or 'studies of the mind', to concentrate on the properties of the soul (while physics is left to study the properties of matter).[142]

Vygotsky (1978) wanted to clarify how higher mental processes are constituted by social processes, and for that reason he wanted to create a psychology which introduced new patterns of explanation: mental phenomena have to find their explanations in social phenomena. Mental processes are founded in human inter-relationships and through the use of language in communication. Internalised inter-relationships become established as intra-relationships, and this means that the social aspect gets primacy to the individual.

The question: 'What creates a personality?' has most often led to two types of answer. One is 'heredity', and among the supporters of this answer we find Hans Christian Andersen with 'The Ugly Duckling'. The other answer is 'environment', and among the supporters of this answer we find another Danish author, Henrik Pontoppidan, who parodies Andersen by telling a tragic story about an eagle that, because of its social conditions, is far from achieving the success of the ugly duckling in the end. Vygotsky suggests a third answer: 'instruction'. It has not to be forgotten that in 1917 about 70% of the population in the Soviet Union were illiterate. How would it be possible to construct the new citizens for the glorious socialist society to be established? Education appeared essential. The idea became particularly important that teaching people to read and write includes much more than supplying them with a particular cultural technique. Literacy can change the learner, as reading and writing also includes a reorganisation of the learner's world-view. There is a resonance between Vygotsky's way of seeing learning and the political aspirations of the new nation.

This brings us to consider the relationship between development and learning. If we follow approaches in psychology inspired by biology, it becomes natural to consider development as prior to learning. This is how Piaget interprets the relationship. For instance, it does not make sense to try to teach a child to run before he or she can walk. It does not make sense to teach a child to make a perspective drawing if the child is still

---

[142] A particular difficulty of Descartes' dualism is to explain the interaction between soul and body. This brought Descartes to suggest the pineal gland as being the unit where the soul could influence the body, for instance where decisions (carried out by the soul) about doing something physically, like walking, was transformed into actual walking (carried out by the body). The opposite route, that the body may have some influence on the soul, was not part of this approach. Maybe it is possible to read some religious priorities into this: the soul could not be substantially influenced by material things. To alter this order of what could influence what, was really a paradigmatic shift in psychology.

struggling with doodles. In such cases teaching must be adjusted to the development of the child. When learning is seen as a biological-like process of growth, such observations can easily become generalised into the claim that learning has to adjust itself to the child's development, biologically as well as epistemologically. Each developmental stage opens for a certain set of learning possibilities, but trying to teach a child something, associated to a stage that the child has not yet reached, is doomed to fail. Vygotsky negates this line of thought. He puts things in the reverse order. When we have to do with higher mental processes, then development, understood as personal development, can follow learning (Vygotsky, 1978, 90). Learning becomes basic, and learning has to be understood in terms of interpersonal relationships. Changing the order of learning and development becomes just one implication of the general principle that social phenomena have priority to individual phenomena.

This idea brings Vygotsky to consider the zone of proximal development. The border of this zone is made up by, on the one side, the actual development of the person, defined by the tasks and problems which the person can solve and manage on his or her own, and, on the other hand, the tasks and problems which the person can manage being supported by a more experienced person, a teacher for instance.[143] In the zone of proximal development significant learning processes take place and the claimed limitation, due to heredity and environment, of what a person can become can be eliminated. Vygotsky states that "the only good kind of instruction is that which marches ahead of the development and leads it; it must be aimed not so much at the ripe as at the ripening functions." (Vygotsky, 1962, 104) Thus, to Vygotsky the important thing is the process of getting to know and the possibilities of learning, not a specification of what can and what cannot be learned at a certain level of development.

With reference to how, as a teacher, to operate in a zone of proximal development, several pedagogues have suggested the metaphor of 'scaffolding' that signals that the students take active responsibility for the learning process with the teacher in the role of the facilitator.[144] The students do the building and control the work, and when the building can remain standing, the scaffold can be removed. The point is that the

---

[143] See Vygotsky (1978, 84f.).

[144] See Wood, Bruner and Ross (1976).

students transform public knowledge to personal knowledge through their active inquiry.[145]

The interest for the zone of proximal development brings the notion of communication into the centre of educational theory, as any operation in the zone of proximal development, scaffolding for instance, includes interaction. Educational approaches which are inspired by Vygotsky share this interest for communication and interaction – not to forget that many other approaches have shown a similar interest in order to understand learning. Here we have reached the basic difference between the mono-logical and the *dia-logical* paradigms. While mono-logical epistemologies identify the resources for learning and getting to know in the individual, the dia-logical paradigm sees processes of learning as based on interaction, communication and dialogue. Our whole study is located in the dia-logical paradigm.

In Vygotsky's presentation of the zone of proximal development, we do not find any clear indication of the nature of the interaction that in fact could take place in this zone. Recent studies, however, have suggested possible forms of interaction, which could realise the potentials of the zone of proximal development. Thus the notion of scaffolding represents a metaphor indicating what could take place.[146] The IC-Model is our suggestion for the kind of scaffolding that could take place in the zone of proximal development.[147] Activities in this zone can include dialogic acts like getting in contact, locating, identifying, etc. However, as we soon shall clarify, we do not intend to park our study in the Vygotskian camp.

We are not aware that Vygotsky paid any particular attention to mathematics.[148] He was concerned about literacy and he discussed the teaching of scientific concepts in general. However, one of the second-generation followers of Vygotsky, Vassily Davydov, has explicitly discussed the teaching and learning of mathematics.[149] Here, mathematical knowledge is considered as a socially constructed and

---

[145] With reference to Vygotsky, Lindfors (1999, 95) distinguishes between 'meaning' which is socially shared, and 'sense' which is the personal conception of things.

[146] See e.g. Lindén (1997); Lindfors (1999) and Cobb, Boufi, McClain and Whitenack (1997).

[147] See Alrø and Skovsmose (1999).

[148] Although the following reference can be found in Vygotsky (1978, 84): "For example, children begin to study arithmetic in school, but long beforehand they have had some experience with quantity – they have had to deal with operations of division, addition, subtraction, and determination of size. Consequently, children have their own preschool arithmetic, which only myopic psychologists could ignore."

[149] See, for instance, Davydov (1977).

accumulated set of knowledge, into which it is the task of teaching to lead the child. Thus, Davydov emphasises that the child's everyday experiences should be included in the educational processes, although they have to be restructured regarding the particular patterns of scientific knowledge.[150] Following this line of thought, Seth Chaiklin (1999) suggests 'subject matter analysis' as a way of ensuring developmental teaching, which acknowledges the Vygotsky inspiration. In the case of mathematics, a subject matter analysis, as indicated by Davydov, nicely fits the Bourbaki-inspired attempts to locate the logical architecture of mathematics. Consequently, it is not surprising that the Davydov approach also fits well the priorities that have celebrated mathematical structures as curriculum headlines. However, much progressive mathematics education has also found inspiration from Vygotsky.[151]

We are inspired by Vygotsky and his interpretation of learning as a collective process, and of locating resources of knowledge production in social processes. In this respect, the Vygotsky inspiration suggests an almost opposite perspective from radical constructivism, which searches for the nucleus of knowledge construction in processes that are strictly individual. We are also inspired by Vygotsky's focus on the role of language in learning and developmental processes. Further, we acknowledge the zone of proximal development that emphasises the resources and possibilities of learning instead of focusing on mistakes and what is not known. With the help of Vygotsky we are inspired to acknowledge the dia-logical nature of knowledge production.[152]

NON-CRITICAL EPISTEMOLOGY

Although we acknowledge the importance of a dia-logical epistemology, we do not simply follow the Vygotsky-inspired socio-cultural approach, as it has been developed in much mathematics education. We find that

---

[150] See the presentation of Davydov in Eriksen (1993).

[151] See, for instance Alrø and Skovsmose (1999); Bartolini Bussi (1998); Cobb, Boufi, McClain and Whitenack (1997); Cobb and Yackel (1998); Eriksen (1993); Høines (1998); Lerman (2000, 2001); Linden (1997); Mellin-Olsen (1987, 1989) and Zack and Graves (2001). Much inspiration can be found in the development of activity theory, see e.g. Chaiklin, Hedegaard and Jensen (eds.) (1999); Chaiklin and Lave (eds.) (1996); Engeström (1998, 1999); Engeström and Middleton (eds.) (1998); Engeström, Miettinen and Punamäki (eds.) (1999); and Hedegaard and Lompscher (eds.) (1999).

[152] Social constructivism opens for this approach, see, for instance, Ernest (1998a).

the interpretation of this approach often includes *non-critical* elements. This claim naturally presupposes some further clarification, and we shall for a moment turn our attention to John Dewey, with whom we also sympathise in his emphasis on inquiry processes. However, elements of Dewey's theory of learning also fit the non-critical paradigm in epistemology, and we shall try to clarify this.[153]

When properly identified, the scientific method contains several qualities, according to Dewey.[154] First, it represents scientific rationality, and here Dewey has, first of all, the natural sciences in mind. According to Dewey, science starts with observations and collection of data. These data then become condensed into guesses and hypotheses, which in turn can be further confirmed or falsified. More data have to be collected, and the process of scientific investigations continues. Science is first of all characterised by a never-ending process of investigations. Strategies are developed, tried out, rejected, improved. In other words: Knowledge is developed.

Secondly, this process of investigation represents the proper way of getting to know, even if the subject of this process is not the scientific community. According to Dewey, there exists a strong similarity between the scientific method and the way children come to learn. Consequently, paying attention to the scientific method also means being able to identify a proper approach to learning and teaching. Dewey does not find any principal difference between a scientific community making investigations and a classroom doing the same. Dewey thus supports the introduction of the experimental method in school, and this has become a key-issue in progressive education. Every learning process must be based on experiences, and the students must participate in actually developing and organising these experiences. The students cannot be spectators they must be actors. Who could imagine a researcher being a spectator of a research process? The students' experiences become essential: "Anything

---

[153] To Dewey, the notion of 'truth' is not the primary notion in epistemology. Instead, the key-term is inquiry. Dewey does not find that reality is constituted by facts which can be 'pictured'. Instead, reality represents problem-situations. Thus, knowledge cannot be understood in terms of true pictures of an 'objective' reality; instead it represents a way of handling problem-situations. Knowledge represents strategies for handling problems. Strategies for handling a problem can be justified, but such a justification is of a different kind than the one developed with reference to a classical theory of truth. The development of strategies is essential to a pragmatic epistemology, and processes of inquiry bring about such strategies. Thus, we see that Dewey shares much of the perspective of radical constructivism.

[154] For a short presentation of this idea, see the introduction in Archambault (ed.) (1964) as well as Dewey (1938).

which can be called a study, whether arithmetic, history, geography, or one of the natural sciences, must be derived from materials which at the outset fall within the scope of ordinary life-experience." (Dewey, 1963, 73) Furthermore: "It is a cardinal precept of the newer school of education that the beginning of instruction shall be made with the experience learners already have; that this experience and the capacities that have been developed during its course provide the starting point for all further learning." (Dewey, 1963, 74) As science cannot import information from outside, experience in education cannot be imported: "When education is based in theory and practice upon experience, it goes without saying that the organized subject-matter of the adult and the specialist cannot provide the starting point." (Dewey, 1963, 83) Dewey emphasises that interaction in education is essential, as any genuine inquiry process presupposes interaction.

Thirdly, Dewey finds an intrinsic resonance between a concern for democracy and an education that has incorporated the scientific method as a defining element. Proper schooling prepares students for the democratic way of life, and this preparation can be related to the scientific method. This method represents proper investigation and, in general terms, a way of approaching a question in a non-dogmatic way. Naturally, Dewey does not claim that any form of actual scientific approach would maintain these qualities. His point is that the scientific method, when developed in a proper way, has qualities that reach far beyond science. An inquiry process represents a genuine anti-dogmatic process that will ensure the development of a democratic way of life. The scientific method thus has a genuine political role to play. Both science and democracy reject external authority. The free thought that is expressed by the inquiry method is in accordance with the spirit of democracy. For that reason, a theory of scientific knowledge production has a grand social and political perspective.

The educational thinking of Dewey does not concern mathematics in particular. However Dewey, more than any other educator and philosopher, has expressed the assumption of modernity in education. In his educational thinking Dewey includes an assumption of harmony between scientific methodology, inquiry based learning processes, and an endeavour for democracy.[155] This idea we will refer to as the Dewey-assumption. We can also refer to it as an assumption of modernity, as modernism sees science and scientific development as a main source for progress in all its aspects: political, economic, and cultural. Clearly

---

[155] See Dewey (1963, 1966) and Archambault (ed.) (1964).

enough, this assumption is in accordance with the Marxist world-view of the 1920s, where the new Soviet Union was constructed in a celebration of technology and science. The relevance of enculturing students into the scientific world-view, as is reflected in the presentation of the notion of zone of proximal development and specified, for instance, within Davydov's thoughts of mathematics education, was just too obvious. The approach of establishing a subject matter analysis of a logical nature as the basic element in identifying a curriculum is an expression of the modernist perspective. The logic of science is presented as sound and healthy, and it is not an educational task to organise a critique of science, but to carry out a logical analysis of science in order to identify its basic elements and to bring these elements into education. In short, the Vygosky-inspired approach to mathematics education embraces the Dewey-assumption. Enculturation becomes an essential educational activity, as the process of enculturation will bring students into science and mathematics and, in particular, into the scientific method and the scientific way of thinking, which will ensure progress in all its aspects.

Bruner (1960) presents a clear example of what the Dewey-assumption might turn into in curriculum thinking. Bruner discusses the basic principles of science and of scientific thinking, and he is far from preparing a critique of science and of scientific thinking. Scientific notions and methodology become a given for education. The new math movement in the 1960s illustrates what this could mean in particular. The concept of 'subject matter analysis' indicates that the particularity of an enculturation can be found by studying scientific theories and concepts, i.e. by studying science 'from within'.

It has been the fashion to contrast Piaget and Vygotsky.[156] While Piaget presented the road to mathematics in such a way that the individual child became the constructor of mathematical knowledge, the Vygotsky-inspired approach emphasised the importance of approaching mathematics as a collective. But both represent modernism in their trust in scientific rationality. The task of education becomes enculturation and not to organise a critique of the content and the form of the enculturation. In this sense we find non-critical elements not only in Piaget's epistemology, but also in Dewey's and Vygotsky's conceptions of learning. These non-critical elements have been part of many studies in mathematics education. However, in the case of Dewey and Vygotsky,

---

[156] One issue of discussion is whether all epistemic qualities can be interpreted as internalised. A Piaget inspired rationalism will refuse this solution. See, for instance, Sfard (1991). Examples of non-critical dia-logical epistemologies are presented in Sfard (2001) and Oers (2001).

we also find critical elements, and we are particularly interested in specifying what a critical epistemology could mean.

CRITICAL EPISTEMOLOGY

As mentioned, Dewey found an intrinsic resonance between education and democracy, in that the processes of learning represent inquiry processes. And in such a process interaction plays an important role. Thus, Dewey's theory of experience, as expressed in *Experience and Education*, contains two ideas that can be condensed into a principle of continuity and a principle of interaction. The principle of continuity states that experience is an on-going process. Previous experiences are the basis for actual experiences that mould the conditions for new experiences. The principle of interaction emphasises that an educational process can only be understood in terms of interaction: "Continuity and interaction in their active union with each other provide the measure of the educative significance and value of an experience." (Dewey, 1963, 44-45) Vygotsky also paid attention to interaction. Consequently, we want to acknowledge the critical potential of Dewey's and Vygotsky's theories of learning, as interaction in terms of dialogue can be seen as basis for critical learning. But Dewey and Vygotsky did not develop critique as an educational task.

We have characterised an epistemology as non-critical if, in some way or another, it embraces the implications of the Dewey-assumption: that it is not an educational task to criticise science, scientific thinking, scientific concepts, but to bring students into this thinking. A critical epistemology, however, is inspired by the challenge of critique as provoked by the D'Ambrosio paradox. It does not rely on the Dewey-assumption. This brings us to a completely new situation in education. Facing this challenge means that it becomes also an educational task to provide a critique of the ideas and the content of what is going to be learned. An educational process cannot be interpreted as a straightforward process of enculturation. When horrors as well as wonders are associated with the content of learning, it becomes essential in education to identify what this could mean. Naturally, we do not claim that this is a simple task, we simply claim that when we have acknowledged the challenge of critique, education is put in a new position.

In the most general terms we can characterise a critical epistemology as a theory of developing or constructing knowledge, where a critique of what is learned is seen as part of the learning process. Thus, a critical epistemology means a theory of a particular form of 'getting to know'. It does not include a theory of how students in the most efficient way come to master some techniques, being mathematical or not. Nor can it be satisfied with identifying zones of proximal development as a fertile ground for enculturing students into (elementary or advanced) scientific knowledge. A critical epistemology is also concerned about how to include a judgement of what is learned as an integral part of the learning process. A critical epistemology is also searching for a competence in 'separating wonders from horrors', when mathematical thinking and techniques are addressed. This explains our interest in considering issues of reliability and responsibility.

To clarify some of the roots of critical epistemology, we shall make a few historical notes about critique. Roughly speaking, one notion of critique can be associated with the Enlightenment and the philosophical thinking that relates to modernism. Another notion of critique appears when critique is no longer seen as a servant of science, but also tries to address the very nature of scientific thinking. This second interpretation of critique is the most relevant to critical education. However, let us first make a few comments on the notion of critique related to modernity.

The Enlightenment, and modernism in general, characterises an attack on all forms of dogmatism.[157] Instead of trusting any sort of external authority, human beings should be put in such a position that they can trust their own faculties. As an early forerunner for the Enlightenment, Francis Bacon outlined a grand picture of the role of reason. By eliminating all preconceptions and *idola*, knowledge can become the vehicle for progress.[158] Bacon emphasised the importance of a criticism of systems of beliefs in order to obtain knowledge. Critique became a tool for clearing the ground for knowledge. While Bacon in this way prepared for empiricism's input to the world-view of the Enlightenment and modernity, another input came from rationalism. Descartes (1993) attacked dogmatism by applying universal doubt to get rid of all thought which *might* be false. Only what might resist universal doubt could serve as the firm ground for the construction of knowledge, and reason became the constructor of knowledge. Much later logical positivism tried to invent a machinery for eliminating unscientific and metaphysical

---

[157] By dogmatism is understood a structure of beliefs which is accepted as true and reliable, because some authority has the power to institutionalise a belief-system as true.

[158] See Bacon (1960, 47-50).

elements from the scientific discourse. Critique became like a process of weeding. In this way the idea was maintained that it is important to do epistemic cleaning – identifying idola, applying universal doubt, eliminating metaphysics – before embarking on the process of constructing knowledge, which could be based on induction (Bacon) or deduction (Descartes) or a hypothetic-deductive approach (as suggested by Hempel, 1965). This notion of critique as 'epistemic cleaning' fits the Dewey-assumption. Knowledge, in particular scientific knowledge, represents epistemic welfare. It must be set free. In this way critique becomes a kind of pre-scientific activity, and certainly not an educational activity.

The notion of critique was developed in a different direction by Critical Theory with particular relevance for education. Thus, Max Horkheimer tried to establish an inter-disciplinary type of research, where sociology, philosophy, history and other disciplines provide an interpretation of social phenomena, which not only could explain the existing state of affairs but also provide an opening for social changes.[159] Critical Theory elaborated a notion of critique that combined the analytical elements with action. Furthermore, from being an activity that clarified the ground for scientific research by eliminating dogmas and ideologies, it became an activity which could address scientific rationality itself. This rationality, for instance in the form of instrumental reason, as discussed by Herbert Marcuse (1991), could turn into an ideology. And consequently it also had to face a critique. In particular, Marcuse criticised instrumentalism within the philosophy of science. Scientific theories, like any other conceptions, might be highly problematic, even if they have demonstrated their instrumental value, their viability. This brings about a new positioning of critique. Now it becomes clear that critique must also address the whole scientific enterprise.

This broader concept of critique is essential when we experience the paradox mentioned by D'Ambrosio. Science and scientific thinking cannot be considered an ultimate progressive force. This is also emphasised by the notion of a risk society including manufactured risks. As Beck remarked, man-made risks "include and combine politics, ethics, mathematics, mass media, technologies, cultural definitions and precepts" (Beck, 1998, 11). A critical epistemology tries to clarify what it could mean, also in an educational context, to face the challenge of critique. It does assume that mathematics also needs to be addressed in a critique. A critical epistemology includes a critique of rationality, also when

---

[159] See, for instance, the chapter 'The Present Situation of Social Philosophy and the Tasks of an Institute for Social Research' in Horkheimer (1993).

rationality refers to mathematics. Mathematics and scientific thinking in general are not considered as models for thought, as was assumed by the Enlightenment. They just represent forms of thought. The supposed intrinsic connection between scientific thinking and progress is not maintained. For that reason critique also becomes an educational task.

A particular task for a critical epistemology is to locate resources for undertaking a critique. We see such resources as grounded in human interaction, and we suggest that dialogue can be seen as a fundamental resource for developing critique as part of learning. Furthermore, we find that carrying out a critique presupposes the involvement of the students, or of any person who performs a critique, and that a critique has very much to do with reflections. Thus, we suggest that a critical epistemology is particularly concerned with the notions of intention, reflection and dialogue.

We see a critical epistemology as dia-logical. This is the reason why we find interesting elements in the conceptions developed by Dewey and Vygotsky. Naturally, we are not claiming that any dia-logical epistemology will turn into a critical one. We only see this turn as a possibility. It is much more difficult (if not impossible) to turn a mono-logical epistemology into a critical epistemology.

Addressing dialogue as a resource for critique has implications for how we see the 'unit' of our analysis. It becomes important to consider processes of interaction, and not first of all processes of isolated contemplation and individualised knowledge construction. This idea is emphasised by Marcelo Borba (1995) when he presents humans-with-media as a relevant unit of research.[160] As it might have been natural to study humans-with-paper-and-pencil when addressing the learning of mathematics, it might now be relevant to study humans-with-computers as a unit. We have not paid much attention to the computer-environment of the landscapes of investigation we have presented. We have more or less taken the computers as well as any other relevant 'media' as being available if necessary. In this way we have recognised humans-with-media as the unit of our study, where the plurality of 'humans' is essential. This is essential, as we see a dia-logical epistemology as a necessary foundation for a critical epistemolology.

---

[160] Borba is inspired by Tikhomirov (1981), who is in line with Vygotsky when emphasising that computers make an integrated part of the learning 'unit', not as extensions of human capacities, but as a restructuring of these capacities. See also Borba and Penteado (2001).

LEARNING MATHEMATICS CRITICALLY

Applications of mathematics and the mathematical way of thinking have found their way into many new areas of social life. In particular, we cannot imagine the development of the information society and its associated economy without mathematics being part of the constituting technologies. Just to indicate the scope of *mathematics in action*: national economies are modelled mathematically in order to facilitate political decision making. Furthermore, these models are connected in a world-wide network; companies make their budgets according to mathematical cost-benefit analysis; insurance strategies are relying on results from probability theory and statistics; medicine tests are based on statistics; according to Thymoszko (1994) war is constituted (but not caused) by mathematics; estimations of risks related to certain productions are carried out by means of mathematics, the risks of operating a nuclear power plant being a well-known example; marketing strategies can be developed by using mathematical models for epidemic growth; any kind of security system for electronic communication is based on number theoretical results; any construction of complex technology, say, an airplane is based on mathematical simulation models, for instance concerning the stability of the construction; any security procedure for, say, take off is based on a network of interrelated formal models; traffic planning is carried out with reference to mathematical models; the identification of environmental effects of technological inventions are often strongly supported by mathematical techniques, the identification of the hole in the ozone layer being an example.

We can continue for a long while, and we have had this richness in mind when we prepared the different landscapes of investigation where the projects 'Terrible small numbers', 'Travel agency', 'Caramel boxes' and 'Batman & Co.' were located. These examples also illustrate the break down of the difference between the classical logic of scientific discovery, technological development, industry and management – as already alluded to by Beck (see Chapter 7).

The broad spectrum of mathematics-based actions related to every-day situations, technology, economy, politics, military, management etc. is not ascribed a quality because of mathematics. This is essential in order to see the paradox mentioned by D'Ambrosio. What mathematics is doing is neither good, nor bad, and certainly not neutral.[161] A critical theory of learning mathematics does not subscribe to the Dewey-

---

[161] This is a slight variation of Kranzberg's law, see Kranzberg (1997).

assumption that a strong connection between scientific methodology, learning in school and democratic development does exist. Nor does such a theory make the opposite claim, that disharmony exists. In the section 'Dialogic teaching and learning – and its significance' in Chapter 4, we emphasised that the relationship between mathematics education and democracy is critical in the sense that mathematics education as a democratic endeavour is a permanent challenge. Facing this challenge is a characteristic of critical mathematics education. Thus, a critical mathematics education also means facing the D'Ambrosio paradox.

We have to face a basic uncertainty about the quality of mathematics in action. The Greek word *poria* means direction, and *a-poria* can be read as 'without direction'. Modernity assumes that the very directedness of progress is pointed out by scientific rationality. This rationality represents a direction, a *poria*. This leads to the intellectual optimist, which we find in modernism. When we give up the Dewey-assumption, we find ourselves in quite a different epistemic situation. We are without direction, and acknowledging this is the characteristic of *aporism*.[162] This uncertainty concerns all aspects of everyday life. We come to live in a mathematics-rich environment, where judgements related to numbers become important for everybody.

Does this mean that mathematics education should teach all these kinds of modelling and techniques? Certainly not! We do not think that the task of mathematics education is simply to prepare people for 'fitting into' a mathematically rich context. This is the approach of simple enculturation. Instead, the educational task is to prepare for a critical citizenship also in a mathematically rich context. In this sense, we see the role of mathematics education as being parallel to the Freire-pedagogy of developing a competence in making a critical reading of social and cultural contexts. Freire has talked about literacy, and we talk about mathemacy as the parallel competence. Mathemacy thus becomes a competence that crystallises the processes of learning mathematics critically. It becomes relevant to discuss conditions for democracy and citizenship in terms, not only of literacy, but also in terms mathemacy. Somehow, this brings us back to Dewey, who definitely was concerned about education and democracy. We also see a strong connection between education and democracy, and we associate the concerns of critical mathematics education with the concerns for democracy in general. But such a connection is not secured by introducing scientific thinking into the classroom. A critical position towards any content

---

[162] For a presentation of aporism, see Skovsmose (1998a, 2000a).

matter issues is necessary. (That many other competencies than mathemacy are necessary is obvious.) It would have been nice if we could conclude this study by claiming that dialogue in fact would ensure the students being involved in critical processes of learning mathematics and address content matter issues by powerful reflections. But this is not the case. As our analyses of the different projects clearly demonstrate, the situation is much more complex. The very notion of dialogue brings ideal elements to epistemology.

The Piagetian approach to epistemology is non-ideal. Piaget tries to identify how the growth of knowledge in fact takes place. He tries to identify certain invariants in this process and in this way to clarify conditions for learning determined by 'nature'. Piaget's epistemology is basically descriptive, presenting aspects of the growth of knowledge which cannot be remoulded by educational enterprises, but which are essential to consider for education. The Vygotskian approach is different, although the notion of the zone of proximal development can be seen as a descriptive concept referring to socially determined conditions for learning. But Vygotsky does not stay in the descriptive camp. He also allows for educational activities to go beyond what might be 'given' by nature. When we indicate that dialogic acts can turn into critical learning, we have no hope of turning our study into a descriptive theory of learning in general. We cannot say much about what will happen, but we try to create a conceptual framework for discussing what *could* happen. In this sense our suggestion of a critical epistemology comes to contain ideal elements, and it comes to deal with educational possibilities.

This has to do with two things. First, dialogue is a fragile process. Dialogic acts can easily turn into non-dialogic acts. Attempts of 'getting in contact' can (sometimes) be experienced as a bit too close and frightening. 'Challenging' questions can (sometimes) become part of an unwelcome evaluation; 'identification' can (sometimes) be experienced as an unpleasant highlighting of misunderstandings; 'thinking aloud' can (sometimes) appear ironic; etc. It is no straightforward process to establish dialogic learning. Secondly, we have to remind ourselves that dialogue, and here we think of successful and genuine dialogue, is unpredictable. It is risky. This means we cannot relate dialogue to a learning process and simultaneously expect some particular outcomes from this. What we can consider is that the inquiring qualities of dialogue may sometimes bring about qualities in learning that we will call critical. Thus, any epistemology, which includes dialogue as an essential element, comes to contain ideal elements. The notion of mathemacy is an example of such an idealisation.

An epistemology that contains terms like dialogue, intention, reflection and critique as fundamental concepts, all of them explosive, may miss descriptive precision, but hopefully it can illuminate educational possibilities.

REFERENCES

Adler, J. (2001a). *Teaching Mathematics in Multicultural Classrooms*. Dordrecht, Boston, London: Kluwer Academic Publishers.

Adler, J. (2001b). Resourcing Practice and Equity: A Dual Challenge for Mathematics Education. In B. Atweh, H. Forgasz and B. Nebres (Eds.), *Sociocultural Research on Mathematics Education* (185-200). Mahwah (New Jersey), London: Lawrence Erlbaum Associates.

Alrø, H. (1995). I forlanger for lidt af jer selv. *Nordic Studies in Mathematics Education, 3*(2), 7-27.

Alrø, H. (1996). Disciplin eller dialog. In H. Alrø (Ed.), *Organisationsudvikling gennem dialog* (211-243). Aalborg: Aalborg Universitetsforlag.

Alrø, H., Blomhøj, B., Bødtkjer, H., Skovsmose, O. and Skånstrøm, M. (2000a). Farlige små tal. *Kvan, 56*, 17-27.

Alrø, H., Blomhøj, B., Bødtkjer, H., Skovsmose, O. and Skånstrøm, M. (2000b). Farlige små tal – almendannelse i et risikosamfund. *Nordic Studies in Mathematics Education, 8*(4), 27-52.

Alrø, H., Blomhøj, B., Bødtkjer, H., Skovsmose, O. and Skånstrøm, M. (2001). Farlige små tal – helt konkret. *Nämnaren, 28*(4), 40-46.

Alrø, H. and Kristiansen, M. (1998). *Supervision som dialogisk læreproces*. Aalborg: Aalborg Universitetsforlag.

Alrø, H. and Lindenskov, L. (1994). Hvad er det de lærer? Hverdag i matematikundervisningen. In G. Nissen and M. Blomhøj (Eds.), *Hul i kulturen: Sæt matematikken på plads* (58-76). Copenhagen: Spektrum Publishers.

Alrø, H. and Skovsmose, O. (1996a). On the Right Track. *For the Learning of Mathematics, 16*(1), 2-9, 22.

Alrø, H. and Skovsmose, O. (1996b). The Students' Good Reasons. *For the Learning of Mathematics, 16*(3), 31-38.

Alrø, H. and Skovsmose, O. (1998). That was not the Intention! Communication in Mathematics Education. *For the Learning of Mathematics, 18*(2), 42-51.

Alrø, H. and Skovsmose, O. (1999). Samtalen som et støttende stillads. In J. T. Hansen and K. Nielsen (Eds.), *Stilladsering – en pædagogisk metafor* (179-201). Århus: Forlaget Klim.

Alrø, H., Skovsmose, O. and Skånstrøm, M. (2000). Mie og Asger: Om samtalen i matematik. *CRIT* (2), 10-21. Copenhagen: Statens Pædagogiske Forsøgscenter.

Appelbaum, P. M. (1995). *Popular Culture, Educational Discourse and Mathematics*. New York: SUNY Press.

Apple, M. (1995). Taking Power Seriously: New Directions in Equity in Mathematics Education and Beyond. In W. Secada, E. Fennema and L. Adajian (Eds.), *New Directions for Equity in Mathematics Education* (329-348). Cambridge: Cambridge University Press.

Archambault, R. D. (Ed.) (1964). *John Dewey on Education: Selected Writings*. Chicago, London: The University of Chicago Press.

Argyris, C. (1988). Empowerment: The Emperor's New Clothes. *Harward Business Review* (May-June).

Atweh, B., Forgasz, H. and Nebres, B. (Eds.) (2001). *Sociocultural Research on Mathematics Education*. Mahwah (New Jersey), London: Lawrence Erlbaum Associates.

Atweh, B., Kemmis, S. and Weeks, P. (Eds.) (1998). *Action Research in Practice: Partnership for Social Justice in Education*. London and New York: Routledge.

Austin, J. L. (1962). *How to Do Things with Words*. Oxford: Oxford University Press.

Austin, J. L. (1970). Other Minds. In J. O. Urmson and G. J. Warnock (Eds.), *Philosophical Papers* (2nd ed.) (76-116). Oxford: Oxford University Press.

Bacon, F. (1960). *The New Organon*. Indianapolis: The Bobbs-Merrill Company.

Bakhtin, M. M. (1990). *The Dialogic Imagination: Four Essays*. Austin: Texas University Press.

Bakhtin, M. M. (1995). *Art and Answerability*. Austin: Texas University Press.

Balacheff, N. and Kaput, J. (1996). Computer-based Learning Environments in Mathematics. In A. Bishop, K. Clements, C. Keitel, J. Kilpatrick and C. Laborde (Eds.), *International Handbook of Mathematics Education* (435-468). Dordrecht, Boston, London: Kluwer Academic Publishers.

Bartolini Bussi, M. G. (1998). Joint Activity in Mathematics Classrooms. In F. Seeger, J. Voigt and U. Waschescio (Eds.), *The Culture of the Mathematics Classroom* (13-49). Cambridge: Cambridge University Press.

Bateson, G. (1972). *Steps to an Ecology of Mind*. New York: Ballantine.

Bauersfeld, H. (1980). Hidden Dimensions in the So-Called Reality of a Mathematics Classroom. *Educational Studies in Mathematics, 11*, 23-41.

Bauersfeld, H. (1988). Interaction, Construction and Knowledge: Alternative Perspectives for Mathematics Education. In T. Cooney and D. Grouws (Eds.), *Effective Mathematics Teaching* (27-46). Virginia: Reston.

Bauersfeld, H. (1992). Classroom Cultures from a Social Constructivists Perspective. *Educational Studies in Mathematics, 23*, 467-481.

Bauersfeld, H. (1995). 'Language Games' in the Mathematics Classroom: Their Function and Their Effects. In P. Cobb and H. Bauersfeld (Eds.), *The Emergence of Mathematical Meaning: Interaction in Classroom Cultures* (271-291). Hillsdale (New Jersey), Hove (UK): Lawrence Erlbaum Associates.

Bauersfeld, H. (1998). About the Notion of Culture in Mathematics Education. In F. Seeger, J. Voigt and U. Waschescio (Eds.), *The Culture of the Mathematics Classroom* (375-389). Cambridge: Cambridge University Press.

Bauman, Z. (1989). *Modernity and the Holocaust*. Cambridge: Polity Press.

Beck, U. (1992). *Risk Society: Towards a New Modernity*. London: SAGE Publications.

Beck, U. (1995a). *Ecological Politics in the Age of Risk*. Cambridge: Polity Press.

Beck, U. (1995b). *Ecological Enlightenment: Essays on the Politics of the Risk Society.* New Jersey: Humanity Press.

Beck, U. (1998). Politics of Risk Society. In J. Franklin (Ed.), *The Politics of Risk Society* (9-22). Cambridge: Polity Press.

Beck, U., Giddens, A. and Lash, S. (1994). *Reflexive Modernization: Politics, Tradition and Aesthetics in the Modern Social Order.* Cambridge: Polity Press.

Berne, M. D. (1964). *Games People Play.* New York: Ballantine Books.

Beth, E. W. and Piaget, J. (1966). *Mathematical Epistemology and Psychology.* Dordrecht: Reidel Publishing Company.

Blomhøj, M. (1995). Den didaktiske kontrakt i matematikundervisningen. *Kognition og pædagogik, 4*(3), 16-25.

Blomhøj, M. (1998). *Edb i gymnasiets matematikundervisning – betydning for undervisning og læring.* Centre for Research in Learning Mathematics, Danish University of Education, Roskilde University Centre, Aalborg University.

Bloor, D. (1976). *Knowledge and Social Imagery.* London: Routledge and Kegan Paul.

Boaler, J. (1997). *Experiencing School Mathematics.* Buckingham: Open University Press.

Bohm, D. (1996). *On Dialogue.* London: Routledge.

Borba, M. (1995). Graphic Calculators, Functions and Reorganization of the Classroom. In M. Borba, T. Souza, B. Hudson and J. Fey (Eds.), *The Role of Technology in the Mathematics Classroom* (53-60). Sevilla, Cruzeiro, Rio Claro: Proceedings of WG 6, ICME-8.

Borba, M. and Penteado, M. G. (2001). *Informática e Educacão Matemática.* Belo Horisonte: Autêntica.

Borba, M. and Skovsmose, O. (1997). The Ideology of Certainty in Mathematics Education. *For the Learning of Mathematics, 17*(3), 17-23.

Bourdieu, P. (1996). *The State Nobility: Elite Schools in the Field of Power.* Cambridge: Polity Press.

Brousseau, G. (1997). *Theory of Didactical Situations in Mathematics: Didactique des mathématiques, 1970-1990* (N. Balacheff, M. Cooper, R. Sutherland and V. Warfield, Trans.). Dordrecht, Boston, London: Kluwer Academic Publishers.

Brown, T. (2001). *Mathematics Education and Language: Interpreting Hermeneutics and Post-Structuralism* (Revised Second Version). Dordrecht, Boston, London: Kluwer Academic Publishers.

Bruner, J. (1960). *The Process of Education.* Cambridge (Massachussets): Harvard University Press.

Buber, M. (1957). Elements of the Interhuman. In M. Buber (Ed.), *The Knowledge of Man: Selected Essays* (62-78). New York: Harper and Row Publishers.

Burton, L. (1996). Mathematics, and its Learning, as Narrative: A Literacy for the Twenty-first Century. In D. Baker, J. Clay and C. Fox (Eds.), *Challenging Ways of Knowing: in English, Mathematics and Science* (29-40). London: Falmer Press.

Burton, L. (Ed.) (1999). *Learning Mathematics: From Hierarchies to Network.* London: The Falmer Press.

Castells, M. (1996). *The Information Age: Economy, Society and Culture. Volume I: The Rise of the Network Society.* Oxford: Blackwell Publishers.

Castells, M. (1997). *The Information Age: Economy, Society and Culture. Volume II: The Power of Identity*. Oxford: Blackwell Publishers.

Castells, M. (1998). *The Information Age: Economy, Society and Culture. Volume III: End of Millennium*. Oxford: Blackwell Publishers.

Cestari, M. L. (1997). *Communication in Mathematics Classrooms – a Dialogical Approach*. Doctoral thesis. Oslo: Oslo University.

Chaiklin, S. (1999). Developmental Teaching in Upper-Secondary School. In M. Hedegaard and J. Lompscher (Eds.), *Learning Activity and Development* (187-210). Aarhus: Aarhus University Press.

Chaiklin, S., Hedegaard, M. and Jensen, U. J. (Eds.) (1999). *Theory and Social Practice: Cultural-Historical Approaches*. Århus: Århus University Press.

Chaiklin, S. and Lave, J. (Eds.) (1996). *Understanding Practice: Perspectives on Activity and Context*. Cambridge: Cambridge University Press.

Christiansen, I. M. (1994). *Classroom Interactions in Applied Mathematics Courses I-II*. Doctoral thesis. Aalborg: Aalborg University.

Christiansen, I. M. (1995). 'Informal Activity' in Mathematics Instruction. *Nordic Studies in Mathematics Education, 2*(3/4), 7-30.

Christiansen, I. M. (1997). When Negotiation of Meaning is also Negotiation of Task. *Educational Studies in Mathematics, 34*(1), 1-25.

Christiansen, I. M., Nielsen, L. and Skovsmose, O. (1997). Ny mening til begrebet refleksion i matematikundervisningen. In J. C. Jacobsen (Ed.), *Refleksive Læreprocesser* (173-190). Copenhagen: Forlaget Politisk Revy.

Cissna, K. N. and Anderson, R. (1994). Communication and the Ground of Dialogue. In R. Anderson, K. N. Cissna and R. C. Arnett (Eds.), *The Reach of Dialogue: Confirmation, Voice and Community* (9-33). Cresskill: Hampton Press.

Clark, D. (Ed.) (2001). *Perspectives on Practice and Meaning in Mathematics and Science Classrooms*. Dordrecht, Boston, London: Kluwer Academic Publishers.

Cobb, P. (1995). Mathematical Learning and Small-Group Interaction: Four Case Studies. In P. Cobb and H. Bauersfeld (Eds.), *The Emergence of Mathematical Meaning: Interaction in Classroom Cultures* (25-129). Hillsdale (NewJersey), Hove (UK): Lawrence Erlbaum Associates.

Cobb, P. and Bauersfeld, H. (Eds.) (1995). *The Emergence of Mathematical Meaning: Interaction in Classroom Cultures*. Hillsdale (NewJersey), Hove (UK): Lawrence Erlbaum Associates.

Cobb, P., Boufi, A., McClain, K. and Whitenack, J. (1997). Reflective Discourse and Collective Reflection. *Journal for Research in Mathematics Education, 8*(3), 258-277.

Cobb, P. and Yackel, E. (1998). A Constructivist Perspective on the Culture of the Mathematics Classroom. In F. Seeger, J. Voigt and U. Waschescio (Eds.), *The Culture of the Mathematics Classroom* (158-190). Cambridge: Cambridge University Press.

Cobb, P., Yackel, E. and Wood, D. (1995). The Teaching Experiment Classroom. In P. Cobb and H. Bauersfeld (Eds.), *The Emergence of Mathematical Meaning: Interaction in Classroom Cultures* (17-24). Hillsdale (NewJersey), Hove (UK): Lawrence Erlbaum Associates.

D'Ambrosio, U. (1994). Cultural Framing of Mathematics Teaching and Learning. In R. Biehler, R. W. Scholz, R. Strässer and B. Winkelmann (Eds.), *Didactics of Mathematics as a Scientific Discipline* (443-455). Dordrecht, Boston, London: Kluwer Academic Publishers.

D'Ambrosio, U. (2001). *Etnomatemática: Elo entre tradiçiõs e a modernidade.* Belo Horisonte: Autêntica.

Davis, B. (1996). *Teaching Mathematics: Toward a Sound Alternative.* New York, London: Garland Publishing.

Davydov, W. (1977). *Arten der Verallgemeinerung im Unterricht.* Berlin: Volk und Wissen Volkseigener Verlag.

Descartes, R. (1993). *Meditations on First Philosophy in Focus.* London, New York: Routledge.

Dewey, J. (1938). The Relation of Science and Philosophy as a Basis for Education. *School and Society, XLVIII*, 470-473. (Reprinted in R. D. Archambault (Ed.) (1964), *John Dewey on Education: Selected Writings* (15-19). Chicago, London: The University of Chicago Press.)

Dewey, J. (1963). *Experience and Education.* New York: Macmillan.

Dewey, J. (1966). *Democracy and Education.* Ontario: The Free Press, Macmillan Publishing Co.

Dowling, P. (1998). *The Sociology of Mathematics Education: Mathematical Myths/Pedagogic Texts.* London: Falmer Press.

Dubinsky, E. (1991). Reflective Abstraction in Advanced Mathematical Thinking. In D. Tall (Ed.), *Advanced Mathematical Thinking* (95-123). Dordrecht, Boston, London: Kluwer Academic Publishers.

Dysthe, O. (1997). *Det flerstemmige klasserum.* Århus: Forlaget Klim.

Dysthe, O. (1998). *The Dialogical Perspective and Bakhtin.* Program for Research on Learning and Instruction. Bergen: University of Bergen.

Eggins, S. and Slade, D. (1997). *Analyzing Casual Conversation.* London, Washington: Casell.

Engeström, Y. (1998). Reorganising the Motivational Sphere of Classroom Culture: The Activity-Theoretical Analysis of Planning in a Teacher Team. In F. Seeger, J. Voigt and U. Waschescio (Eds.), *The Culture of the Mathematics Classroom* (76-103). Cambridge: Cambridge University Press.

Engeström, Y. (1999). Innovative Learning in Work Teams: Analyzing Cycles of Knowledge Creation in Practice. In Y. Engeström, R. Miettinen and R.-L. Punamäki (Eds.), *Perspectives on Activity Theory* (377-404). Cambridge: Cambridge University Press.

Engeström, Y. and Middleton, D. (Eds.) (1998). *Cognition and Communication at Work.* Cambridge: Cambridge University Press.

Engeström, Y., Miettinen, R. and Punamäki, R.-L. (Eds.) (1999). *Perspectives on Activity Theory.* Cambridge: Cambridge University Press.

Eriksen, D. (1993). *Personlige og sociale sider ved elevernes tilegnelse af faglig viden og kunnen i folkeskolens matematikundervisning.* Doctoral thesis. Copenhagen: Royal Danish School of Educational Studies.

Ernest, P. (1998a). *Social Constructivism as a Philosophy of Mathematics.* Albany: State University of New York Press.

Ernest, P. (1998b). The Culture of the Mathematics Classroom and the Relations between Personal and Public Knowledge: An Epistemological Perspective. In F. Seeger, J. Voigt and U. Waschescio (Eds.), *The Culture of the Mathematics Classroom* (245-268). Cambridge: Cambridge University Press.

Fasheh, M. (1993). From a Dogmatic, Ready-Answer Approach of Teaching Mathematics towards a Community-Building, Process Orientated Approach. In C. Julie, D. Angelis and Z. Davis (Eds.), *Political Dimensions of Mathematics Education 2: Curriculum Reconstruction for Society in Transition* (15-19). Cape Town: Maskew Miller Longman.

Fasheh, M. (1997). Mathematics, Culture, and Authority. In A. B. Powell and M. Frankenstein (Eds.), *Ethnomathematics: Challenging Eurocentrism in Mathematics Education* (273-290). Albany: State University of New York Press.

Feyerabend, P. (1975). *Against Method*. London: Verso.

Fosse, T. (1996). Hva venter de seg – av skolens matematikk? In M. J. Høines (Ed.), *De små teller også*. Bergen: Caspar.

Frankenstein, M. (1987). Critical Mathematics Education: An Application of Paulo Freire's Epistemology. In I. Shor (Ed.), *Freire for the Classroom* (180-210). Portsmouth: Boyton and Cook.

Frankenstein, M. (1989). *Relearning Mathematics: A Different Third R – Radical Maths*. London: Free Association Books.

Frankenstein, M. (1995). Equity in Mathematics Education: Class in the World Outside the Class. In W. Secada, E. Fennema and L. Adajian (Eds.), *New Directions for Equity in Mathematics Education* (165-190). Cambridge: Cambridge University Press.

Franklin, J. (Ed.) (1998). *The Politics of Risk Society*. Cambridge: Polity Press.

Freire, P. (1972). *Pedagogy of the Oppressed*. New York: Herder and Herder.

Freire, P. (1974). *Cultural Action for Freedom*. London: Pinguin Books.

Gadamer, H.-G. (1989). *Truth and Method* (2nd revised edition). London: Sheed and Ward.

Gadotti, M. (Ed.) (1996). *Paulo Freire: Uma Biobibliografia*. Sao Paulo: Cortez Editora.

Gellert, U., Jablonka, E. and Keitel, C. (2001). Mathematical Literacy and Common Sense in Mathematics Education. In B. Atweh, H. Forgasz and B. Nebres (Eds.), *Sociocultural Research on Mathematics Education* (57-73). Mahwah (New Jersey), London: Lawrence Erlbaum Associates.

Gergen, K. J. (1973). Social Psychology as History. *Journal of Personality and Social Psychology, 26*, 309-320.

Gergen, K. J. (1997). *Virkelighed og relationer*. Copenhagen: Dansk psykologisk Forlag.

Giddens, A. (1990). *The Consequences of Modernity*. Cambridge: Polity Press.

Giddens, A. (1998). Risk Society: The Context of British Politics. In J. Franklin (Ed.), *The Politics of Risk Society* (23-34). Cambridge: Polity Press.

Glasersfeld, E. v. (Ed.) (1991). *Radical Constructivism in Mathematics Education*. Dordrecht, Boston, London: Kluwer Academic Publishers.

Glasersfeld, E. v. (1995). *Radical Constructivism. A Way of Knowing and Learning*. London: Falmer Press.

Habermas, J. (1984, 1987). *The Theory of Communicative Action I-II*. London, Cambridge: Heinemann, Polity Press.

Hannaford, C. (1998). Mathematics Teaching is Democratic Education. *Zentralblatt für Didaktik der Mathematik, 1998*(6), 181-187.

Hedegaard, M. and Lompscher, J. (Eds.) (1999). *Learning Activity and Development*. Aarhus: Aarhus University Press.

Hempel, C. G. (1965). *Aspects of Scientific Explanation*. New York: The Free Press.

Hermansen, M. (1996). *Læringens univers*. Århus: Forlaget Klim.

Hermansen, M. (1998). *Fra læringens horisont: En antologi*. Aarhus: Forlaget Klim.

Herrlitz, W. (1987). 'Gamma, Herr Jensen': Zur Analyse von Handlungsfiguren in der Unterrichtskommunikation, *Jahrbuch der Deutschdidaktik 1986-87* (69-83). Königstein.

Høines, M. J. (1998). *Begynneroplæringen* (3. ed.). Bergen: Casper Forlag.

Høines, M. J. (2002). *Fleksible språkrom: Matematiklæring som tekstutvikling*. Bergen: Institut for praktisk pedagogikk, det psykologiske fakultet, Universitetet i Bergen.

Horkheimer, M. (1993). *Between Philosophy and Social Science: Selected Early Writings*. Cambridge, Massachusetts: The MIT Press.

Isaacs, W. (1994). Dialogue and Skillful Discussion. In P. Senge, C. Roberts, R. B. Ross, B. J. Smith and A. Kleiner (Eds.), *The Fifth Discipline Fieldbook* (357-380). London: Nicholas Brealey.

Isaacs, W. (1999a). *Dialogue and the Art of Thinking Together*. New York: Doubleday.

Isaacs, W. (1999b). Dialogue. In J. Stewart (Ed.), *Bridges not Walls. A Book about Interpersonal Communication* (7th ed.) (58-65). Boston: McGraw-Hill College.

Jaworski, B. (1994). *Investigating Mathematics Teaching: A Constructivist Enquiry*. London: The Falmer Press.

Johnston, B. and Yasukawa, K. (2001). Numeracy: Negotiating the World Through Mathematics. In B. Atweh, H. Forgasz and B. Nebres (Eds.), *Sociocultural Research on Mathematics Education* (279-294). Mahwah (New Jersey), London: Lawrence Erlbaum Associates.

Jungwirth, H. (1991). Interaction and Gender – Findings of a Microethnographical Approach to Classroom Discourse. *Educational Studies in Mathematics, 22*(3), 263-284.

Keitel, C. (1989). Mathematics and Technology. *For the Learning of Mathematics, 9*(1), 7-13.

Keitel, C. (1993). Implicit Mathematical Models in Social Practice and Explicit Mathematics Teaching by Applications. In J. de Lange (Ed.), *Innovation in Maths Education by Modelling and Applications* (19-30). New York: Ellis Horwood.

Keitel, C., Kotzmann, E. and Skovsmose, O. (1993). Beyond the Tunnel-Vision: Analysing the Relationship between Mathematics, Society and Technology. In C. Keitel and K. Ruthven (Eds.), *Learning from Computers: Mathematics Education and Technology* (243-279). Berlin: Springer.

Khuzwayo, H. (1998). Occupation of Our Minds: A Dominant Feature in Mathematics Education in South Africa. In P. Gates (Ed.), *Proceedings of the First International Mathematics Education and Society Conference* (219-232). Nottingham: Centre for the Study of Mathematics Education.

Khuzwayo, H. (2000). *Selected Views and Critical Perspectives: An Account of Mathematics Education in South Africa from 1948 to 1994*, Doctoral thesis. Aalborg: Aalborg University.

Knijnik, G. (1998). Ethnomathematics and Political Struggles. *Zentralblatt für Didaktik der Mathematik, 1998*(6), 188-194.

Kranzberg, M. (1997). Technology and History: 'Kranzberg's Laws'. In T. S. Reynolds and S. H. Cutcliffs (Eds.), *Technology and the West: A Historical Anthology from Technology and Culture* (5-20). Chicago: University of Chicago Press.

Kristiansen, M. and Bloch-Poulsen, J. (2000). *Kærlig rummelighed i dialoger: Om interpersonel organisationskommunikation.* Aalborg: Aalborg Universitetsforlag.

Krummheuer, G. (1983). Das Arbeitsinterim im Mathematikunterricht. In H. Bauersfeld et al. (Eds.), *Lernen und Lehren von Mathematik* (57-106). Köln: IDM Band 6.

Krummheuer, G. (1995). The Ethnography of Argumentation. In P. Cobb and H. Bauersfeld (Eds.), *The Emergence of Mathematical Meaning: Interaction in Classroom Cultures* (229-269). Hillsdale (NewJersey), Hove (UK): Lawrence Erlbaum Associates.

Krummheuer, G. (2000a). Studies of Argumentation in Primary Mathematics Education. *Zentralblatt für Didaktik der Mathematik, 2000*(1), 155-161.

Krummheuer, G. (2000b). Mathematics Learning in Narrative Classroom Cultures: Studies of Argumentation in Primary Mathematics Education. *For the Learning of Mathematics, 20*(1), 22-32.

Lakatos, I. (1976). *Proofs and Refutations: The Logic of Mathematical Discovery.* Cambridge: Cambridge University Press.

Lakoff, R. (1975). *Language and Woman's Place.* New York: Harper and Row.

Lemke, J. L. (1990). *Talking Science: Language, Learning and Values.* New Jersey: Ablex Publishing Corporation.

Lerman, S. (Ed.) (1994). *Cultural Perspectives on the Mathematics Classroom.* Dordrecht, Boston, London: Kluwer Academic Publishers.

Lerman, S. (1998). Cultural Perspectives on Mathematics and Mathematics Learning. In F. Seeger. J. Voigt and U. Waschescio (Eds.), *The Culture of the Mathematics Classroom* (290-307). Cambridge: Cambridge University Press.

Lerman, S. (2000). The Social Turn in Mathematics Education Research. In J. Boaler (Ed.), *Multiple Perspectives on Mathematics Teaching and Learning* (19-44). Westport: Ablex Publishing.

Lerman, S. (2001). Cultural, Discursive Psychology: A Sociocultural Approach to Studying the Teaching and Learning of Mathematics. *Educational Studies in Mathematics*, 46, 87-113.

Levinson, S. C. (1983). *Pragmatics.* Cambridge: Cambridge University Press.

Lindén, N. (1997). *Stilladser om børns læring.* Århus: Forlaget Klim.

Lindenskov, L. (1992). *Hverdagsviden og matematik.* Doctoral thesis. Roskilde: Roskilde University Centre.

Lindfors, J. W. (1999). *Children's Inquiry. Using Language to make Sense of the World.* New York: Teachers College, Columbia University.

Lins, R. (2001). The Production of Meaning for Algebra: A Perspective Based on a Theoretical Model of Semantic Fields. In R. Sutherland, T. Rojano, A. Bell and R. Lins (Eds.), *Perspectives on School Algebra* (37-60). Dordrecht, Boston, London: Kluwer Academic Publishers.

Lyotard, J.-F. (1984). *The Post-Modern Condition: A Report on Knowledge.* Manchester: Manchester University Press.

Maas, U. and Wunderlich, D. (1972). *Pragmatik und sprachliches Handeln*. Frankfurt am Main: Athenaion.

Marcuse, H. (1991). *One-Dimensional Man: Studies in the Ideology of Advanced Industrial Society*. London: Routledge.

Markova, I. and Foppa, K. (Eds.) (1990). *The Dynamics of Dialogue*. New York: Harvester Wheatsheaf. Barnes & Noble Books.

Markova, I. and Foppa, K. (Eds.) (1991). *Assymetries in Dialogue*. New York: Harvester Wheatsheaf. Barnes & Noble Books.

Mellin-Olsen, S. (1977). *Indlæring som social proces*. Copenhagen: Rhodos.

Mellin-Olsen, S. (1981). Instrumentalism as an Educational Concept. *Educational Studies in Mathematics, 12*, 351-367.

Mellin-Olsen, S. (1987). *The Politics of Mathematics Education*. Dordrecht: Reidel Publishing Company.

Mellin-Olsen, S. (1989). *Kunnskapsformidling*. Bergen: Caspar Forlag.

Mellin-Olsen, S. (1991). *Hvordan tænker lærere om matematik*. Bergen: Høgskolen i Bergen.

Mellin-Olsen, S. (1993). Dialogue as a Tool to Handle Various Forms of Knowledge. In C. Julie, D. Angelis and Z. Davis (Eds.), *PDME II Report*, 243-252. Cape Town: Maskew Miller Longman.

Moll, L. C. (Ed.) (1990). *Vygotsky and Education: Institutional Implications and Applications of Sociohistorical Psychology*. Cambridge: Cambridge University Press.

Naidoo, A. (1999). *The Impact of the Experience of Novice Teachers on the Mathematics Curriculum at a South African College of Education*. Doctoral thesis. Aalborg: Aalborg University.

Nickson, M. (1992). The Culture of the Mathematics Classroom: An Unknown Quantity? In D. A. Grouws (Ed.), *Handbook of Research on Mathematics Teaching and Learning* (101-114). New York: MacMillan Publishing Company.

Nickson, M. (2002). Social and Critical Mathematics Education: Underlying considerations. In L. Haggerty (Ed.), *Teaching Mathematics in Secondary Schools* (229-240). London: Routledge Falmer.

Nielsen, L., Patronis, T. and Skovsmose, O. (1999). *Connecting Corners: A Greek-Danish Project in Mathematics Education*. Århus: Systime.

Oers, B. van (2001). Educational Forms of Initiation in Mathematical Culture, *Educational Studies in Mathematics*, 46, 59-85

Penteado, M. G. (2001). Computer-based Learning Environments: Risks and Uncertainties for Teachers. *Ways of Knowing, 1*(2), 23-35.

Piaget, J. (1970). *Genetic Epistemology*. New York: Columbia University Press.

Pimm, D. (1987). *Speaking Mathematically: Communication in Mathematics Classrooms*. London: Routledge.

Polanyi, M. (1966). *The Tacit Dimension*. New York: Doubleday.

Porter, T. M. (1995). *Trust in Numbers: The Pursuit of Objectivity in Science and Public Life*. Princeton, New Jersey: Princeton University Press.

Powell, A. and Frankenstein, M. (Eds.) (1997). *Ethnomathematics: Challenging Eurocentrism in Mathematics Education*. Albany: State University of New York Press.

Rawl, J. (1971). *A Theory of Justice*. New York: Oxford University Press.

Richards, J. (1991). Mathematical Discussion. In E. v. Glaserfeld (Ed.), *Radical Constructivism in Mathematics Education* (13-52). Dordrecht, Boston, London: Kluwer Academic Publishers.

Rogers, C. R. (1958). The Characteristics of a Helping Relationship. *Personnel and Guidance Journal 37*, 6-16.

Rogers, C. R. (1961). *On Becoming a Person: A Therapist's View of Psychotherapy*. London: Constable.

Rogers, C. R. (1962). The Interpersonal Relationship: The Core of Guidance. *Harward Educational Review, 32*(4).

Rogers, C. R. (1994). *Freedom to Learn* (3rd ed.). New York: Macmillan College Publishing Company.

Rogers, C. R. and Farson, R. E. (1969). Active Listening. In R. C. Huseman, C. M. Logue and D. L. Freshley (Eds.), *Readings in Interpersonal and Organizational Communication* (480-496). Boston: Holbrook.

Searle, J. (1969). *Speech Acts*. Cambridge: Cambridge University Press.

Searle, J. (1983). *Intentionality: An Essay in the Philosophy of Mind*. Cambridge: Cambridge University Press.

Secada, W., Fennema, E. and Adajian, L. (Eds.) (1995). *New Directions for Equity in Mathematics Education*. Cambridge: Cambridge University Press.

Seeger, F., Voigt, J. and Waschescio, U. (Eds.) (1998). *The Culture of the Mathematics Classroom*. Cambridge: Cambridge University Press.

Senge, P. (1990). *The Fifth Discipline: The Art and Practice of the Learning Organization*. New York: Doubleday.

Sfard, A. (1991). On the Dual Nature of Mathematical Conceptions: Reflections on Processes and Objects as Different Sides of the Same Coin. *Educational Studies in Mathematics, 22*, 1-36.

Sfard, A. (2000). Steering (Dis)course between Metaphor and Rigor: Using Focal Analysis to Investigate the Emergence of Mathematical Objects. *Journal for Research in Mathematics Education, 31*(3), 296-327.

Sfard, A. (2001). There is More to Discourse Than Meets the Ears: Looking at Thinking as Communication to Learn More About Mathematical Learning. *Educational Studies in Mathematics, 46*, 13-57.

Sigel, I. E. and Kelley, T. D. (1988). A Cognitive Developmental Approach to Questioning. In J. T. Dillon (Ed.), *Questioning and Discussion: A Multidisciplinary Study* (105-134). Norwood: Ablex.

Sinclair, J. M. and Coulthard, M. (1975). *Towards an Analysis of Discourse*. London: Oxford University Press.

Skott, J. (2000). *The Images and Practice of Mathematics Teachers*. Doctoral thesis. Copenhagen: Royal Danish School of Educational Studies.

Skovsmose, O. (1994). *Towards a Philosophy of Critical Mathematical Education*. Dordrecht, Boston, London: Kluwer Academic Publishers.

Skovsmose, O. (1998a). Aporism: Uncertainty about Mathematics. *Zentralblatt für Didaktik der Mathematik, 1998*(3), 88-94.

Skovsmose, O. (1998b). Critical Mathematics Education: Some Philosophical Remarks. In C. Alsini, J. M. Alvarez, B. Hodgson, C. Laborde and A. Pérez (Eds.), *8th International Congress on Mathematical Education: Selected Lectures* (413-425). Sevilla: S.A.E.M. THALES.

Skovsmose, O. (1998c). Linking Mathematics Education and Democracy: Citizenship, Mathematics Archaeology, Mathemacy and Deliberative Interaction. *Zentralblatt für Didaktik der Mathematik, 1998*(6), 195-203.

Skovsmose, O. (1999). *Mathematical Agency and Social Theorising*. Centre for Research in Learning Mathematics, Danish University of Education, Roskilde University Centre, Aalborg University.

Skovsmose, O. (2000a). Aporism and Critical Mathematics Education. *For the Learning of Mathematics, 20*(1), 2-8.

Skovsmose, O. (2000b). Cenários para investigação. *Bolema* (14), State University of São Paulo at Rio Claro, 66-91.

Skovsmose, O. (2000c). Escenarios de investigación. *Revista EMA, 6*(1), 1-25.

Skovsmose, O. (2001a). Landscapes of Investigation. *Zentralblatt für Didaktik der Mathematik, 2001*(4), 123-132.

Skovsmose, O. (2002). Landscapes of Investigation. In L. Haggarty (Ed.), *Teaching Mathematics in Secondary Schools: A Reader* (115-128). London: Routledge Falmer.

Skovsmose, O. and Borba, M. (in press). Research Methodology and Critical Mathematics Education. In R. Zevenbergen and P. Valero (Eds.), *Researching the Socio-political Dimensions of Mathematics Education: Issues of Power in Theory and Methodology*, Dordrecht, Boston, London: Kluwer Academic Publishers.

Skovsmose, O. and Nielsen, L. (1996). Critical Mathematics Education. In A. J. Bishop, K. Clements, C. Keitel, J. Kilpatrick and C. Laborde (Eds.), *International Handbook of Mathematics Education I-II* (1257-1288). Dordrecht, Boston, London: Kluwer Academic Publishers.

Skovsmose, O. and Valero, P. (2001). Breaking Political Neutrality: The Critical Engagement of Mathematics Education with Democracy. In B. Atweh, H. Forgasz and B. Nebres (Eds.), *Sociocultural Research on Mathematics Education,* (37-55). Mahwah (New Jersey), London: Lawrence Erlbaum Associates.

Skovsmose, O. and Valero, P. (2002). Democratic Access to Powerful Mathematical Ideas. In L. English (Ed.), *Handbook of International Research in Mathematics Education* (383-407). Mahwah (New Jersey), London: Lawrence Erlbaum Associates.

Skovsmose, O. and Yasukawa, K. (2000). *Mathematics in a Package: Tracking Down the 'Formatting Power of Mathematics' Through a Socio-Mathematical Excavation of PGP*. Centre for Research in Learning Mathematics, Danish University of Education, Roskilde University Centre, Aalborg University.

Steffe, L. P. (1991). The Constructivist Teaching Experiment: Illustrations and Implications. In E. v. Glasersfeld (Ed.), *Radical Constructivism in Mathematics Education* (177-194). Dordrecht, Boston, London: Kluwer Academic Publishers.

Steinbring, H. (1998). Mathematical Understanding in Classroom Interaction: The Interrelation of Social and Epistemological Constrains. In F. Seeger, J. Voigt and U. Waschescio (Eds.), *The Culture of the Mathematics Classroom* (344-372). Cambridge: Cambridge University Press.

Steinbring, H. (2000). Interaction Analysis of Mathematical Communication in Primary Teaching: The Epistemological Perspective. *Zentralblatt für Didaktik der Mathematik, 2000*(5), 138-148.

Stewart, J. (Ed.) (1999). *Bridges Not Walls. A Book about Interpersonal Communication* (7th ed.). Boston: McGraw-Hill College.

Stewart, J. and Logan, C. (1999). Emphatic and Dialogic Listening. In J. Stewart (Ed.), *Bridges Not Walls. A Book about Interpersonal Communication* (7th ed.) (217-237). Boston: McGraw-Hill College.

Stillman, G. and Balatti, J. (2001). Contributions of Ethnomathematics to Mainstream Mathematics Classroom Practice. In B. Atweh, H. Forgasz and B. Nebres (Eds.), *Sociocultural Research on Mathematics Education* (313-328). Mahwah (New Jersey), London: Lawrence Erlbaum Associates.

Streeck, J. (1979). 'Sandwich. Good for you.' – Zur pragmatischen und konversationellen Analyse von Bewertungen im institutionellen Diskurs der Schule. In J. Dittmann (Ed.), *Arbeiten zur Konversationsanalyse* (235-257). Tübingen.

Struve, J. and Voigt, J. (1988). Die Unterrichtsszene im Menon-Dialog. *Journal für Mathematikdidaktik, 9*(4), 259-285.

Stubbs, M. (1976). *Language, Schools and Classrooms*. London: Methuen.

Stubbs, M. (1983). *Discourse Analysis. The Sociolinguistic Analysis of Natural Language*. Oxford: Basil Blackwell.

Tarp, A. (2001). Mathematics Before or Through Applications: Top-down and Bottom-up Understandings of Linear and Exponential Functions. In J. F. Matos, W. Blum, K. Houston and S. P. Carreira (eds.): *Modelling and Mathematics Education* (119-129). Chichester: Horwood Publishing.

Tikhomirov, O. K. (1981). The Psychological Consequences of Computerization. In J. V. Wertsch (Ed.), *The Concept of Activity in Soviet Psychology*. New York: M. E. Sharpe.

Tymoczko, T. (1994). Humanistic and Utilitarian Aspects of Mathematics. In D. F. Robitaille, D. H. Wheeler and C. Kieran (Eds.), *Selected Lectures from the 7th International Congress on Mathematics Education* (327-339). Sainte-Foy: Les Presses De L'Université Laval.

Valero, P. (1998a). Deliberative Mathematics Education for Social Democratization in Latin America. *Zentralblatt für Didaktik der Mathematik, 1998*(6).

Valero, P. (1998b). Socialization or learning? A view on the Danish Folkeskole. *CRIT* (4), 20-29. Copenhagen: Statens Pædagogiske Forsøgscenter.

Valero, P. and Vithal, R. (1999). Research Methods of the "North" revisited from the "South". *Perspectives in Education*, 18(2), 5-12.

Vithal, R. (1998a). Data and Disruptions: The Politics of Doing Mathematics Education Research in South Africa. In N. A. Ogude and C. Bohlmann (Eds.), *Proceedings of the Sixth Annual Meeting of the South African Association for Research in Mathematics and Science Education* (475-481). UNISA.

Vithal, R. (1998b). Democracy and Authority: A Complementarity in Mathematics Education? *Zentralblatt für Didaktik der Mathematik, 1998*(6), 27-36.

Vithal, R. (2000a). *In Search of a Pedagogy of Conflict and Dialogue for Mathematics Education*. Doctoral thesis. Aalborg: Aalborg University.

Vithal, R. (2000b). Re-searching Mathematics Education from a Critical Perspective. In J. V. Matos and M. Santos (Eds.), *Proceedings of the Second International Mathematics Education and Society Conference* (87-116). Centro de Investigação em Educação de Faculdade de Ciências. Lisbon: University of Lisbon.

Vithal, R., Christiansen, I. M. and Skovsmose, O. (1995). Project Work in University Mathematics Education: A Danish Experience: Aalborg University. *Educational Studies in Mathematics, 29*(2), 199-223.

Vithal, R. and Skovsmose, O. (1997). The End of Innocence: A Critique of 'Ethnomathematics'? *Educational Studies in Mathematics, 34*, 131-157.

Voigt, J. (1984). *Interaktionsmuster und Routinen im Mathematikunterricht.* Beltz: Weinheim.

Voigt, J. (1985). Patterns and Routines in Classroom Interaction. *Recherches en Didactique des Mathematique, 6*, 69-118.

Voigt, J. (1989). The Social Constitution of the Mathematics Province: A Microethnografical Study in Classroom Interaction. *The Quarterly Newsletter of Laboratory of Comparative Human Cognition, 11*(2), 27-35.

Voigt, J. (1994). Negotiation of Mathematical Meaning and Learning Mathematics. *Educational Studies in Mathematics, 26*, 275-298.

Volmink, J. (1994). Mathematics by All. In S. Lerman (Ed.), *Cultural Perspectives on the Mathematics Classroom* (51-68). Dordrecht, Boston, London: Kluwer Academic Publishers.

Vygotskij, L. S. (1962). *Thought and Language.* Cambridge, Massachusetts: The MIT Press.

Vygotsky, L. (1978). *Mind in Society.* Cambridge, Massachusetts: Harvard University Press.

Wedege, T. (1999). To Know or not to Know – Mathematics, that is a Question of Context. *Educational Studies in Mathematics, 39*, 229-249.

Wedege, T. (2000). *Matematikviden og teknologiske kompetencer hor kortuddannede voksne.* Doctoral thesis. Roskilde: Roskilde University Centre.

Wells, G. (1999). *Dialogic Inquiry. Towards a Sociocultural Practice and Theory of Education.* Cambridge: Cambridge University Press.

Wittgenstein, L. (1953). *Philosophical Investigations.* Oxford: Basil Blackwell.

Wood, D. (1995). An Emerging Practice of Teaching. In P. Cobb and H. Bauersfeld (Eds.), *The Emergence of Mathematical Meaning: Interaction in Classroom Cultures* (203-227). Hillsdale (NewJersey), Hove (UK): Lawrence Erlbaum Associates.

Wood, D., Bruner, J. S. and Ross, G. (1976). The Role of Tutoring in Problem Solving. *Journal of Child Psychology, 17*, 89-100.

Wood, T. (1994). Patterns of Interaction and the Culture of Mathematics Classroom. In S. Lerman (Ed.), *Cultural Perspectives on the Mathematics Classroom* (149-168). Dordrecht, Boston, London: Kluwer Academic Publishers.

Wright Mills, C. (1959). *The Sociological Imagination.* Oxford: Oxford University Press.

Wunderlich, D. (1975). *Linguistische Pragmatik.* Wiesbaden: Athenaion.

Yackel, E. (1995). Children's Talk in Inquiry Mathematics Classrooms. In P. Cobb and H. Bauersfeld (Eds.), *The Emergence of Mathematical Meaning: Interaction in Classroom Cultures* (131-162). Hillsdale (NewJersey), Hove (UK): Lawrence Erlbaum Associates.

Yasukawa, K. (1998). Looking at Mathematics as Technology: Implications for Numeracy. In P. Gates (Ed.), *Proceedings of the First International Mathematics Education and Society Conference* (351-359). Nottingham: Center for the Study of Mathematics Education, Nottingham University.

Young, R. (1992). *Critical Theory and Classroom Talk*. Clevedon: Longdun Press Ltd.

Zack, V. and Graves, B. (2001). Making Mathematical Meaning Through Dialogue: '*Once* you Think of It, the Z Minus Three Seems Pretty Weird'. *Educational Studies in Mathematics, 46*, 229-271.

Zevenbergen, R. (2001). Mathematics, Social Class, and Linguistic Capital: An Analysis of Mathematics Classroom Interaction. In B. Atweh, H. Forgasz and B. Nebres (Eds.), *Sociocultural Research on Mathematics Education* (201-215). Mahwah (New Jersey), London: Lawrence Erlbaum Associates.

NAME INDEX

277

SUBJECT INDEX

Mathematics Education Library

Managing Editor: A.J. Bishop, Melbourne, Australia

1. H. Freudenthal: *Didactical Phenomenology of Mathematical Structures.* 1983
   ISBN 90-277-1535-1; Pb 90-277-2261-7

2. B. Christiansen, A. G. Howson and M. Otte (eds.): *Perspectives on Mathematics Education.* Papers submitted by Members of the Bacomet Group. 1986.
   ISBN 90-277-1929-2; Pb 90-277-2118-1

3. A. Treffers: *Three Dimensions.* A Model of Goal and Theory Description in Mathematics Instruction The Wiskobas Project. 1987   ISBN 90-277-2165-3

4. S. Mellin-Olsen: *The Politics of Mathematics Education.* 1987
   ISBN 90-277-2350-8

5. E. Fischbein: *Intuition in Science and Mathematics.* An Educational Approach. 1987
   ISBN 90-277-2506-3

6. A.J. Bishop: *Mathematical Enculturation.* A Cultural Perspective on Mathematics Education. 1988   ISBN 90-277-2646-9; Pb (1991) 0-7923-1270-8

7. E. von Glasersfeld (ed.): *Radical Constructivism in Mathematics Education.* 1991
   ISBN 0-7923-1257-0

8. L. Streefland: *Fractions in Realistic Mathematics Education.* A Paradigm of Developmental Research. 1991   ISBN 0-7923-1282-1

9. H. Freudenthal: *Revisiting Mathematics Education.* China Lectures. 1991
   ISBN 0-7923-1299-6

10. A.J. Bishop, S. Mellin-Olsen and J. van Dormolen (eds.): *Mathematical Knowledge: Its Growth Through Teaching.* 1991   ISBN 0-7923-1344-5

11. D. Tall (ed.): *Advanced Mathematical Thinking.* 1991   ISBN 0-7923-1456-5

12. R. Kapadia and M. Borovcnik (eds.): *Chance Encounters: Probability in Education.* 1991   ISBN 0-7923-1474-3

13. R. Biehler, R.W. Scholz, R. Sträßer and B. Winkelmann (eds.): *Didactics of Mathematics as a Scientific Discipline.* 1994   ISBN 0-7923-2613-X

14. S. Lerman (ed.): *Cultural Perspectives on the Mathematics Classroom.* 1994
    ISBN 0-7923-2931-7

15. O. Skovsmose: *Towards a Philosophy of Critical Mathematics Education.* 1994
    ISBN 0-7923-2932-5

16. H. Mansfield, N.A. Pateman and N. Bednarz (eds.): *Mathematics for Tomorrow's Young Children.* International Perspectives on Curriculum. 1996
    ISBN 0-7923-3998-3

17. R. Noss and C. Hoyles: *Windows on Mathematical Meanings.* Learning Cultures and Computers. 1996   ISBN 0-7923-4073-6; Pb 0-7923-4074-4

Mathematics Education Library

18. N. Bednarz, C. Kieran and L. Lee (eds.): *Approaches to Algebra*. Perspectives for Research and Teaching. 1996   ISBN 0-7923-4145-7; Pb ISBN 0-7923-4168-6

19. G. Brousseau: *Theory of Didactical Situations in Mathematics*. Didactique des Mathématiques 19701990. Edited and translated by N. Balacheff, M. Cooper, R. Sutherland and V. Warfield. 1997   ISBN 0-7923-4526-6

20. T. Brown: *Mathematics Education and Language*. Interpreting Hermeneutics and Post-Structuralism. 1997   ISBN 0-7923-4554-1
Second Revised Edition. 2001   Pb ISBN 0-7923-6969-6

21. D. Coben, J. O'Donoghue and G.E. FitzSimons (eds.): *Perspectives on Adults Learning Mathematics*. Research and Practice. 2000   ISBN 0-7923-6415-5

22. R. Sutherland, T. Rojano, A. Bell and R. Lins (eds.): *Perspectives on School Algebra*. 2000   ISBN 0-7923-6462-7

23. J.-L. Dorier (ed.): *On the Teaching of Linear Algebra*. 2000

     ISBN 0-7923-6539-9

24. A. Bessot and J. Ridgway (eds.): *Education for Mathematics in the Workplace*. 2000

     ISBN 0-7923-6663-8

25. D. Clarke (ed.): *Perspectives on Practice and Meaning in Mathematics and Science Classrooms*. 2001   ISBN 0-7923-6938-6; Pb ISBN 0-7923-6939-4

26. J. Adler: *Teaching Mathematics in Multilingual Classrooms*. 2001

     ISBN 0-7923-7079-1; Pb ISBN 0-7923-7080-5

27. G. de Abreu, A.J. Bishop and N.C. Presmeg (eds.): *Transitions Between Contexts of Mathematical Practices*. 2001   ISBN 0-7923-7185-2

28. G.E. FitzSimons: *What Counts as Mathematics?* Technologies of Power in Adult and Vocational Education. 2002   ISBN 1-4020-0668-3

29. H. Alrø and O. Skovsmose: *Dialogue and Learning in Mathematics Education*. Intention, Reflection, Critique. 2002   ISBN 1-4020-0998-4

30. K. Gravemeijer, R. Lehrer, B. van Oers and L. Verschaffel (eds.): *Symbolizing, Modeling and Tool Use in Mathematics Education*. 2002   ISBN 1-4020-1032-X

31. G.C. Leder, E. Pehkonen and G. Törner (eds.): *Beliefs: A Hidden Variable in Mathematics Education?* 2002   ISBN 1-4020-1057-5; Pb ISBN 1-4020-1058-3

KLUWER ACADEMIC PUBLISHERS – DORDRECHT / BOSTON / LONDON